Globalization and Dynamics of Urban Production

SCIENCES

Geography and Demography, Field Director – Denise Pumain

Socio-Economic Geography of the Fabric of Cities,
Subject Head – Natacha Aveline-Dubach

Globalization and Dynamics of Urban Production

Coordinated by
Natacha Aveline-Dubach

WILEY

First published 2023 in Great Britain and the United States by ISTE Ltd and John Wiley & Sons, Inc.

Apart from any fair dealing for the purposes of research or private study, or criticism or review, as permitted under the Copyright, Designs and Patents Act 1988, this publication may only be reproduced, stored or transmitted, in any form or by any means, with the prior permission in writing of the publishers, or in the case of reprographic reproduction in accordance with the terms and licenses issued by the CLA. Enquiries concerning reproduction outside these terms should be sent to the publishers at the undermentioned address:

ISTE Ltd
27-37 St George's Road
London SW19 4EU
UK

www.iste.co.uk

John Wiley & Sons, Inc.
111 River Street
Hoboken, NJ 07030
USA

www.wiley.com

© ISTE Ltd 2023

The rights of Natacha Aveline-Dubach to be identified as the author of this work have been asserted by her in accordance with the Copyright, Designs and Patents Act 1988.

Any opinions, findings, and conclusions or recommendations expressed in this material are those of the author(s), contributor(s) or editor(s) and do not necessarily reflect the views of ISTE Group.

Library of Congress Control Number: 2022952097

British Library Cataloguing-in-Publication Data
A CIP record for this book is available from the British Library
ISBN 978-1-78945-138-2

ERC code:
SH1 Individuals, Markets and Organisations
  SH1_2 International management; international trade; international business; spatial economics
  SH1_9 Industrial organisation; strategy; entrepreneurship
SH2 Institutions, Values, Environment and Space
  SH2_9 Urban, regional and rural studies

Contents

Introduction xi
Natacha AVELINE-DUBACH

    I.1. Market finance's stranglehold on the city xiv
    I.2. Diversity of modes of capital accumulation in real estate xvii
    I.3. What are the consequences for contemporary capitalisms? xix
    I.4. References xx

Part 1. Sectoral Reconfigurations of Property Markets and Urban (Re)Development 1

Chapter 1. The Financialized City and the Extraction of Urban Rent 3
Thierry THEURILLAT

    1.1. Institutionalization of direct connections between the urban built environment and financial markets 5
        1.1.1. Securitization as a connector from the urban built environment to market finance 6
        1.1.2. The consolidation of the driving role of the urban built environment thanks to connections to global investment circuits 8
        1.1.3. Space at the heart of the valorization and extraction of value by the Global City 9
    1.2. Territorialized chains of financialized urban production: a transcalary and multiactor re-intermediation 11
        1.2.1. Financialization through the extraction of urban rent by financial landowners 12
        1.2.2. Financialization through the extraction of urban rent via household property 15
        1.2.3. The financialization of urban development strategies through municipal land 17
    1.3. Conclusion 19
    1.4. References 21

Chapter 2. Real Estate Developers: Coordinating Actors in the Production of the City 27
Julie POLLARD

2.1. The real estate developer, a multi-faceted player 29
   2.1.1. What is a real estate developer? 29
   2.1.2. The diversity of real estate developer profiles 31
2.2. The changing role of real estate developers: between market and politics . . . 34
   2.2.1. Is financialization (re)shaping real estate developers? 34
   2.2.2. How (and why) do developers integrate "social" objectives? 36
   2.2.3. Are environmental issues transforming the practices of
real estate developers? 39
2.3. References 41

Chapter 3. Housing, Ownership, Assets and Debt: Geographical Approaches 47
Renaud LE GOIX

3.1. Introduction: a renewed interest in housing finance and home ownership . . . 47
3.2. Is residential real estate becoming a financialized asset? 49
   3.2.1. Geographical approaches to the financialization of real estate 49
   3.2.2. Property and inflationary mechanisms 50
   3.2.3. Asset-based welfare 53
3.3. Geographical analysis of property market regimes 54
   3.3.1. The value of property in space, renewal of a critical analysis 54
   3.3.2. The limits of classical approaches to prices in the city 55
   3.3.3. Market regimes 57
3.4. Property and socio-spatial segregation 60
   3.4.1. The role of credit and intermediation in inequality and segregation . . . 60
   3.4.2. The new market mechanisms, a strengthening of the relationship
between property and inequality 62
   3.4.3. Sharing ownership 63
3.5. Conclusion 65
3.6. References 65

Chapter 4. Logistics Urbanization, Between Real Estate Financialization and the Rise of Logistics Urban Planning 73
Nicolas RAIMBAULT and Adeline HEITZ

4.1. Introduction 73
4.2. Logistics development in the outer-suburbs: a dynamic of sprawl
and financialization of logistics real estate 75
   4.2.1. An increase in the number of warehouses to supply major cities 76
   4.2.2. The logistics sprawl of metropolitan areas on a global scale 78
   4.2.3. Financialized production of outer-suburban logistics zones 82

4.2.4. The challenges of regulating the diffuse urbanization of economic
activities 85
4.3. Logistics development in urban centers: urban logistics 85
    4.3.1. The rise of logistics real estate in urban centers: urban logistics
    facilities. 86
    4.3.2. Towards a logistics urban planning 89
    4.3.3. The rise of a logistics real estate market in urban centers 92
4.4. Logistics spaces in the inner suburbs: the case of intermediate logistics
as a blind spot in logistics urban planning 93
    4.4.1. Permanence and mutations of intermediate logistics activities in
    the suburbs 94
    4.4.2. Intermediate logistics, a blind spot in public policy 96
4.5. Conclusion 97
4.6. References 98

Chapter 5. The City–Port Relationship in the Metropolitan Fabric 105
Jean DEBRIE

5.1. The shift in city-port relations and the reconfiguration of intra-urban
scales. 105
5.2. The levels of the port metropolis 106
    5.2.1. The terminalization movement 106
    5.2.2. The docklandization movement 109
5.3. The city–port interfaces, support for major urban projects. 111
    5.3.1. Standardization versus differentiation (forms/functions) 111
5.4. Who governs the port metropolis? 117
5.5. Conclusion: "Creating the city with the port?" The agenda of the
port metropolis 118
5.6. References 120

**Part 2. Regional Dynamics of Capital Accumulation in East Asian,
Middle Eastern and West African Real Estate Markets** 125

**Chapter 6. Land Value Capture and Its Large-Scale Application in
Northeast Asia** 127
Natacha AVELINE-DUBACH

6.1. Introduction 127
6.2. Origins and contemporary forms of LVC 130
    6.2.1. Circulation of LVC models between the West and the East. 130
    6.2.2. Contemporary approaches to LVC 133
6.3. LVC strategies in East Asia. 137
    6.3.1. Flexible and consensual LVC practice in Japan 137
    6.3.2. An LVC regime based on land concessions in Hong Kong 142
    6.3.3. Optimization of the LVC by local governments in China 145

6.4. Conclusion 149
6.5. References 151

Chapter 7. The Dual Regionalization of Real Estate Financialization in Southeast Asia 155
Gabriel FAUVEAUD

7.1. Introduction 155
7.2. The oligopolistic preconditions for the organization of real estate markets in Southeast Asia 156
7.3. A privatization of land tenure. 159
7.4. Regionalization and internationalization of real estate development 161
7.5. Towards a rescaling of real estate production and urban governance 163
7.6. Financialization of the regional real estate market 166
7.7. China and the new geopolitics of real estate in Southeast Asia 169
7.8. Conclusion 172
7.9. References 173

Chapter 8. Real Estate in the Middle East: An Economy Shaped by Rents 177
Myriam ABABSA

8.1. Introduction 177
8.2. The financialization of economies and real estate in the Middle East. 180
   8.2.1. Arab metropolises as engines of economic development 181
   8.2.2. Half of foreign investments are in real estate in the Middle East 182
   8.2.3. Capital invested in real estate and Arab real estate investment trust . . 187
   8.2.4. Households' indebtedness for mortgages in the Middle East 189
   8.2.5. The legalization of informal settlements through the titling of "dead capital". 191
8.3. Egypt and Jordan: the squandering of public land and the construction of new cities. 192
   8.3.1. The new cities of Cairo. 192
   8.3.2. The Abdali project, Amman 195
   8.3.3. Rental renewals and their current outcomes in Cairo and Amman 196
8.4. Saudi Arabia: tax innovation to finance housing 198
8.5. Lebanon and Syria: reconstruction policies as a means of consolidating elites 200
   8.5.1. Lebanon, land of investor exemptions and subsidies 200
   8.5.2. Syria confiscates refugees' property and deploys a policy of territorial revenge 204
8.6. Conclusion 208
8.7. References 209

Chapter 9. Building Cities in West Africa: Construction Boom and Capitalism 213
Armelle CHOPLIN

    9.1. Construction boom and cement industry. 216
    9.2. City-making: actors and sectors 218
    9.3. Concrete, towers and megaprojects 220
    9.4. "Social" housing programs 224
    9.5. Self-build and incremental urbanization 227
    9.6. Conclusion 228
    9.7. References 229

Conclusion 235
Olivier CREVOISIER and Natacha AVELINE-DUBACH

    C.1. The emergence of the international dimension of real estate 236
    C.2. Real estate, a highly sought-after asset 237
    C.3. The diversity of capital accumulation dynamics in real estate 237
    C.4. From sectorial and induced real estate to the integrated and driving production of urban construction 239
    C.5. The financialized urban construct as a concrete scene of the global city . . . 240
    C.6. Social consequences and the need for rethinking public policies . . . . `240
    C.7. References 241

List of Authors 243

Index 245

Introduction

The Accumulation of Capital in the Urban Fabric

Natacha AVELINE-DUBACH[1,2]
[1] *UMR Géographie-cités, CNRS, Aubervilliers, France*
[2] *CNRS@CREATE, Singapore*

The past three decades have seen a phenomenal increase in real estate values in several regions of the world. This began with a remarkable convergence of residential booms during the 1990s in the countries of the Organization for Economic Co-operation and Development (OECD), with the exception of Germany and Japan (Aalbers 2016). The outbreak of the global financial crisis in 2007–2008 seemed to mark the end of this wave of speculative euphoria. Yet, despite the dramatic economic and social cost of the financial crash, real estate markets quickly returned to growth. While some countries suffered the shock of a severe crisis (Ireland, Spain and the Baltic States), the upward momentum resumed in Europe (Tutin 2014) and North America (Lambie-Hanson et al. 2019). Even the Covid-19 pandemic, which harmed economies and reduced employment levels – and whose effects continue to this day – was unable to adversely affect the extraordinarily resilient real estate markets. The result is a growing disconnect between real estate prices and the financial capacity of economic actors, primarily households, to occupy built-up space in major metropolitan areas. According to the International Monetary Fund (IMF's) Global House Price Index, house prices worldwide rose by an average of almost 70% between 2000 and 2020, without the Covid-19 pandemic

Globalization and Dynamics of Urban Production,
coordinated by Natacha AVELINE-DUBACH. © ISTE Ltd 2023.

having significantly affected prices at the time of writing[1]. In many metropolises, the middle classes are having to give up on any plans for home ownership, while rents are absorbing a growing share of their income (Christophers 2021).

This disjunction between real estate prices and the financial capacity of economic agents, which is widespread on several continents, is not new. A first wave of synchronous real estate cycles swept the planet in the 1980s, leading to financial crises everywhere and ending in a long depression in Japan (Renaud 1997; Aveline 2004). The theory of the "speculative bubble" was then used to interpret these episodes of exuberant rise in asset prices[2] (initially financial, then by extension in land and real estate). This theory, which became very fashionable in the 1990s and was widely reported in the media during the global subprime mortgage crisis, is based on the assumption that assets have an intrinsic or "fundamental" value, reflecting local economic performance. In the case of real estate, this value is most often calculated using macroeconomic and demographic variables (municipal/regional GDP, household income, population growth, etc.) or financial parameters (expected future rental flows, interest rates) (Aveline-Dubach 2019). By comparing these estimated values with the actual values of transactions recorded on the market, we obtain the size of the bubble, i.e. the purely speculative part of the price structure. In principle, this anomaly cannot last for long, since markets should theoretically return to equilibrium. Hence, the bubble hypothesis can only be validated after endogenous or exogenous market "restoring forces" have removed the speculative mechanism.

From the outset, heterodox economists challenged the idea that assets have an intrinsic value, transcending the institutional nature of markets and the logic of actors (inter alia Stiglitz 1990; Orléan 1999, 2011). However, the brutality of the decline phases of real estate cycles had lent credence to the idea of a return to an equilibrium and conferred a heuristic significance to the bubble theory. This is no longer the case today; the bubble hypothesis does not explain the surprising resilience of real estate in the face of a sustained price disconnection, even if some have dared to use the oxymoron of "robust bubble" (Timbeau 2013). Moreover, this theory has recently come under fire from urban and housing scholars (geographers, sociologists and political scientists), who consider that it too conveniently masks the responsibility of public action.

---

1. See: https://www.imf.org/external/research/housing/images/globalhousepriceindex_lg.png [Accessed January 18, 2022].
2. An asset is an investment medium. It is a security, property or anything that can be bought, held and then sold to earn a return or gain value. Its main characteristics are profitability, risk and liquidity.

Several authors in this field had already highlighted the effects of the deregulation of financial markets, mortgage credit and neoliberal urban policies[3] in the formation of real estate cycles (see the pioneering work of Harvey (1985), Aalbers (2008) and Corpataux et al. (2009)). However, the growing driving role of the real estate and mortgage credit markets in the growth dynamics of national economies has more recently led some authors to accuse the public authorities of having constructed a "particular logic of asset inflation" (Adkins et al. 2021, p. 553). Ryan-Collins (2021) emphasizes the major responsibility of central banks in this respect, because while they are mandated to regulate consumer price inflation, they are not committed to controlling asset price inflation. He adds that the quantitative easing policies carried out by central banks to boost growth in Japan, the United States and Europe have only increased tension in asset markets by encouraging massive capital allocation.

How did we get here? This book will provide answers by reporting on the tremendous rise in real estate investment around the world, a phenomenon largely underpinned by the geographic and sectoral expansion of market finance.

To understand how these complex connections between capital (financial or banking) and real estate are established, it is necessary to examine their anchoring in the material setting of the city, or what is commonly called the "urban built environment"[4]. The contributions in this book therefore approach these changes from a multiscale perspective, paying particular attention to the methods of financing and operational implementation of real estate production on a metropolitan scale. Based on a body of empirical work, they show how, largely under the impetus of the central and local state, the growing and multifaceted influences of the logics and practices of market finance in several property subsectors (residential, logistics, port) are taking shape. These developments increase the dependence of a growing number of economic actors on inflated property values, a process that ostensibly contributes to the exacerbation of social inequalities.

However, the institutional construction of asset inflation is not based exclusively on the financialization of urban production and household real estate debt.

---

3. This term has become generic in the work of critical geography on the city. It describes the entrepreneurial strategies pursued by local governments to develop the attractiveness of their territory in the context of increased competition, accompanied by spatial planning policies that accommodate the private sector. Its relevance as a category of analysis is nevertheless debated and its application to the French case has been discussed by several authors (inter alia Morange and Fol 2014; Pinson and Journel 2017).
4. As defined by Beauregard (1994), the built environment includes all buildings, structures and landforms that have been created for human use and satisfaction.

Moreover, the process of financialization is far from being generalized, even if the expansion of financial circuits is taking place on a global scale. The focus of the international literature on the major Western economies, particularly the Anglo-American ones, tends to obscure the great diversity of urban contexts and the political and institutional arrangements that condition the accumulation of capital in the built environment.

Thus, in Northeast Asia, it is not financialization which has propelled real estate prices to global upper limits, but rather large-scale land value capture strategies pursued by local governments or private actors to provide urban infrastructure. On the contrary, some regions are still only moderately targeted by market finance. This is the case in Sub-Saharan Africa, which has been immune to the financial wave until now, but which is now its last frontier.

In order to analyze these multiple forms of capital accumulation in the urban fabric, we have structured this book into two parts. The first part presents a series of contributions which deals with the way in which finance has come to occupy a central place in the processes of urban production in North America and Europe, subjecting the built environment of major cities to the imperatives and movements of global finance market players and exposing finance in turn to the cycles of real estate production. This evolution is related to the rise of the proprietary ideology and situated in the context of sectoral reconfigurations within a globalized economy.

The second part moves away from the major Western countries, which are the original foci of both the financial industry and the conceptual frameworks of urban issues. It briefly outlines the distinctive, but rather convergent regional dynamics of capital accumulation in the metropolitan areas of four major sub-continents: Northeast Asia (Japan, China and Hong Kong), Southeast Asia (Indonesia, the Philippines, Thailand, Cambodia and Vietnam), the Middle East (Egypt, Saudi Arabia, Jordan, Syria and Lebanon) and West Africa (the urban corridor connecting the cities of Abidjan, Accra, Lom, Cotonou, Porto-Novo and Lagos).

I.1. Market finance's stranglehold on the city

The book begins with an analytical framework proposed by Thierry Theurillat to explain, using a territorial approach, how the financial industry has made the built environment a driving force in the growth of contemporary capitalisms by creating "a continuum linking land, urban construction, planning and urban governance policies and market finance" aimed at exploiting urban rent. According to this analysis, the creation of rent takes place in the major metropolises of industrialized countries, especially the financial capitals (the "global cities"), which concentrate the leading functions of the economy and to which local and regional investment systems are centralized. Urban rent is then extracted through the securitization of urban objects, real estate debts and, more recently, municipal debts, all of which are a vehicle for a growing number of global investment circuits seeking to satisfy exclusive criteria of return and risk. The value of these investment vehicles depends on the collective opinions of financial market participants and can deviate considerably from that of the underlying real estate objects. These deterritorialization mechanisms facilitate the mobility and liquidity of capital. The financial industry massively exploits this to invest the ever-increasing savings of the aging populations of industrialized countries, companies and governments, and also to divert liquid assets injected into economies by central banks towards jobs deemed more profitable. The real estate industry plays a pivotal role in the urban anchoring of this capital, especially property developers who act as negotiators with local actors.

In this context, the developer's functions are being transformed. Julie Pollard reports on the empirical variety of figures of this urban operator and emphasizes its eminently relational role at the interface of a dense network of actors who intervene in the different phases of the real estate project. The developer's role as a mediator in the local anchoring of financial capital leads it to internalize the requirements and criteria of investors, thus facilitating the alignment of spatial planning rules with the interests of the financial industry. By diversifying their resources through this access to finance capital, developers are led to carry out organizational restructuring of varying intensities, depending on the country and the sector, and to engage in large-scale urban projects. Faced with the growing importance of environmental standards and policies, they are navigating between a strategy of adaptation under constraint and negotiation–resistance. Some of them are developing differentiation strategies using sustainable development labels and certifications, the strong marketing dimension of which can sometimes amount to *greenwashing*. However, not all of these players are focused on maximizing profit. Julie Pollard mentions the emergence of developers who are genuinely committed to a social objective and ready to reduce their profit margins. Others, who are more conventional, are sometimes forced to do so by local housing policies or make the choice to increase their "symbolic capital" (corporate image) by occasionally delivering affordable projects.

The magnitude of the disconnection between housing prices and household incomes in metropolitan markets cannot leave territorial actors indifferent. Renaud Le Goix sheds light on some of the drivers of this disconnection. He highlights the widely held interpretation of rising prices as being the exclusive result of a shortage of residential supply. This diagnosis is based on the frame of reference of market equilibrium, without consideration for other factors, encouraging public authorities to liberalize urban planning and construction rules ever more. Such supply-side measures not only do not re-establish "market equilibrium" but tend, on the contrary, to reinforce speculative expectations and, consequently, to support the rise in prices. In fact, the large-scale expansion of real estate or mortgage credit has been a powerful inflationary factor for residential values. The rapid proliferation in household debt has been stimulated by government measures to promote home ownership (public subsidies and tax incentives), as well as by wider access to credit (low rates, extanded debt maturity) as house prices have soared. Le Goix points to the link between the expansion of the proprietary ideology promoted by the state and the dismantling of social welfare in industrialized countries. Households are encouraged to accumulate capital in real estate assets to compensate for the erosion of the welfare state (a process known as "asset-based welfare"). This results in greater social inequalities, as households not only have socially stratified access to credit, but also derive very unequal benefits from their properties depending on their nature and location.

In addition to the residential and tertiary activities traditionally targeted by finance (offices, retail), the latter is also taking over the built spaces of productive sectors that are subject to a profound reshaping of global value chains. This is the case of the logistics sector, whose recent changes are discussed by Nicolas Raimbault and Adeline Heitz. The explosion of e-commerce, recently reinforced by the Covid-19 pandemic, has led to an intense production of logistics buildings in major cities. While the routing of products requires an organization of flows on three different scales within urban areas, the bulk of logistic built-up space in the suburbs is constructed in the form of gigantic warehouses that serve as "parcel factories". This category of property is now largely owned by international firms specializing in logistics asset management, which tend to control the entire real estate value chain from the development of the logistics zone to the rental management of warehouses. Many local authorities are interested in such initiatives since it allows them to carry out their economic development at low cost, but Nicolas Raimbault and Adeline Heitz point out a series of undesirable effects: selection of companies to be located by the real estate industry, extensive soil artificialization, increase in greenhouse gas emissions and longer commuting time of employees.

The organization of freight flows also depends on the points where territories are connected to international trade, as is the case with ports that occupy vast tracts of land in coastal and river cities. Like the operators of mass transit systems and airport infrastructures (Maulat and Pedro Forthcoming), port authorities have become active managers of their land holdings, making increasing use of financial techniques and standards. Jean Debrie addresses the spatio-temporal fragmentation of port land holdings following the dislocation of the city–port relationship. Relying on a diversity of case studies, Debrie shows that the "terminalization" of ports (relocation of port activities away from urban cores) has enabled the real estate development of urban harbor fronts, transforming them into central places bearing new forms of urbanity. By working on the systematic requalification or "docklandization" of these brownfields, port infrastructure managers have become key actors in urban redevelopment. Like their railway counterparts, they are now the major providers of urban land through which the accumulation of capital in real estate is taking place with varying degrees of intensity depending on local political and economic arrangements.

I.2. Diversity of modes of capital accumulation in real estate

While the United States and then Europe were the initial centers of financialization of urban production, Asia has become the major growth pole. However, the diversity of capitalisms and the different stages of development in the region are an obstacle to the ubiquitous penetration of finance. China has refused to connect its real estate markets to global investment channels, preferring to develop its own investment vehicles so as not to weaken the state's capacity for regulatory action (Aveline-Dubach 2019; Theurillat 2022; Wu 2021). On the contrary, India is considered unsafe and difficult to connect to global financial circuits (Halbert and Rouanet 2014). In fact, only Japan and Singapore have a level of financialization of real estate comparable to that of the major Western economies (Haila 2015; Aveline-Dubach 2020).

However, Japan shares with China and Hong Kong an experience of massive capital accumulation in real estate that has materialized in strong residential price inflation. Natacha Aveline-Dubach attributes this to strategies of meta-capture of land value (*macro-value capture*) common to these countries/regions. Unlike the logic of urban rent extraction for the sole benefit of financial investors mentioned by Theurillat, the strategy of land value capture (LVC) practiced in this region, of which macro-value capture is an extreme form, aims to recoup from the beneficiaries (predominantly the landowners) all or part of the value (the urban rent) generated by the construction of infrastructure or public facilities via real estate projects. This provides a strong incentive to multiply property development projects by attracting the savings of economic actors, primarily households, through housing investment. These practices are underpinned by the so-called "developmental state" approach, a common feature of the countries in the region (White 1988), whereby the state concentrates its financial efforts on industrial development while making property development a major pillar of its growth model. Macro-value capture was well suited to growing cities, but it has generated an over-accumulation of national savings in the built environment – notably in the form of a dangerous residential vacancy – that risks weighing heavily on economies subject to rapid ageing processes.

Neighboring countries in Southeast Asia are also experiencing intense capital accumulation in real estate, albeit within different configurations of state–economy relations. Gabriel Fauveaud identifies common characteristics in the dynamics of real estate investment in the region, beyond the conventional dichotomy between "crony capitalisms" and planned economies in transition. Fauveaud explains this relative convergence by a double regionalization of real estate investment, first intra-Asia and then intra-Southeast Asia. In this region, where land ownership used to be largely in the public domain, the World Bank played a leading role in implementing reforms to commodify land and formalize property rights. These transnational investment initiatives have also fostered the emergence of national real estate conglomerates, sometimes in an oligopolistic situation due to collusion between political and economic elites. Large developers are playing a pivotal role in the growing entrenchment of market finance in the region's urban megaprojects, where condominiums for a wealthy regional customer base are driving up prices in the residential markets. The financial centers of Hong Kong and Singapore, in particular, are hubs for such real estate investments. Singapore is also notable for the "export" of its urban model and its significant investment of sovereign wealth in regional real estate. Fauveaud points to China's recent rise in power since the launch of the Belt and Road Initiative, with multiform investments from Chinese companies and households contributing to the rise in property prices.

In the Middle East, we find certain features similar to those of Southeast Asia, as shown in Myriam Ababsa's contribution. To explain this, we can cite the generalized movement of commodification of large public land holdings driven by international donors (IMF and World Bank), the privatization of urban production and spatial planning resulting from symbiotic relationships between governments and real estate players, and the contribution of regional sovereign wealth funds to the financing of urban megaprojects. However, Ababsa highlights a more advanced process of financialization in this region. The four major regional sovereign wealth funds (from the UAE, Kuwait and Saudi Arabia) and the private equity funds owned by ruling family clans are pursuing the same objective of extracting urban rent by taking advantage of the low prices of public land and the state's infrastructure investment in new cities and other flagship projects. Here, it is not real estate returns that are targeted (a large part of the buildings being vacant), but the prospects of capital gain on land whose holding has a cost close to zero. The middle classes are excluded from these projects, and more modest households are being massively evicted from the formal private rental sector by the deregulation of below-market lease contracts.

West Africa is still little coveted by financial investors, but Armelle Choplin reveals, as in the Middle East, upstream strategies for positioning foreign investors on land intended for large urban projects. These projects are located in the centers of major cities along the urban corridor of more than 1,000 km linking Abidjan to Lagos, and are highly publicized and reserved for local elites and members of African diasporas. However, they are not yet developed, or are even still in the pipeline. Financial investors benefit from advantageous conditions for land acquisitions or long-term leases because governments, which aim at a "Dubaization" of their capital, manage to expropriate the informal occupants at low cost. The allegedly "affordable" housing promoted by the World Bank is also being targeted by foreign actors, some of whom are considering making it investable by global financial players through the establishment of future investment channels. However, a large part of housing construction is carried out by the households themselves, operating in an incremental way according to their financial capacities on the outskirts of cities. Armelle Choplin describes in detail these self-construction processes that make the concrete block the major resource, the "poor man's lingot". Savings are certainly placed first in the land, but it is the concrete that gives value to the house. This is not only because it makes the home less vulnerable to rain and eviction, but also because it gives its owner a "right to the city". These self-construction processes that capitalize on the building material, contrary to any financial logic, invite us to rethink the definition of value to better take into account the well-being of the *homo urbanus*.

I.3. What are the consequences for contemporary capitalisms?

In this book's conclusion, Olivier Crevoisier and Natacha Aveline-Dubach note the rising prominence of real estate in the growth dynamics of contemporary capitalisms, echoing Aalbers' (2017) hypothesis that a new regime of capital accumulation of 'financial-real estate' is emerging. They situate its origin in the bursting of the 'dot-com bubble' of the years 2000-2002, following which real estate imposed itself as a strategic asset to restore investors' confidence in the face of the stock market crash. Crevoisier and Aveline-Dubach highlight the role of the ageing population and the erosion of social protection in increasing demand for real estate investment. This transition to a new mode of accumulation is marked by a shift from *commodities* to *subscription fees*: those who wish to take advantage of the opportunities and resources offered by the city, especially the "Global City", must pay fees in the form of overpriced real estate or rents, as is the case for digital platforms. This goes hand in hand with a reversal of the logic of real estate investment, which no longer simply anticipates the need generated by economic growth but seeks to induce it by providing an urban infrastructure for targeted activities and populations. States bear a heavy responsibility for this dangerous development, and it is up to them to implement adequate policies to foster the creation of more inclusive physical and social environments.

I.4. References

Aalbers, M.B. (2008). The financialization of home and the mortgage market crisis. *Competition & Change*, 12(2), 148–166.

Aalbers, M.B. (2016). *The Financialization of Housing: A Political Economy Approach*. Routledge, London.

Adkins, L., Cooper, M., Konings, M. (2021). Class in the 21st century: Asset inflation and the new logic of inequality. *Environment and Planning A: Economy and Space*, 53(3), 548–572.

Aveline, N. (2004). Property markets in Tokyo and the management of the last boom-bust cycle. In *Property Markets and Land Policies in Northeast Asia: The Case of Five Cities: Tokyo, Seoul, Shanghai, Taipei and Hong Kong*, Aveline, N. and Li, L.-H. (eds). Maison Franco-Japonaise/Center for Real Estate and Urban Economics HKU, Hong Kong.

Aveline-Dubach, N. (2019). China's housing booms: A challenge to bubble theory. In *Theories and Models of Urbanization*, Batty, M. and Pumain, D. (eds). Springer, Cham.

Aveline-Dubach, N. (2020). The financialization of real estate in megacities and its variegated trajectories in East Asia. In *Handbook of Megacities and Megacity-Regions*, Sorensen, A. and Labbé, D. (eds). Edward Elgar Publishing, Cheltenham.

Beauregard, R.A. (1994). Capital switching and the built environment: United States, 1970–89. *Environment and Planning A*, 26(5), 715–732.

Christophers, B. (2021). A tale of two inequalities: Housing-wealth inequality and tenure inequality. *Environment and Planning A: Economy and Space*, 53(3), 573–594.

Corpataux, J., Crevoisier, O., Theurillat, T. (2009). The expansion of the finance industry and its impact on the economy: A territorial approach based on Swiss pension funds. *Economic Geography*, 85(3), 313–334.

Haila, A. (2015). *Urban Land Rent: Singapore as a Property State*. Wiley-Blackwell, Hoboken.

Halbert, L. and Rouanet, H. (2014). Filtering risk away: Global finance capital, transcalar territorial networks and the (un) making of city-regions: An analysis of business property development in Bangalore, India. *Regional Studies*, 48(3), 471–484.

Harvey, D. (1985). *The Urbanization of Capital*. Basil Blackwell, Oxford.

Konings, M., Adkins, L., Rogers, D. (2021). The institutional logic of property inflation. *Environment and Planning A: Economy and Space*, 53(3), 448–456.

Kuznets, P.W. (1988). An East Asian model of economic development: Japan, Taiwan, and South Korea. *Economic Development and Cultural Change*, 36(3), 11–43.

Lambie-Hanson, L., Li, W., Slonkosky, M. (2019). Institutional investors and the US housing recovery. Working paper, Federal Reserve Bank of Philadelphia, WP 19-45. DOI: 10.21799/frbp.wp.2019.45.

Maulat, J. and Pedro, M. (Forthcoming). De nœud de réseau à actif immobilier : l'évolution des modèles économiques des lieux de transport. In *Les transports et leurs lieux*, Frétigny, J.-B. (ed.). ISTE Éditions, London.

Orléan, A. (1999). *Le pouvoir de la finance*. Odile Jacob, Neuilly-sur-Seine.

Orléan, A. (2011). *L'empire de la valeur, refonder l'économie*. Le Seuil, Paris.

Pinson, G. and Journel, C.M. (2017). *Debating the Neoliberal City*. Taylor & Francis, London.

Renaud, B. (1997). The 1985 to 1994 global real estate cycle: An overview. *Journal of Real Estate Literature*, 5(1), 13–44.

Ryan-Collins, J. (2021). Breaking the housing–finance cycle: Macroeconomic policy reforms for more affordable homes. *Environment and Planning A: Economy and Space*, 53(3), 480–502.

Stiglitz, J.E. (1990). Symposium on bubbles. *Journal of Economic Perspectives*, 4(2), 13–18.

Theurillat, T. (2022). Urban growth, from manufacturing to consumption and financialization: The case of China's contemporary urban development. *Regional Studies*, 56(8), 1–15.

Timbeau, X. (2013). Les bulles "robustes". *Revue de l'OFCE*, 2, 277–313.

Tutin, C. (2014). Statuts d'occupation, endettement des ménages et exubérance des marchés du logement. In *Colloque Annuel ASRDLF 2014*.

White, G. (1988). *Developmental States in East Asia*. Springer, Cham.

Wu, F. (2021). The long shadow of the state: Financializing the Chinese city. *Urban Geography*, 0(0), 1–22.

PART 1

Sectoral Reconfigurations of Property Markets and Urban (Re)Development

1

The Financialized City and the Extraction of Urban Rent

Thierry THEURILLAT
Institut du Management des Villes et du Territoire (IMVT),
Haute École de Gestion-Arc (HES-SO), Neuchâtel, Switzerland

How can we explain the central role of real estate and, more broadly, of the urban built environment in today's economy? Research on the *financialization of urban production* has highlighted the ever-stronger interconnections between the urban landscape and financial markets. This phenomenon explains, in particular, surging urbanization and the rise in land and property prices observed on a global scale since at least the beginning of the 2000s.

The crisis of American mortgage debts (subprimes) sold on the financial markets was undeniably a trigger for society's realization about the hold of market finance on economies. Over the last 10 years, it has led the research community to extend and renew the debates of the 1990s (Haila 1988; Beauregard 1994; Coakley 1994; Charney 2001), which were influenced by David Harvey's theories and concepts of "the tendency to treat land as a financial asset by landowners" (1982, p. 347) and "urbanization of capital and capital switching" (1978, 1985).

The field of literature that we describe as the *financialization of urban production* brings together researchers in urban geography and, more broadly, in urban studies. Despite the diversity of theoretical approaches, whether neo-Marxian,

---

For a color version of all the figures in this chapter, see www.iste.co.uk/avelinedubach/globalization.zip.

institutionalist, relationalist or cultural, this heuristic field shares a certain number of common points and foundations relating to definitions, conceptualizations and questioning as well as analytical and methodological approaches. The main heuristic objective is to analyze the functioning of market finance outside of the trading room and to take into account the way it is implemented in territories (Corpataux and Crevoisier 2016).

Manuel Aalbers' (2016, p. 2) definition of financialization is now a reference. This states: "the growing domination of actors, markets, practices, calculations and discourses, at various scales, causing a structural transformation of economies, firms (including financial institutions), states and households". The research community on the financialization of urban production has been concerned with measuring the phenomenon of financialization as a globalizing process affecting the transformation of the urban built environment and with understanding its concrete implications, from the perspective of both processes and outcomes, according to territorial contexts (Halbert and Attuyer 2016).

This results in variations and degrees of financialization depending on the more or less liberalized contexts of urban policies and financial systems. At the same time, researchers have highlighted the need to understand the financialization of the urban built environment as a second circuit of capital[1] as a continuum linking land, real estate and infrastructure, urban planning and governance policies and market finance at once.

This chapter presents a territorial approach to the financialization of urban production by highlighting both the ways in which *market finance creates and extracts urban rent*. Urban rent is defined here in a simple way as income from the ownership of a "land asset". However, our territorial reading of rent is based on the distinction and interdependent interactions between financial and real markets. The first part presents the modalities of deterritorialization and transformation of the urban built environment into liquid financial products through direct connections with financial markets enabled by securitization. The creation of financial value for the

---

1. In David Harvey's approach, the urban built environment, i.e. the infrastructure necessary for economic production (factories, roads, etc.) and consumption (houses, stores, etc.) constitutes the second of the three circuits of capital accumulation and circulation. The urbanization of capital is seen as a shift from the primary circuit of production to that of ownership in order to overcome the over-accumulation inherent in the dynamics of capitalism, i.e. the search for profits in a competitive environment between capitalist firms. As for the third circuit, it is composed of the technological sector (science and innovation) and the social sector, which serve the reproduction of capital. The financial system plays a major role in circulating surplus capital.

holders of financial securities linked to the urban built environment depends then on the collective and self-fulfilling opinions of participants in financial markets and can be totally amplified compared to the value of real estate objects in the real markets. The second part reveals the way in which financialized logic is applied in real markets of the urban built environment and the role of various intermediary actors of the territorialized chain and the impacts of market finance on urban production.

1.1. Institutionalization of direct connections between the urban built environment and financial markets

First of all, financialization means the ever stronger connection of the urban built environment to market finance (see Figure 1.1). It is disrupting the "traditional" local and regional real estate investment system by modifying the flows of financing and the types of owners by connecting them to a globalized system organized centrally by the financial metropolises. It is in this context that the urban structure has become a central element of financialized accumulation over the last 20 years. Varying from country to country, the types of connection to market finance are based on three main characteristics that make it possible to deterritorialize the urban built environment: securitization, insertion into global investment circuits and control of the financialized space of value creation and extraction by the Global City.

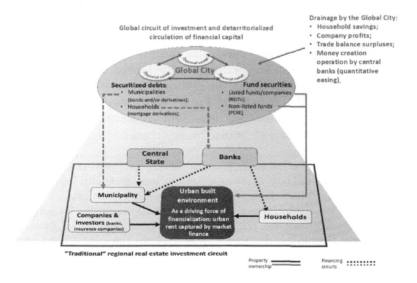

Figure 1.1. *The connections of the urban built environment to market finance (source: Own development)*

1.1.1. *Securitization as a connector from the urban built environment to market finance*

The first characteristic of financialization refers to establishing direct connections between the urban built environment and financial markets through securitization, i.e. the creation of securities (paper securities) sold as financial products to different types of investors (institutional investors such as pension funds or investment funds, or private individuals, for example) on the financial markets. The connection of the urban structure to market finance via securitization thus makes it possible to extract urban rent almost instantaneously on the financial markets. Two forms of financialized extraction of urban rent can be distinguished.

First of all, the extraction of urban rent by financiers can relate directly to urban property. This has long attracted "classic" investors such as banks, insurance companies and pension funds (Harvey 1985; Fainstein 2001). More recently, however, we have seen the appearance of new investors and the scale of their direct investments in urban property (see Figure 1.2)[2]. The dissociation between property ownership and use, encouraged by tax incentives in various countries, has led to the emergence of the rental market for commercial property (offices, shops) and the securitization of urban property on financial markets. To varying extents depending on the country, the buildings of many service sector companies have been outsourced and sold to various real estate investment vehicles. Firstly, the latter consist mainly of real estate funds and real estate investment trusts (REITs), which are listed on the stock exchange and open to all types of investors (individuals and institutions). Secondly, private equity real estate funds (PEREs), which are not listed on the stock exchange and are intended for a limited number of investors (institutional and wealthy individuals), are also typical examples of the real estate financial industry. By taking over the real estate portfolios of large companies or traditional investors, most of these new investment vehicles have very close ties to them as they may be affiliated with, or used by, large banks.

> The development of the real estate financial industry goes hand in hand with new management techniques and investment strategies. The more traditional logic (known as the passive management) of real estate investment to protect against inflation has given way to a logic of active management. Dynamic calculation methods (discounted cash flow) have been widely adopted. They make it possible to create a real estate value according to future yield projections. Their more or less long-term values (long-term rents

---

2. Urban ownership by financiers has become a major phenomenon that extends to a growing number of urban objects such as multi-functional real estate complexes and mega-projects, large urban development projects and infrastructure. See Aalbers (2019) for an overview of financialized urban objects.

> or capital gains on disposal) are thus discounted according to market segments (corporate real estate, residential real estate; regional markets) and types of risk (according to the gradient "low-risk or core" to "high-risk or opportunistic").
>
> In this context, the active management logic consists of adopting a diversification strategy by constantly recomposing its real estate portfolio according to the evolution of the markets. Strategically, REITs are positioned more on investments based on rents and expected capital gains upon resale in the long term. Consequently, existing properties or properties under development where the return is assured (so-called "core" properties with existing tenants) are their preferred target. As for private funds (PEREs), which are generally set up for a limited period of time (3–6 or even 10 years), they are positioned more on yields and short-term value growth and focus on the rehabilitation and development of real estate projects (so-called value-added or opportunistic properties).

Box 1.1. *Market finance and active investment logic*

Secondly, the extraction of urban rent by market finance is based on debt. Subprime products are well-known examples of the securitization of mortgage debt. These products have their origins in the policies of facilitating access to private property for households implemented in different countries, especially since the 1990s (Aalbers and Christophers 2014; Fernandez and Aalbers 2016). Private property has rapidly become the main source of household wealth, changing in the process its traditional value for investment (property rent). At the same time, private household property has become a very important investment outlet and money creation medium (via mortgage debt)[3] for banks. However, and this is where financialization comes in, private property policies have been directly financed by the financial markets in some countries (the United States and the United Kingdom are the leading examples). In this context, the manufacture of subprime products was based on two main elements. On the one hand, banks used investment vehicles to move mortgages allocated to households off their balance sheets. Then, the mortgages were transformed into sophisticated financial securities and purchased en masse by institutional investors (pension funds, insurance funds and mutual funds) on a global scale. As a result, due to the rise in prices of mortgage debt derivatives (subprime) in the financial markets, banks have been pushed to issue more and more mortgage debt derivatives while outsourcing risk to the financial markets. The more

---

3. According to the institutionalist view of money, commercial banks have the capacity to create scriptural/fiduciary money independently of savers' deposits. Therefore, from an institutionalist perspective, it is the credits that make the deposits and not the other way around as advanced by the neoclassical view of money. Bank credits are based on visions of the future (projects, enterprises, etc.) and thus make it possible to open economic circuits upstream of future activities.

recent creation of other derivatives backed by collateral that is ever more distant from urban objects (e.g. taxes from urban development) also falls under the same logic of a direct connection to financial markets and the city's grip on the financing of urban production (Weber 2015).

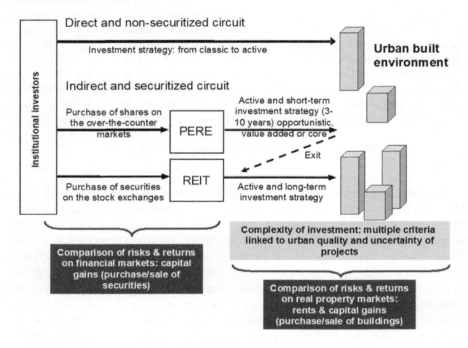

Figure 1.2. *The investment logic of specialized funds, REITs and PEREs (source: Based on Theurillat and Crevoisier (2013) and Aveline-Dubach (2016))*

1.1.2. *The consolidation of the driving role of the urban built environment thanks to connections to global investment circuits*

The second characteristic of financialization is that it has reinforced the driving role of the urban construct in the dynamics of contemporary capitalism and urban growth (Aalbers and Christophers 2014). First, policies of liberalization and open borders have not only facilitated the circulation of financial capital, but also accelerated the massive drainage of investment into financial markets over the past 20 years (Theurillat et al. 2010). Different investment channels have formed into a veritable "money wall" on a global scale (Fernandez and Aalbers 2016) in search of investment opportunities. This money wall has various components. Firstly, it is based on the growing old-age savings mainly in developed countries. The drainage of these household savings into the financial markets has been institutionalized by the establishment of funded pension systems, via the development of institutional investors such as pension funds (e.g. in the United States, Great Britain, Canada, the Netherlands and Switzerland) or by the development of mutual investment funds as complements to pay-as-you-go pension systems (e.g. in Germany, France and Italy, where pension funding comes directly from employees). At the same time, sovereign wealth funds have been set up (e.g. China, Norway, Saudi Arabia, Russia) to manage commercial surpluses or surpluses from raw materials (oil, gas). Finally, the money wall has been completed by massive monetary injections (*Quantitative Easing*) into the economy by central banks, via commercial banks or interventions of security purchases on financial markets, following the various financial and economic crises that have caused the mass of liquid assets to skyrocket.

Secondly, in recent decades, the urban built environment has become both one of the main catalysts of global securities trading and its main recipient. So much so that for many scholars, the centrality of real estate/urban construct in contemporary economies is no longer in doubt (Aalbers and Christophers 2014). However, the degrees or variations of its financialization are subject to interpretation. The United States and Great Britain seem to be the two countries where the connections between real estate and market finance have been the most advanced, which makes it possible to speak of a "regime of financialized accumulation driven by real estate" (Hofman and Aalbers 2019). This would then follow the previous regime of financialized accumulation centered on companies. In all cases, financialized accumulation refers to the growth of prices on financial markets rather than to the growth of activities in the real economy (Boyer 2000).

1.1.3. *Space at the heart of the valorization and extraction of value by the Global City*

The third characteristic of financialization is based on the fact that space is at the heart of market finance's power to create and extract value through the liquidity/mobility of capital (Corpataux and Crevoisier 2005). Through securitization, market finance has the capacity to accelerate the future, i.e. *to transform future income rights (annuities) in the more or less long term linked to property or to debts with a whole series of immobile, territorialized and illiquid assets as collateral (land, buildings; companies; government or household debts; etc.) into totally deterritorialized, mobile and liquid assets (financial products) that can be valued and extracted on the financial markets in an almost instantaneous manner by investors.* This vast operation of deterritorialization and valorization implies the setting up of a financial industry whose objective consists of establishing a logic of the investor/shareholder seeking to optimize their investment portfolio made up of securities (financial products).

Firstly, by formatting the legislative framework and the techniques for calculating and evaluating investments according to its own criteria (Corpataux et al. 2009), the market finance makes it possible to decontextualize and deterritorialize the value of investments made over the long term and according to multiple criteria (see Figure 1.2). In this way, investors can focus on two unique criteria: financial return and risk. According to the precepts of modern portfolio theory, the return on a financial asset is given instantaneously by its price on the financial markets. As for the risk, it is considered as probabilizable and can be reduced for each investor thanks to the diversification of the portfolio of assets (financial products). From then on, market finance makes it possible to escape from the complexity of real markets where there are multiple uncertainties (production, market, political, climatic, etc.). Facilitated by liquidity, which gives the possibility of withdrawal at any time (exit)[4], investing in the financial markets becomes a pure exercise in financial engineering where the aim is to maximize returns while minimizing risks by mixing investment portfolios. An optimal portfolio must cover the entire universe of financial products such as traditional products (financial securities: corporate shares, government bonds, etc.) and increasingly sophisticated products (derivatives: foreign exchange, financial securities and debt risks[5]).

Secondly, in order to function and create value, market finance constantly needs new spaces and new sectors to extend its hold and constitute a financialized space made totally abstract and deterritorialized within which financial capital can circulate easily (Corpataux et al. 2009). This space has expanded as a result of the seizure of an ever-increasing number of countries and their economic sectors on a global scale since the 1980s, made possible by financial liberalization and border opening reforms. Spatial expansion is the counterpart of financial innovations so that investors can break free from territorial constraints and carry out "capital switching" on a global scale within the financialized space by mixing cities, countries or continents.

---

4. Withdrawal can take place almost immediately on publicly organized listed markets but not so quickly on unlisted and private markets, known as over-the-counter markets.
5. Originally, derivatives were linked to risks, for example currency risks, which were then borne by investors in the financial markets, typically hedge funds (e.g. the three-month evolution of the exchange rate of the euro against the US dollar is today defined between two parties, one of which prices the rate downwards and the other upwards). There are now derivatives on all kinds of price movements in the financial markets where there is no need to own the securities (or underlying), for example the stocks or corporate bonds, treasury bills or currencies being bet on.

Moreover, the creation of economic value is carried out centrally by the financial industry according to opinions. Today, the financial industry, composed of the main banks and various investment vehicles (which intervene in various credit, wealth management or investment operations), is organized on an international scale and is located in the world's financial centers, which are closely interconnected and constitute the Global City (Sassen 1991). The price values on financial markets reflect *financial conventions* (Orléan 2011), i.e. shared visions of the future within the financial industry, a company, a sector of activity or even the economy of a country at a given time. For example, these past years, the financial values of companies such as Tesla or digital startups have been driven up by favorable market opinions in favor of renewable energies and the platform economy (Srnicek 2017). Financial markets therefore function as self-fulfilling forces that not only creates financial value by imposing itself on all investors at a given moment, but also performs reality (Callon 2007).

Finally, the drainage of investment flows (linked to pensions, trade surpluses, etc., as mentioned above) to the financial centers and the financialization of a growing number of sectors of the economy (companies, households, states, urban built environment) in various countries benefit the Global City. The financialization of the economy places the Global City in the lead and amplifies its power to create and extract economic value produced in the regions. The extraction of economic value by shareholders has mainly benefited the financial multinationals (Ioannou et al. 2021). It has also been the basis for (non-financial) corporate strategies and has led to the formation of monopolies on a global scale in most sectors of activity (Birch 2020). On the contrary, regions and firms, especially industrial ones, which are not or only marginally connected to the investment circuits of market finance have clearly been penalized (Jeannerat and Theurillat 2021).

1.2. Territorialized chains of financialized urban production: a transcalary and multiactor re-intermediation

Over the last 10 years, the way in which the value of the urban built environment is created in territories and extracted by market finance has been increasingly documented, in very different institutional and territorial contexts, both in the North and in the South. The result is a diversity of situations and variations in the financialization of urban production according to the types of connections established between market finance, cities and the urban construct. Three perspectives of analysis have been privileged. The first perspective concerns the hold of financiers on the ownership of urban objects, while the second perspective concerns the policies for accessing household property. In both cases, the links between the real estate and financial industries at the root of the reconfiguration of investment channels in the urban built environment are highlighted. The third perspective questions the role of municipalities in the financialization of urban planning and governance.

1.2.1. *Financialization through the extraction of urban rent by financial landowners*

The direct intervention of financiers in the city has been facilitated by the development of rental real estate, generally more focused on commercial real estate (offices and shops) than on residential real estate.

In general, close links can be observed between the globalization of firms, the investment of financiers in urban property and the stimulation of real estate markets in financial metropolises (Sassen 2010). Financial capital is mainly oriented towards large metropolises that agglomerate multinationals in the upper tertiary sector and commercial groups that are the tenants of buildings held by financial landowners (Charney 2001; Theurillat et al. 2015). Within metropolises, central spaces or new urban development hubs are favored (Guironnet and Halbert 2018). In many countries, the creation of a real estate finance industry is seen as an imperative means of anchoring global financial capital, and thus contributing to the (re)construction of the value of the urban built environment. Urban regeneration operations are precisely part of the objective of making the main metropolises competitive on a global scale (Fainstein 2001).

The anchoring of financial capital in the city is drastically changing the core business of the real estate industry. The large development companies, which can be listed on the stock exchange and, depending on the country, backed by banks, have in particular oriented their strategies towards the ever-increasing investment demand of their new clientele, the real estate finance industry. By having the indispensable knowledge of local real estate markets and their institutional and political aspects, the major developers have positioned themselves as privileged intermediaries in the creation of rent for financiers.

In Chicago, the local real estate industry was driven by a direct connection to market finance throughout the 2000s (Weber 2015). The securitization of their debts on the financial markets was a powerful lever to build business centers for large local firms without really taking into account the demand for use, which led to real estate overproduction. In France, Switzerland and the United States, real estate development groups have been at the center of networks of actors and competencies on land and urban planning aspects as well as on legal, economic and financial aspects so as to produce Large Urban Development Projects (LUDPs) that allow for the absorption of large amounts of liquidity from financial institutions (Theurillat and Crevoisier 2013, 2014; Guironnet et al. 2016).

Developers have an essential relational role between urban objects, territorial actors (such as municipalities and communities) and investors. In addition to taking into account the needs of users (main tenants), they act as negotiators with territorial actors, particularly with public authorities (Theurillat 2011). By internalizing the requirements of their financial clients in terms of profitability (rents and capital gains on disposal), the promoters' negotiation work covers all the issues that can hinder the securing of investments. The anchoring of capital in the city can be facilitated by entrepreneurial policies of municipalities that are favorable to investment, as in the case of LUDPs in the Paris and Lyon regions in France (Guironnet 2019). Negotiations can be hindered by the intervention of organizations representing community interests, as in the case of an LUDP in the city of Zurich in Switzerland (Theurillat and Crevoisier 2013). In the case of an LUDP in London, developers used communication experts to negotiate with local communities (Brill 2020).

By being at the center of the relational work, developers have positioned themselves as central actors in a new chain of production of large urban projects and urban governance featured by market finance. In Hong Kong, Singapore and Japan, large urban projects have resulted in close configurations between real estate investment funds and major national real estate groups which have become key stakeholders in urban planning and governance (Smart and Lee 2003; Haila 2015; Aveline-Dubach 2020a).

The relational work of intermediation and negotiation of developers relies on a whole chain of real estate specialists, first and foremost among which are real estate consulting firms (Guironnet and Halbert 2018). Today, this is dominated in particular by a few multinationals such as CBRE, JLL, DTZ alongside more national players. Their analyses, mainly aimed at investors, both national and international and large tenants (multinationals in the tertiary sector or retail), make it possible to open up local urban rent markets by making them transparent and liquid, i.e. visible to investors. The creation of the financial value of the urban built environment consists in formatting operations, i.e. the selection and assembly of objects by categories (by size, market segment and types of tenants) so that their characteristics and uncertainties (linked to construction, pollution, institutions, opposition from the local community, etc.) of future investment returns can be fully translated and reduced in terms of returns (long-term rents or capital gains on disposal based on discounted cash flow methods) and risks (core, value-added or opportunistic; see

Figure 1.2). At the same time, this operation of formatting and representing urban objects makes it possible to position certain cities and their real estate objects on the investors' map and thus to develop opinions favorable to investments within the financialized investment sector of urban production. In the end, benchmarking of real estate markets by segment, region and country enables financial actors to stick to a deterritorialized comparison of the levels of urban rent to be extracted.

The intermediation role of the real estate industry is even more fundamental in anchoring international investment flows. The connection of urban objects to the global circulation of financial capital relies on "trans-scalar territorial networks" (Halbert and Rouanet 2014) to filter all the risks inherent in the creation of urban rent. Bangalore's inclusion as a "world-class city" on the international investor map was an assemblage and formatting operation of large urban projects articulated around a network of regional and national actors composed of developers, real estate and legal advisors and politicians. However, the filtering of investment risk in emerging markets such as India, which are operated by the regional–national network of actors, is also subject to reversal, as was the case after 2008 (Searle 2018). The transformation of territorialized objects into "liquid" objects could not take place, leading to the bankruptcy of some local developers. The access of financiers to local real estate markets can also be prevented, or at least drastically curtailed (David and Halbert 2014). In Mexico City, the central area remained in the hands of the local real estate industry, forcing developers connected to international investors to prospect for peripheral areas. In China, the extraction of rent from real estate objects (mainly offices) by foreign investors is conditioned by putting cities on the map from analyses of multinational real estate investment consulting firms and by establishing partnerships with local investors or developers, as well as by strict control of capital outflow (profits) (Aveline-Dubach 2013).

The financial crisis of 2008 did not deter investors from real estate. On the contrary, the post-crisis period has stimulated the expansion of financiers' direct intervention in the city as landlords in some countries. Corporate real estate has strengthened in Ireland and France (Wijburg and Aalbers 2017a; Waldron 2018), but it is mainly residential rental property which constitutes a new stage of financialization. Urban rent now comes from household housing, as in Germany, Japan and the United States (Fields and Uffer 2016; Wijburg and Aalbers 2017b; Aveline-Dubach 2020a). Investment in residential real estate reveals a continuum between private funds whose investment model is based on short-term value creation (capital gains) and the sale of rehabilitated buildings to publicly traded funds and investment companies (REITs) that rely on long-term income (rents) (Wijburg et al. 2018) (see Figure 1.2).

In the end, the formatting of buildings allowing the extraction of real estate rent by financiers based on direct urban property in the more or less long term (rents and/or capital gains) is an operation of spatial, economic and social selection. Firstly, market finance produces "custom-made" parts of the city. LUDPs such as business centers, shopping or leisure complexes, as well as gentrified residential neighborhoods in central or suburban spaces (Fainstein 2016; Scott 2019) are emblematic of the "financialized city". Secondly, rent extraction by financiers can amplify accumulation by dispossession (Harvey 2005). Maximizing returns can imply the eviction of former tenants, as in the case of the restructuring of social housing in Berlin or New York by private equity funds (Fields and Uffer 2016) or the rehabilitation of commercial space in social developments by REITs in Hong Kong (Aveline-Dubach 2016). In other urban contexts, the extraction of LUDP rent by financial actors is secured in the long term, coming from the lease of large tenants, multinational firms or large retail groups. (Theurillat and Crevoisier 2014; Guironnet et al. 2016). Thirdly, the huge masses of liquidity in the hands of the real estate financial industry amplifies and accelerates speculation and pushes for ever greater mismatches with real demand. In the cases of the United States, Spain and Ireland, urban areas have been developed without taking into account the demand for built space. In the case of Switzerland, while investment is secured in the long term, based on very high occupancy rates, the availability of financial capital has nevertheless led to the explosion of large shopping and leisure malls.

1.2.2. *Financialization through the extraction of urban rent via household property*

The second perspective on the analysis of financialization emphasizes the policies that encourage individual property ownership. The logic of financialization can be ensured by a direct connection to financial markets. The securitization of mortgages in the United States has been one of the most emblematic forms of individual property extraction by market finance. This drastically boosted the construction of large residential neighborhoods in most US cities throughout the 2000s (Aalbers 2012). In Spain, the access to global financial capital of large developers, either through their listing on the stock market or through their privileged links with international real estate investment funds (PEREs), was at the origin of the huge speculative bubble and urban production during the 1990s. Driven by a tourism-oriented urban development model, this finance capital accumulation resulted in the construction of large neighborhoods and residential complexes sold to retirees from northern European countries (Coq-Vuelta 2013).

In some eastern and southern European countries, the privatization of household property is characteristic of "subordinated financialization" (Fernandez and Aalbers 2020), i.e. an indirect connection to market finance and to global investment flows boosted by massive liquidity injections from central banks (the Fed and the European Bank) and seeking primarily to invest in emerging countries. In Brazil, the massive issuance of domestic bonds by the central bank was the source of one of the world's largest home ownership and urban development programs, which functioned as a powerful subsidy to the real estate industry. The government bonds that resulted from the Brazilian central bank's trading of huge amounts of foreign capital were used by banks as collateral for borrowing in the interbank markets and for massive mortgage lending to households.

However, in many countries, policies of privatization of household property ownership are characteristic of bank-based residential capitalism (Schwartz and Seabrooke 2009). China is iconic in this respect. The privatization of urban household property ownership since 1998 has been one of the major investment outlets for state-owned banks. Moreover, bank loans to households have been at the origin of the emergence of a powerful real estate industry at a local level and the creation of large real estate groups operating at a national level (Theurillat et al. 2016; Theurillat 2021). At the same time, speculation in household real estate has been institutionally encouraged and is organized through interprovincial investment channels. The coupling of money creation through real estate and household investments has been at the origin of the development of huge gentrified neighborhoods and new towns throughout the country, while a structural lack of affordable housing prevails. For some authors, the logic of massive household investment in real estate, which was then assimilated into a form of financialization (Forrest and Hirayama 2015), is characteristic of several South Asian countries and responds to the absence or poor development of social security coverage and pension systems.

Ultimately, the connection of the built environment to market finance and to the circulation of capital on a global scale increases rent extraction, which is carried out mainly by the banking system and is institutionally encouraged by policies of privatization of household property. Dependence on financial markets can further reinforce the predatory nature of the banking system (Minsky 1982), seeking an ever-increasing number of clients, and thus subjecting them to the changing views of the market. At the same time, market finance increases 10-fold the abundance of liquidity and the capacity to create money, which are at the origin of both the explosion of urban production on a global scale and the formation of speculative bubbles. All of these factors have created ever greater discrepancies between land and property prices and the purchasing power of individuals.

1.2.3. *The financialization of urban development strategies through municipal land*

The United States is emblematic of the active role played by municipalities (local authorities and their development agencies) in connecting urban objects to market finance and in the emergence of financialized urbanism (Peck and Whiteside 2016). In a structural context marked by significant budget cuts by the federal government since the 1980s, which has become even more pronounced in the post-2008 period, the financing of American cities has become increasingly dependent on the issuance of municipal bonds on financial markets or the securitization of tax incremental financing (or TIF (see Chapter 8)). The latter are directly dependent on urbanization, i.e. urban growth driven by real estate and infrastructure development projects to attract capital (businesses and investors). To this end, different types of investment vehicles have been created in increasingly sophisticated combinations of financial engineering, opaque institutional arrangements and highly selective future income-formatting resulting in the redefinition of urban centralities (Ashton et al. 2016; Kirkpatrick 2016). This speculation on urban growth makes the provision of public goods and services and urban planning strategies increasingly dependent on financial market opinions. In other words, the connection of real estate to financial markets is accelerating and amplifying the so-called entrepreneurial strategies of American cities. A new phase of financialized urbanism is taking shape, with urban growth becoming a machine for extracting debt from the financial markets (Peck and Whiteside 2016). Subjected to the opinions of the financial markets, the decline in competitiveness of American cities can lead to situations of bankruptcy (as in the case of Detroit) and the intervention of technocrats responsible for implementing structural adjustment plans which amplify the privatization of urban assets.

In Britain, it is also a context of fiscal austerity and budget constraints that has led municipalities to focus their urban development strategies on real estate, using land as an "asset", a collateral that can be monetized (Ward and Swyngedouw 2018). This strategy of financing urban development through debt can result in municipalities establishing direct connections to financial markets. The securitization of tax revenues (tax incremental financing or TIF), the creation of real estate investment vehicles by municipalities where real estate revenues are used as collateral for bank loans or the issuance of municipal bonds facilitated by loose monetary policies are all instances where the urban built environment becomes an important financialized collateral. The ever-increasing dependence of municipal public finances on financial markets marks the emergence of financialized urban governance in Britain (Christophers 2019).

The nature of the variations and interactions between entrepreneurial and financialized urbanism is also being questioned in continental Europe. This debate is a continuation of the debate on new neoliberal urban policies which have emerged since the early 1990s (Brenner and Theodore 2002). An entrepreneurial governance has gradually been established in European cities to replace the managerial urban governance which characterized the Fordist period in most Western countries, and was based on the financing and distribution of wealth between territories by national governments (Pinson 2020). Based on the decentralization of fiscal, economic and planning powers, urban policies are conditioned by the priority given to urban growth. In this context, the transformation of the urban fabric, particularly through major urban projects, becomes a crucial lever for improving the competitiveness of cities within a globalized hierarchy (Brenner 2004). This leads to the formation of growth coalitions led by a small number of actors (development agencies and real estate companies) and marked by an opacity of decisions and interests (Lauermann 2018).

The use of land and real estate leverage by municipalities to recreate urban value, as well as the nature of connections with actors and markets, vary territorially according to the types of financial and budgetary constraints. In Belgium and Holland, municipalities' real estate-led development strategies are characteristic of entrepreneurial urbanism (Van Loon et al. 2018). However, in the Dutch case, although no direct connection between municipal finances and financial markets has been established, municipal land strategies take financialized forms. In order to use land as collateral for municipal borrowing from banks, municipalities have developed strategies to raise land and real estate prices through massive land acquisitions and urbanization expansion (rezoning of agricultural land) to accelerate real estate development. In France (the Paris region) and Italy (Milan), urban planning has become an instrument for connecting to financial actors (REITs, PEREs) to secure the profitability of large urban development projects (Guironnet et al. 2016; Savini and Aalbers 2016). This connection to market finance is based on discourses of urban competitiveness in which urban revitalization operations financed by market finance actors are considered essential to the re-creation of urban value.

The debate on variations in entrepreneurial urbanism and its amplification by financialization also concerns other continents. China is a good example of these variations. It has no financial real estate markets and the state plays a central role. On the one hand, urban growth policies driven by land are referred to as Chinese-style entrepreneurial urbanism (He and Wu 2009) or state entrepreneurialism (Wu 2017). Based on a planning monopoly that allows agricultural land to be transformed into urban land and its use rights to be sold for real estate projects, land is the main financial lever for municipalities. It is therefore the basis for strategies of land monetization, i.e. the creation and extraction of urban rent, activated around growth coalitions between local governments and the real estate industry (see Chapter 8). Moreover, this strategy of urban development through land is based on debt. Indeed, municipalities have borrowed massively through their investment and urban development companies from banks and increasingly from the bond market and investment funds to finance the servicing of land and the construction of social infrastructure of all kinds (museums, sports complexes, etc.) (Theurillat et al. 2016). As a result, the financialization of Chinese urbanization is characterized by a dependence on future revenues expected from extensive urban development based on the massive construction of real estate and infrastructure projects, which can then take the form of bubbles whose collapse poses a constant risk to urban production in China (Aveline-Dubach 2020b).

1.3. Conclusion

This chapter has presented a territorial approach to the financialization of urban production based on the growing literature within urban studies. It firstly revealed the way in which the urban built environment is transformed into totally deterritorialized financial products. As a result of securitization and insertion into global financial circuits, financial capital can easily circulate within a financialized space that allows investors to avoid the complexity of investments in the real economy by focusing on the constitution of portfolios of financial products on the basis of criteria of risk and financial returns. This investment logic is the basis for the submission of cities and regions to the opinions of financial markets and the extraction of urban rent by the financial centers of the Global City. However, researchers have questioned and revealed the way in which the process of financialization takes place in different institutional and territorial contexts. Their work highlights *the continuum of relations between land and urban planning, real estate markets, urban policies and governance and market finance.* Thus, the unveiling of the territorialization of the financialization of urban construction reveals long chains of re-intermediation involving a multiplicity of specialized actors in the real estate financial industry (major investors, large real estate development groups, multinational consulting firms), at different scales, as well as the role played by local public authorities. Moreover, with the ever more advanced and complex boundaries of the hold of market finance on urban production, researchers show very diverse connections between urban construction and financial markets and more or less neoliberal and financialized types of urban governance.

Taking into account territorial context proves to be fundamental since the territory reveals the instituted actors in presence capable of acting in return on the institutions and of establishing relationships at different scales (Theurillat 2011; Crevoisier 2014). The territorial approach also allows for the development of meso-level theories, allowing for a way out of the debate between generalization and idiosyncrasy, based on comparative empirical frameworks. However, the way in which the territorial context is interpreted and used to establish theories is the subject of a new debate. Today, we can roughly distinguish between two "schools" of thought in urban geography.

The first "school" inserts the territorial context into globalizing processes while taking into account varieties or diversities. This is the case with the conceptual and comparative approach proposed by Manuel Aalbers, which has become an essential reference for any author who seeks to position themselves in the debate on the financialization of urban production. The diversity or variation of financialization forms are considered to be degrees or even stages. Financialization can take place without the presence of well-developed financial markets or direct connections between the urban construct and financial markets. In this case, financialization is more about the practices, instruments and calculations that shape actors and institutions. This leads to considering "assetization", i.e. urban development strategies through land (land value capture), where land is the monetized collateral, as a potential step towards financialization (Fernandez and Aalbers 2016). Thus, we find varied and hybrid models of assetization–financialization and neoliberalization depending on institutional and territorial contexts. The objective is, indeed, to show "the general picture displaying common trajectories of territorial transformations moving in the same direction, from different starting points, at different times and at a different pace" (Aalbers 2017). Even though there is no "pure" financialization, the American and English models of market finance and neoliberal governance function as the benchmarks of the literature on the financialization of urban production. The researchers thus contribute to a comparative approach by positioning themselves and comparing their work with that of other territorial contexts, certainly according to different theoretical approaches, but from the angle of a globalizing, varied and hybrid financialization process in progress. In terms of impacts, financialization is seen as a speculative process of urban rent extraction causing a drastic increase in land and real estate values which can lead to crises, and accentuate the gentrification of certain urban spaces.

The second "school" takes the diversity of territorial contexts very seriously. Jennifer Robinson spearheads a conceptual and methodological approach which has been described as post-neoliberal and post-colonial. Firstly, the range of globalizing conceptualizations produced out of American and British empirical analyses and framing other institutional and territorial contexts makes it impossible to account for existing realities and the transformations taking place (Parnell and Robinson 2012;

Robinson et al. 2021). Moreover, the observation of very significant territorial differences and variations is considered a crucial starting point for (re)constructing a theory of the urban, based on comparative empirical studies carried out in cities located in different continents in order to move away from conceptual frameworks derived mainly from Anglo-American empirical cases. The words "specificity as a tool for diversity" invite us to go beyond the fetishism of financialization and neoliberal competitiveness by considering the processes and consequences resulting from the diversity of financing circuits and the diversity of policies and institutional arrangements at work in the creation and extraction of urban rent (Fainstein 2016). Urban production is thus not necessarily associated with the prioritization of urban growth and competitiveness or with speculation and maximization of rent extraction by financiers.

Without taking a position in this debate, this chapter defines financialization as the *creation and extraction of urban rent by market finance*, emphasizing both the distinction and the dialectic that operate between the real and financial real estate markets, and showing the multiple forms and degrees of connection between market finance, cities and urban objects. It is, indeed, the centralization of decisions and the formation of self-fulfilling opinions on the financial markets that make it possible to both create and extract value from the urban built environment and economic activities by directing flows towards this or that sector of activity or this or that city and region. However, the debate on the conceptual limits of financialization and the renewal of urban theories must be enriched. By placing the focus on the territorial context, these two schools of thought are concerned with the creation and extraction of urban rent as part of the internal dynamics of transformation of the urban construct, i.e. within the second circuit of capital (Ward and Aalbers 2016). The origin of urban rent is not really questioned; at least, the explanation given is that urban rent is the driving role of real estate today for urban development. However, the creation of wealth in cities and regions, at the origin of urban rent, is now being debated by researchers concerned with urban and regional development (Crevoisier and Rime 2020). The urban value can no longer be approached solely in terms of the competitiveness of exporting activities (goods and services). It is also based on the attractiveness of people, who are increasingly mobile as residents and consumers, which places consumption, leisure activities and, more generally, services to people at the heart of the creation of urban value and the dynamics of real estate markets.

1.4. References

Aalbers, M.B. (2010). Global intercity networks and commodity chains: Any intersections? *Global Networks*, 10(1), 150–163.

Aalbers, M.B. (2012). *Subprime Cities: The Political Economy of Mortgage Markets*. Wiley-Blackwell, Oxford.

Aalbers, M.B. (2016). *The Financialization of Housing: A Political Economy Approach*. Routledge, London.

Aalbers, M.B. (2017). The variegated financialization of housing. *International Journal of Urban and Regional Research*, 41(4), 542–554.

Aalbers, M.B. (2019). Financial geography III: The financialization of the city. *Progress in Human Geography*, 44(3), 595–607 [Online]. Available at: https://doi.org/10.1177%2F0309132519853922.

Aalbers, M.B. and Christophers, B. (2014). Centering housing in political economy. *Housing, Theory and Society*, 31(4), 373–394.

Ashton, P., Doussard, M., Weber, R. (2016). Reconstituting the state: City powers and exposures in Chicago's infrastructure leases. *Urban Studies*, 53(7), 1384–1400.

Aveline-Dubach, N. (2013). Finance capital launches an assault on Chinese real estate. *China Perspectives*, 2, 29–39.

Aveline-Dubach, N. (2016). Embedment of "liquid" capital into the built environment: The case of REIT investment in Hong Kong. *Issues and Studies*, 52(4), 1–32.

Aveline-Dubach, N. (2020a). The financialization of real estate in megacities and its variegated trajectories in East Asia. In *Handbook on Megacities and Megacity-Regions*, Labbé, D. and Sorensen, A. (eds). Edward Elgar, Cheltenham.

Aveline-Dubach, N. (2020b). China's housing booms: A challenge to bubble theory. In *Theories and Models of Urbanization*, Pumain, D. (ed.). Springer, Cham.

Beauregard, R. (1994). Capital switching and the built environment: United States 1970–1989. *Environment and Planning A*, 26(5), 715–732.

Birch, K. (2020). Technoscience rent: Toward a theory of rentiership for technoscientific capitalism. *Science, Technology, & Human Values*, 45(1), 3–33.

Boyer, R. (2000). Is a finance-led growth regime a viable alternative to Fordism? A preliminary analysis. *Economy and Society*, 29, 111–145.

Brenner, N. (2004). *New States Spaces. Urban Governance and the Rescaling of Statehood*. Oxford University Press, Oxford.

Brenner, N. and Theodore, N. (2002). Cities and the geographies of "Actually existing Neoliberalism". *Antipode*, 34, 349–379.

Brill, F. (2020). Complexity and coordination in London's Silvertown Quays: How real estate developers (re)centred themselves in the planning process. *EPA: Economy and Space*, 52(2), 362–382.

Callon, M. (2007). What does it mean to say that economics is performative? In *Do Economists Make Markets? On the Performativity of Economics*, Mackenzie, D., Muniesa, F., Siu, L. (eds). Princeton University Press, Princeton.

Charney, I. (2001). Three dimensions of capital switching within the real estate sector: A Canadian case study. *International Journal of Urban and Regional Research*, 25(4), 740–758.

Christophers, B. (2019). Putting financialisation in its financial context: Transformations in local government-led urban development in post-financial crisis England. *Transactions of the Institute of British Geographers*, 44(3), 571–586.

Coakley, H. (1994). The integration of property and financial markets. *Environment and Planning A: Economy and Space*, 26(5), 697–713.

Coq-Vuelta, D. (2013). Urbanisation and financialisation in the context of a rescaling state: The case of Spain. *Antipode*, 45(5), 1213–1231.

Corpataux, J. and Crevoisier, O. (2005). Increased capital mobility/liquidity and its repercussions at regional level: Some lessons from the experiences of Switzerland and UK. *European and Urban Regional Studies*, 4(12), 315–334.

Corpataux, J. and Crevoisier, O. (2016). Lost in space: A critical approach to ANT and the social studies of finance. *Progress in Human Geography*, 40(5), 610–628.

Corpataux, J., Crevoisier, O., Theurillat, T. (2009). The expansion of the finance industry and its impact on the economy: A territorial approach based on Swiss pension funds. *Economic Geography*, 85(3), 313–334.

Corpataux, J., Crevoisier, O., Theurillat, T. (2017). The territorial governance of the finance industry. In *Handbook on the Geographies of Money and Finance*, Martin, R. and Pollard, J. (eds). Edward Elgar Publishers, London.

Crevoisier, O. (2014). Beyond territorial innovation models: The pertinence of the territorial approach. *Regional Studies*, 48(3), 551–561.

Crevoisier, O. and Rime, D. (2020). Anchoring urban development: Globalisation, attractiveness and complexity. *Regional Studies*, 58(1), 36–52.

David, L. and Halbert, L. (2014). Finance capital, actor-network theory and the struggle over calculative agencies in the business property markets of Mexico City Metropolitan Region. *Regional Studies*, 48(3), 516–529.

Fainstein, S. (2001). *The City Builders: Property Development in New York and London 1980–2000*. University Press of Kansas, Lawrence.

Fainstein, S. (2016). Financialization and justice in the city. *Urban Studies*, 53(7), 1503–1508.

Fernandez, R. and Aalbers, M.C. (2016). Financialization and housing: Between globalization and varieties of capitalism. *Competition and Change*, 20(2), 71–88.

Fernandez, R. and Aalbers, M.C. (2020). Housing financialization in the global south: In search of a comparative framework. *Housing Policy Debate*, 30(4), 680–701.

Fields, D. and Uffer, S. (2016). The financialisation of rental housing: A comparative analysis of New York City and Berlin. *Urban Studies*, 53(7), 1486–1502.

Forrest, R. and Hirayama, Y. (2015). The financialisation of the social project: Embedded liberalism, neoliberalism and home ownership. *Urban Studies*, 52(2), 233–244.

Guironnet, A. (2019). Cities on the global real estate marketplace: Urban development policy and the circulation of financial standards in two French localities. *Urban Geography*, 40(10), 1527–1547.

Guironnet, A. and Halbert, L. (2018). Produire la ville pour les marchés financiers. *Espaces et Sociétés*, 3(174), 17–34.

Guironnet, A., Attuyer, K., Halbert, L. (2016). Building cities on financial assets: The financialization of property markets and its implications for city governments in the Paris city-region. *Urban Studies*, 53(7), 1442–1464

Haila, A. (1988). Land as a financial asset. *Antipodes*, 20(2), 79–101.

Haila, A. (2015). *Urban Land Rent: Singapore as a Property State*. John Wiley & Sons, New York.

Halbert, L. and Attuyer, K. (2016). The financialisation of urban production: Conditions, mediations and transformations. *Urban Studies*, 53(7), 1347–1361

Halbert, L. and Rouanet, H. (2014). Filtering risk away: Global finance capital, transcalar territorial networks, and the (un)making of city-regions: An analysis of business property development in Bangalore, India. *Regional Studies*, 48(3), 471–484.

Harvey, D. (1978). The urban process under capitalism: A framework for analysis. *International Journal of Urban and Regional Research*, 2(1–4), 101–131.

Harvey, D. (1982). *The Limits to Capital*. Blackwell, Oxford.

Harvey, D. (1985). *The Urbanization of Capital*. Basil Blackwell, Oxford.

Harvey, D. (2005). *A Brief History of Neoliberalism*. Oxford University Press, Oxford.

He, S. and Wu, F. (2009). China's emerging neoliberal urbanism: Perspectives from urban redevelopment. *Antipode*, 41(2), 282–304.

Hofman, A. and Aalbers, M.B. (2019). A finance- and real estate-driven regime in the United Kingdom. *Geoforum*, 100, 89–100.

Ioannou, S., Wójcik, D., Pazitka, W. (2021). Financial centre bias in sub-sovereign credit ratings. *Journal of International Financial Markets, Institutions & Money*, 70, 101261 [Online]. Available at: https://eprints.whiterose.ac.uk/175018/1/1-s2.0-S1042443120301451-main.pdf.

Jeannerat, H. and Theurillat, T. (2021), Old industrial spaces challenged by platformized value capture 4.0. *Regional Studies*, 55(10), 1738–1750.

Kirkpatrick, O. (2016). The new urban fiscal crisis: Finance, democracy, and municipal debt. *Politics & Society*, 44(1), 45–80.

Lauermann, J. (2018). Municipal statecraft: Revisiting the geographies of the entrepreneurial city. *Progress in Human Geography*, 42(2), 205–224.

Minsky, H. (1982). *Can "It" Happen Again?*. Routledge, Oxford.

Orléan, A. (2011). *L'empire de la valeur. Refonder l'économie*. Le Seuil, Paris.

Parnell, S. and Robinson, J. (2012). (Re)theorizing cities from the global south: Looking beyond neoliberalism. *Urban Geography*, 33(4), 593–617.

Peck, J. and Whiteside, H. (2016). Financializing detroit. *Economic Geography*, 92(3), 235–268.

Pinson, G. (2020). *La ville néolibérale*. PUF, Paris.

Robinson, J., Harrison, P., Shen, J., Wu, F. (2021). Financing urban development, three business models: Johannesburg, Shanghai and London. *Progress in Planning*, 154 [Online]. Available at: https://www.ncbi.nlm.nih.gov/pmc/articles/PMC7539139/.

Sanfelici, D. and Halbert, L. (2016). Financial markets, developers and the geographies of housing in Brazil: A supply-side account. *Urban Studies*, 53(7), 1465–1485.

Sassen, S. (1991). *The Global City*. Princeton University Press, Princeton.

Savini, A. (2016). The de-contextualisation of land use planning through financialisation: Urban redevelopment in Milan. *European Urban and Regional Studies*, 23(4), 878–894.

Schwartz, H.M. and Seabrooke, L. (eds) (2009). *The Politics of Housing Booms and Busts*. Palgrave Macmillan, Basingstoke.

Scott, A.J. (2019). Land redevelopment and the built environment in third-wave cities: Review and synthesis. *Journal of Urban Technology*, 26(1), 57–81.

Searle, L. (2018). The contradictions of mediation: Intermediaries and the financialization of urban production. *Economy and Society*, 47(4), 524–546.

Smart, A. and Lee, J. (2003). Financialization and the role of real estate in Hong Kong's regime of accumulation. *Economic Geography*, 79(2), 153–171.

Srnicek, N. (2017). *Platform Capitalism*. Polity Press, London.

Theurillat, T. (2011). La ville négociée : entre financiarisation et durabilité. *Géographie, economie et société*, 13(3), 225–254.

Theurillat, T. (2017). The role of money in China's urban production: The local property industry in Qujing, a fourth-tier city. *Urban Geography*, 38(6), 834–860.

Theurillat, T. (2021), Urban growth, from manufacturing to financialization: The case of China's contemporary urban development. *Regional Studies*, 56(8), 1244–1258.

Theurillat, T. and Crevoisier, O. (2013). The sustainability of a financialized urban megaproject: The case of Sihlcity in Zurich. *International Journal of Urban and Regional Research*, 37(6), 2052–2073.

Theurillat, T. and Crevoisier, O. (2014). Sustainability and the anchoring of capital: Negotiations surrounding two major urban projects in Switzerland. *Regional Studies*, 48(3), 501–515.

Theurillat, T., Corpataux, J., Crevoisier, O. (2010). Property sector financialization: The case of Swiss pension funds (1992–2005). *European and Planning Studies*, 18(2), 189–212.

Theurillat, T., Rérat, P., Crevoisier, O. (2015). The real estate markets: Players, institutions and territories. *Urban Studies*, 52(8), 1414–1433.

Theurillat, T., Lenzer, J., Zhan, H. (2016). The increasing financialization of China's urbanization. *Issues & Studies*, 52(4), 1640002 [Online]. Available at: https://www.worldscientific.com/doi/abs/10.1142/S1013251116400026.

Van Loon, J., Oosterlynck, S., Aalbers, M. (2018). Governing urban development in the low countries: From managerialism to entrepreneurialism and financialization. *European Urban and Regional Studies*, 26(4), 400–418.

Waldron, R. (2018). Capitalizing on the state: The political economy of real estate investment trusts and the "resolution" of the crisis. *Geoforum*, 90, 206–218.

Ward, C. and Aalbers, M. (2016). "The shitty rent business": What's the point of land rent theory? *Urban Studies*, 53(9), 1760–1783.

Ward, C. and Swyngedouw, E. (2018). Neoliberalisation from the ground up: Insurgent capital, regional struggle, and the assetisation of land. *Antipode*, 50(4), 1077–1097.

Weber, R. (2015). *From Boom to Bubble: How Finance Built the New Chicago*. University of Chicago Press, Chicago.

Wijburg, G. and Aalbers, M.B. (2017a). The internationalisation of commercial real estate markets in France and Germany. *Competition and Change*, 21(4), 301–320.

Wijburg, G. and Aalbers, M.B. (2017b). The alternative financialization of the German housing market. *Housing Studies*, 32(7), 968–989.

Wijburg, G., Aalbers, M.B., Heeg, S. (2018). The financialisation of rental housing 2.0: Releasing housing into the privatised mainstream of capital accumulation. *Antipode*, 50(4), 1098–1119.

Wu, F.L. (2017). State entrepreneurialism in urban China. In *Debating the Neoliberal City*, Pinson, G. and Journel, C.M. (eds). Routledge, Abingdon.

2

Real Estate Developers: Coordinating Actors in the Production of the City

Julie POLLARD

LAGAPE, Institut d'études politiques, Université de Lausanne, Switzerland

Among the works that today question the role of private economic actors in the material production of cities, a central place is given to private property developers. This chapter examines the changing roles of these actors over the last two decades. It discusses changes in the characteristics of real estate developers and their participation in the development of cities, focusing primarily on Europe and North America.

Real estate developers and, more broadly, the dynamics of real estate development have given rise to a diverse body of research, in terms of theoretical perspectives, disciplinary entries, methodological choices and the fields investigated. Several contributions proposing reviews of the literature show the dynamics of research on this subject since the 1980s (Gore and Nicholson 1991; Healey 1991; Ball 1998; Coiacetto 2001; Guy and Henneberry 2008; Ballard and Butcher 2020). Initially dominated by classical economic and financial analyses aimed at modeling the calculations and choices of developers to shed light on the functioning of real estate markets, research has gradually diversified to add more institutional and sociological depth to these actors and processes, leading to the development of more critical approaches.

Following Gore and Nicholson (1991) and Healey (1991), Guy and Henneberry (2008) identify four main streams of research: approaches centered on the description of the different stages of the development process; decision-making or behavioral approaches that analyze the interaction between the practices of actors and the broader process of real estate development; mainstream economic approaches and urban political economy approaches that are positioned at a more macro level and place the development process in parallel with other processes of economic production, and finally, institutionalist models centered on the organizations and networks that structure real estate development. The approaches also vary according to national contexts, with work centered on the United States and the United Kingdom being largely dominant. Research published in French is much less abundant, although we should note the seminal work of Topalov (1973), which adopts a Marxist perspective, and a renewed interest in real estate developers since the 2010s. The national research traditions may therefore have appeared relatively fragmented.

In the work carried out over the last 20 years, greater importance has been given to the articulation of economic logics and social and political logics in order to understand real estate development processes (Guy and Henneberry 2000; Fainstein 2001; Guy et al. 2002). The weight of public regulation, the embeddedness of actors in local and national configurations and the empirically observed diversity of these actors, in terms of profiles and strategies, are at the heart of the work carried out. For example, *The City Builders*, a reference book by Fainstein (2001), enriches knowledge on real estate developers by showing how their development is linked both to the transformation of financial markets and to government policies. Fainstein also highlights the significance of "non-economic" motivations – such as religious beliefs or male competition – that drive the management strategies of property development firms. In other national contexts (urban regions of India, Indonesia and China), Shatkin (2017) underlines the variable and determining role of states in structuring real estate markets and facilitating real estate developers' activities.

The recent period has been marked by a renewed interest in these actors at the international level. This renewal is based, in part, on case studies carried out in the south (such as Shatkin's work). Recent contributions include a special issue of the journal *Environment and Planning A* (Ballard and Butcher 2020), as well as a set of recent articles in the journal *Geoforum* (see, in particular: Brill 2022; Geva and Rosen 2018; Hyde 2022; Robin 2022; Domaradzka 2022). Building on these contributions, this chapter is structured in two parts. The first part describes these actors by presenting their characteristics and the diversity of their profiles. The second part explores how the developers are considered as actors – in interaction with others – in processes of urban development[1]. Three axes are proposed to

---

1. This implies placing their internal business operations, their relationship to risk and their forms of rationality in second place.

explore the recent dynamics: financialization of real estate, social issues and environmental issues.

2.1. The real estate developer, a multi-faceted player

2.1.1. *What is a real estate developer?*

The real estate developer (or property developer) is often presented as a decisive player in the making of the city. They initiate and coordinate projects. As Charney (2007, p. 1179) puts it, the developer "acts as a proactive agent who makes things happen". In concrete terms, the real estate developer initiates a real estate project, plans its development and oversees the various stages until the project's achievement. Their tasks include: prospecting for land, setting up a legal support company for the project[2], raising the funds for the project, choosing an architect and a construction company, filing the necessary authorizations (building permits in particular) and marketing the operation. Real estate operations may involve housing, offices and commercial premises or serviced residences[3]. This approach, based on the concrete activities developed – *what the developer does* – is necessarily reductive and subject to variation according to national and local contexts. For example, in the United States, developers can sell the projects they have built or retain ownership and manage them for rental purposes – the roles of investor and developer thus overlap. In Spain, the developer carries out activities related to development and land management. The land is treated not only as an *input* of the activity of development, but also as an *output:* it often happens that the developer buys a piece of land solely with the aim of reselling it and realizing a capital gain. In France, urban development and real estate development have historically been distinct, and developers do not integrate the management activities of the housing they build[4]. Real estate development involves a large number of players whose skills may overlap, with boundaries sometimes blurring or even shifting. Some large firms are both developers and investors; others are both developers and builders (Ball 2002). The real estate development activity may be carried out by actors who are

---

2. A real estate project can be carried out directly by the development company: but most often, it is carried out by an ad hoc legal structure – in France, generally a real estate company (*société civile immobilière* (SCI)).
3. In France, in 2020, housing construction represents approximately 80% of the production of real estate developers (in terms of revenue) (source: Fédération des promoteurs immobiliers).
4. However, recent developments have led to a growing involvement of real estate developers upstream of their traditional activities, either directly in the development – since the opening of development to the competitive sector – or in the definition of urban projects in a partnership approach with the urban development structure. This extension of the sphere of intervention of real estate developers in France also extends to rental management activities.

not – or not solely – real estate developers, making it difficult to identify the role of real estate development:

> A development role may be context dependent, for instance, a building firm is a developer when it acquires land, subdivides it and builds houses on it for sale, but not when it is contracted to build houses on a client's land. Furthermore, development functions may be mixed up with others like property construction, finance, investment and management (Coiacetto 2009, p. 123).

On a more theoretical level, in his seminal work on real estate developers, Topalov considers the developer as "a social agent who ensures the management of a circulating real estate capital in its phase of transformation into housing merchandise" (Topalov 1973, p. 15). This conception, centered on the economic calculation of developers, is marked by the central place given to the actors' modes of financing – which have evolved considerably since the 1960s, particularly with the financialization of real estate and the rise of tax exemption schemes. In order to define these actors, we suggest taking into consideration their economic activity of transformation (1) and their role as relational actors (2).

1) The developer is, first and foremost an **economic actor**, whose activities are spatialized and aimed at making a profit. They initiate and supervise the production process of real estate operations, at the intersection of financial, land and real estate markets. They are in charge of "project management – which implies in particular the management of the capital they managed to raise for the development project – but also the definition of the final product and land prospecting" (Trouillard 2014, p. 26). The profit margin achieved by the developer corresponds to the difference between the funds invested in the project, and the revenues resulting from the sale of the property units. Analytically, this margin is subject to contrasting interpretations. Some consider that the adjustment variable lies in the price of land, according to the countdown calculation model[5] (Topalov 1973). For others, the price of the land is given to the developer, which impacts the price level of the project. Coulondre (2017) enriches this reflection by arguing that the creation of profit by developers is also played out in the *qualification* of the buildings. In order to generate profit, the developer works to define, in a strategic manner, the *qualities* of their project for several categories of stakeholders. For instance, in order to convince local elected officials, they may emphasize the architectural interest of the project; and in order to

---

5. Schematically, in this perspective: the developer estimates their revenue by defining the selling price of their project, from which they subtract various types of costs, notably related to construction, and in relation to which they set a targeted promotion margin. The remaining amount corresponds to the sum that can be allocated to the acquisition of the land.

attract buyers, they may communicate on the social composition of the neighborhood (Coulondre 2017). Such arguments may enable the developer to obtain less expensive land and/or have high sales prices accepted.

2) This leads us to consider that developers are also **"relational entrepreneurs"** (Coulondre 2017), at the heart of a network of actors that they weave and structure. The relational work of developers is described by Ballard and Butcher (2020, p. 267): "Much of the work of developers is not in the production of the material environment per se, but is in fact directed to building, sustaining, managing and responding to relationships and networks". This work refers to the role of coordinating other actors that the developer exercises. Their activities place them in a position of interface for a set of actors, who intervene in different phases of the real estate project: funders (financial establishments, investment funds), designers (architects, research departments), builders (construction companies) and marketers (central sales offices, real estate agents). Second and most importantly, the notion of relational entrepreneurs echoes the fact that the economic activities of developers are inserted into a dense set of local, regional and/or national regulations (construction law, urban planning rules, real estate development law, etc.) that they incorporate into their logic of action and on which they may seek to act (Leffers 2018; Pollard 2018). In this political and institutional environment, interactions with local elected officials are central to the activities of real estate developers. The notion of relational entrepreneurs thus also refers to the integration of developers into local governance systems.

2.1.2. The diversity of real estate developer profiles

The first works developed in the 1970s and 1980s, adopting mainly economic perspectives with little empirical basis, were largely aimed at developing models simulating the decision-making of developers (see Coiacetto (2001)). These models have remained relatively abstract, considering the developer an ideal-typical figure.

From the 2000s onwards, the developer's role has been understood more in its complexity, taking into account the uncertainty and interpretation processes in decision-making, as well as the variety of developer profiles. Research addresses the heterogeneity of developers in various ways: size of the actors (and/or of the projects carried out), internal structuring of the company, location strategies, financing methods, determination of target populations or preferred modes of occupation and articulation of economic motivations with other types of motivations (social, in particular) (Rosen 2017). These variations are also dependent on the institutional and political contexts in which developers operate (Guy and Henneberry 2008).

> The coexistence between large internationalized actors and a multitude of small, dispersed, atomized actors with unsustainable structures is noted in different national contexts (Coiacetto 2009; Henneberry and Parris 2013; Trouillard 2014).
>
> In the French case, despite a movement towards corporate concentration, Trouillard (2014) observes the persistence of many small companies, whose lifespan may correspond to that of a single project. He explains this by the fact that size does not bring economies of scale and that the tasks remain the same, anchored in the territories.
>
> Working on the Australian case, Coiacetto (2009) and Ruming (2010) also point to the variability and complexity of the property development industry. The industry is characterized by an oligopolistic structure, combined with the presence of many small players, and a high level of business creation and demise. The smallest operators are able to develop their activities on their own, and often lead only one project.

Box 2.1. *The structure of the real estate development industry*

A body of work documents the variety of developer profiles, and articulates these profiles with specific strategies, including spatial location (on the French case, see: Topalov 1973; Trouillard 2014).

The pioneering research of Topalov (1973) differentiates actors according to their modes of financing, i.e. combinations of capital which they most frequently manage. Each developer is considered as "an element of a system of places where the production and circulation of housing goods take place [...]. Each identifiable position that defines a type of developer has a corresponding operating logic, i.e. general objectives specific to the type and a set of means to achieve them" (Topalov 1973, pp. 3, 21). Topalov distinguishes between real estate agencies-developers, contractors-developers, technicians-developers, financiers-developers, coordinating bank subsidiaries[6] and coordinating *outsiders* (i.e. actors whose exclusive activity is real estate development). For each type of developer identified, there is a specific logic of land and real estate action. These profiles emerged from the period of the developers' structuring, observed by Topalov in the 1960s.

The perspective opened by Topalov has been developed, updated, and discussed by a body of work focusing on the articulation between types of capital and developers' development strategies in a variety of local and national contexts (see, for example, Romainville 2017; Shimbo 2019). Romainville's (2017) work on

---

6. The developer-financiers are regularly involved in real estate development, while the coordinating bank subsidiaries are involved on a more occasional basis depending on the strategies of the parent company.

Brussels highlights and differentiates the investment strategies of financialized[7] and non-financialized developers. While the former – described as more risk-averse and favoring large, standardized projects – invest largely in the most expensive business districts and peripheral residential areas of the Brussels urban region, the smaller, independent developers turn to the more central and less expensive districts of the urban area, particularly those where gentrification dynamics are observed.

In the French case, Topalov's typological ambition can be reconsidered in light of the intense recomposition of real estate development: dynamics of professionalization, concentration and, more broadly, profound financial changes. Among the largest French developers, subsidiaries of banking groups (such as BNP Paribas Real Estate or Sogeprom) or construction groups (such as Bouygues Immobilier, Eiffage Immobilier or Vinci Immobilier) still dominate, as well as some independent developers (such as Nexity) (Pollard 2018). Many of the largest companies have origins that date back to the 1950s–1960s. However, this does not preclude substantial (and, for some, frequent) changes in these firms. We note, for example, Initial Public Offerings (IPOs), radical changes in the shareholding of these players or affiliation with large groups. These developments can make it difficult to typologize developers, especially in a way that is based on sources of financing. Moreover, to some observers, the importance of tax exemption schemes since the end of the 1990s has led to the emergence of a new type of developers, whose activities are focused exclusively on the production and sale of housing to households benefiting from such tax breaks.[8] (Vergriete 2013).

Other authors, adopting a typological approach, propose to move away from financing methods to distinguish categories of actors. Trouillard (2014) constructs a typology, on a basis that is both quantitative and inductive, focusing on differentiating the location strategies of developers. He takes into account all the developers active in the Paris region (1984–2012) and distinguishes five classes of developers: hyper-central developers, developers of privileged central spaces, developers of popular central spaces, peri-urban and new town developers, and developers of the greater Parisian periphery. The first and last classes are mainly made up of small developers, who are highly specialized in terms of territory, while the "intermediate" classes include the largest developers in the Paris region. Another example is based on a detailed study of two cities on the Australian east coast;

---

7. In her analysis, financialized developers include subsidiaries of financial companies and publicly traded companies (or companies with at least one listed shareholder).
8. These developers generally offer buyers a global package, integrating, in addition to the traditional activities of the developer, downstream activities: management and rental guarantee of the housing.

Coiacetto (2001) identifies six categories[9] of developers. In this work, he shows how each category of actor can be associated with its own practices, development strategies and also specific representations.

The interest of these typological approaches is to give substance to the empirical variety of actors, while seeking to envisage characteristics common to some of them and identify regularities in their strategies. In the rest of this chapter, we consider developers more in terms of their *interactions*, in order to account for their participation in the urban production processes.

2.2. The changing role of real estate developers: between market and politics

In order to shed light on recent developments in the role of real estate developers in the material building of the city, three lines of research are presented here. These reflect the diversity of research conducted on real estate developers today. In a transversal manner, they question the power of developers, their insertion into networks of actors and the regulatory capacities of public actors.

2.2.1. *Is financialization (re)shaping real estate developers?*

Since the 2000s, a significant body of work has focused on the effects of the rise of financial investors (pension funds, insurance companies, sovereign wealth funds, hedge funds, etc.) and of the consultancy industry (see, for example, Lorrain 2011; Halbert and Attuyer 2016; Aalbers 2017) on urban developments. The financialization of real estate can be understood as a "globalized phenomenon of expanding finance into real estate, resulting both in the use of financial asset management techniques – commonly applied to securities – to real estate assets and in the financing of real estate on the global capital market" (Nappi-Choulet 2009, p. 31). The ownership of real estate by financial investors is not new. However, we now see these players investing in large real estate funds, which own diversified and internationalized portfolios of real estate assets (Van Loon and Aalbers 2017; Aalbers 2019). This trend largely concerns office real estate, but it is also developing beyond, towards commercial real estate, hotel real estate (Aalbers 2019) or large urban projects (Theurillat 2011). Financialization refers to many processes (Drozdz et al. 2020), which impact real estate developers in different ways.

---

9. The following types are presented: Passive Local Property Owning Developers, "Means To A Mission" Developers, Specialised Client Developers, Showpiece Developers, "Eye On The Street" Builder-Developers and Value Adding Opportunity Developers.

Financialization primarily concerns **buildings produced by developers, and purchased by financial investors,** who turn them into investment vehicles, dependent on the **financial** markets. Producing buildings for financial actors results in a reshaping of the role of developers, due to the standards and expectations of these actors. Theurillat and Crevoisier refer to real estate developers as anchoring actors to express the fact that their (new) role is to "anchor" international investment in specific urban contexts for the production of financialized real estate projects (Theurillat 2011; Theurillat and Crevoisier 2014). Developers thus occupy an intermediary position within negotiations between international actors and local public, or sometimes private actors. They contribute to "negotiating the territorial articulation of external logics, linked to the mobility of capital, with in situ logics" (Theurillat 2011, p. 238). Other authors have delved into this role of developers as "anchors" of international investments, both connected to international financial networks and inserted into local contexts, particularly in the metropolises of southern countries (David and Halbert 2014; Searle 2016; Brill 2022). In the field of commercial real estate, a body of work shows how developers anticipate and integrate investors' standards. Guironnet (2016) thus observes that

> the intermediary situation of these players, whose role is *not* to keep the buildings as assets, feeds the anticipation and internalization of the investment criteria of asset managers. In some cases, it is reinforced by professional movements between marketing and real estate development professions, which reinforce the claimed knowledge of investors' expectations.

Second, financialization refers to developers' **methods of financing**, and therefore to a financing circuit that mobilizes capital from the financial markets. It is the perspective adopted by Romainville (2017) to explore the financialization of housing in Brussels. The international financialized developers[10] that she analyzes, who set up in Brussels from the 2000s onwards, have specific project development strategies (affluent peripheral neighborhoods and standardized architectural forms. In a completely different context, Rouanet and Halbert (2016) show how developers based in Bangalore (India) mobilize international financial capital to develop much more geographically extensive growth strategies. This mode of financing has enabled them to acquire a dominant position in the transformation of cities, and influence certain reforms and urban growth policies. The articulation of different financing channels available to real estate developers is one of the aspects

---

10. Companies listed on the stock exchange are thus systematically considered to be among the financialized developers (Romainville 2017, p. 629). These financialized actors are closely linked to the production of financialized housing *(rental) property*, even though this remains very limited in Brussels.

finely documented by Weber (2015) in her analysis of the production of tertiary real estate in Chicago during the millennial boom – from the late 1990s to the late 2000s. Weber explains the overproduction of office space not only by the abundance of capital available on the financial markets for developers, but also by particularly favorable instruments put in place by the local government, as well as by the practices and interactions between real estate professionals – in particular, between real estate developers and intermediaries such as brokers (Weber 2015).

The expanding dynamics of financialization should not mask the importance of **local and sectoral variations**: the financialization of real estate development is not an inexorable or homogeneous movement. Van Loon (2016), who compares the financing of real estate developers in Belgium and the Netherlands, highlights the contrast between Dutch developers, who have financialized their activities, and Belgian developers, who operate largely on the basis of their own funds. Furthermore, the role of institutional investors varies greatly from one country to another, and also according to the sectors considered. While in the United States and in numerous European countries, financial actors are playing an increasing role in residential real estate (Fields and Uffer 2016; Aalbers 2017; Romainville 2017), in France, housing has long appeared – and still largely remains – the "left behind of financialization" (Nappi-Choulet 2012). Rental investment by individuals, made particularly attractive by the tax exemption schemes put in place by the state, has had a decisive role in the production of residential real estate (Pollard 2018). In other sectors in France, tertiary real estate (Guironnet 2016) and logistics real estate[11] (Raimbault (2016), see also Chapter 4), financialization is much more advanced. In these sectors, the role of the central state and local authorities has been decisive in the deployment of new financial instruments (Wijburg 2019).

2.2.2. *How (and why) do developers integrate "social" objectives?*

In the context of housing crisis, marked by exacerbated difficulties in access to housing for the middle and working classes in both North America and Europe, the interventions of real estate developers have diversified. Public policies that rely on implementation by private real estate developers are gaining momentum (Christophers 2014; Geva and Rosen 2018; Hyde 2022; Domaradzka 2022; Pollard 2022). Developers are thus expanding their sphere of activity to new territories and/or new categories of population. There are many "social" challenges in response to which real estate developers are called upon to act: contribution to urban requalification, production of affordable housing, property development in

---

11. Financialization takes a specific form in this sector due to the role of "global fund developer-managers" (Raimbault 2016).

unattractive neighborhoods or even in *shrinking cities*. Why might they have an interest in positioning themselves in the face of such issues?

A first set of works proposes explanations based on the **increasing complexity of real estate development**, both in the way profit is defined and in the diversity of the companies' profiles. Extending the analyses – organizational and economic – of the practices and behaviors of real estate developers, these works enrich the conceptualization of the economic calculations of developers, and in particular their conception of profit "maximization" (Guy et al. 2002; Rosen 2017; Hyde 2022; Garboden and Jan-Trettien 2020). Some authors emphasize that it is actors with particular profiles who will intervene in a priori less attractive territories. Based on a study in Manchester (United Kingdom), Guy et al. (2002) show the importance of independent local developers, who will be able to design and make financially profitable projects in less valued locations, in line with a local urban aesthetic and culture. Rosen (2017) distinguishes profiles of developers in Toronto (Canada) and identifies a type of developer: *socially conscious developers*. These developers build a specific approach to profitability and profit, integrating the idea of "social benefit". This leads them to accept lower margins on the condition that social objectives are also achieved: "Profit is gauged not only by economic gain, but also by service to the public. Daniels (*one of the developers studied*) is thus content with relatively lower profit margins since its social objectives are part and parcel of its profit" (Rosen 2017, p. 621). For their part, Garboden and Jan-Trettien (2020) emphasize the variety of activities that can be undertaken by developers operating in urban regeneration areas, in order to ultimately promote profit creation. Based on a survey in a neighborhood of Baltimore (USA) – presented as a shrinking city – they observe how developers engage in various community-building activities: organization of drinks parties, creation of shared gardens, neighborhood clean-up days, etc. Motivations and activities interpreted as directly profitable are thus intermingled with others that are more indirect or longer term. The narratives of developers may also change. Domaradzka (2022) explains, in the Polish case, that the rise of social and political mobilizations carried out in the name of the right to the city has led developers to integrate and reinterpret this narrative in their discourse. She points out that this notion is used by developers to re-assert their dominant position locally and their "right to profit from the city" (Domaradzka 2022, p. 182).

A second entry focuses on the **weight of policy instruments** – be they regulatory, economic or fiscal, communicational, etc. – that frame or guide the intervention of real estate developers. These instruments can, for example, compel or encourage developers to produce affordable or social housing. Gimat and Pollard (2016) show that, in the French case, real estate developers have been increasingly responsible for the production of social housing from the 2000s onwards. In order to compel real estate developers to introduce quotas of social housing into their projects, local governments have regulatory instruments at their disposal (e.g. the introduction of social mix sectors in local urban plans), and also more flexible instruments, such as "developer charters" or other "best practices" that the developer must comply with in order to obtain a building permit. The study also explains why developers have an interest in the production of social housing: counter-cyclical nature of social housing construction, guaranteed and secure sales, etc. (Gimat and Pollard 2016). On a completely different note, the work of Christophers (2014) highlights the use of economic modeling tools to assess the potential for integrating affordable housing into new developments in the United Kingdom. He describes the performative effect of these instruments that lead local governments to integrate, upstream, in their practices and representations, the profit norms set by property developers and support the developers' model of capital accumulation (property-led urbanized capital accumulation).

A third line of research looks at **negotiation practices** and **exchange processes**, between real estate developers and local governments. This work emphasizes public–private partnerships – whether formal or informal – and the intermingling of strategies and expectations of developers and public actors. This refers, in particular, to the conditions of concrete implementation of policy instruments. Indeed, starting with official urban plans and documents, the participation of developers is achieved through mutual adaptations and renegotiations over time. In the British urban planning system, *"development contributions"* have been introduced as a means of generating public revenue and involving developers in the financing of policies of general interest (affordable housing, education, health, transport, public facilities, etc.) (Elsmore 2020; see also Chapter 6). The analysis of Elsmore (2020), based on the Southwark district (London, the United Kingdom), reveals that these contributions often serve developers' interests by improving the quality of the projects and the urban amenities of the districts. In his analysis in Toronto and Vancouver (Canada), Hyde (2022) shows how local policy-makers engage in processes to "trade" more building rights (and the rights to build buildings of higher density) with developers in return for including social or affordable housing in projects. These exchanges mask the economic calculations of profit maximization behind an "altruistic" language of reciprocity and giving. The logic of "giving back to get ahead" corresponds to a logic of accumulation for the private sector: developers increase their symbolic capital and enhance their reputation in this way, which leads to new profit opportunities in later phases. Hyde points out that these policies of capturing land value, which tend to develop in North American cities, can be interpreted in a perspective of neoliberalization of the supply of certain social services. The temporal dimension of the negotiations appears central. A similar logic is found in the work of Citron (2017), who observes the articulation of land development activities with real estate activities downstream. The largest French real estate developers are increasingly active in land development. This requires significant investments and involves a high level of risk for limited gains. But such activities are strategic for developers: they create future real estate development opportunities (Citron 2017). This implicitly assumes that all (or part) of the land charges[12] will later be de facto reserved for the developer.

All of these studies highlight the benefits that developers derive from their "social" interventions, and the *ultimate* subjugation of social objectives to developers' profit objectives (Geva and Rosen 2018; Leffers 2018; Elsmore 2020). This research also considers a number of **perverse effects** of the increasing intervention of private developers in the implementation of social dimensions of housing production, such as the gentrification of working-class neighborhoods or the increasing involvement of developers in local decision-making processes without any democratic control (Hyde 2022).

2.2.3. Are environmental issues transforming the practices of real estate developers?

Issues related to sustainable development echo in the real estate and construction sector: construction of energy-efficient housing, environmental impact studies for development projects, development of eco-neighborhoods, implementation of new construction standards, promotion of the wood industry in construction, etc. Based on the observation that the sector weighs heavily on CO_2 emissions and energy consumption, a series of public policies have been developed to encourage real estate developers to adopt more environmentally friendly practices. What are the effects of the instruments put in place? Are environmental concerns changing the practices of developers?

The growing concern for environmental issues is reflected in the evolution of **public regulation**, both at the national and local levels. A variety of instruments have been put in place to change the practices of developers: regulatory instruments (e.g. thermal regulations); economic and fiscal instruments (development of eco-conditionalities – e.g. subsidies or tax deductions reserved for buildings deemed to be virtuous); conventional and incentive instruments (e.g. mobilization of sectoral actors through the establishment of partnerships) and norms and standards

---

12. The land cost corresponds to the overall cost of acquiring a plot of land in a given real estate project. This cost includes the price of the land itself, and also the costs related to its acquisition (notary and real estate agency fees, taxes related to the transaction, etc.) and its development.

(e.g. development of labels and prizes for the construction of exemplary buildings). A body of work, focusing primarily on the condition of emergence of these new norms, points to the reluctance of developers with regard to these new imperatives (Beuschel and Rudel 2009; Storbjörk et al. 2018). Taburet (2012, p. 327) thus writes about French developers: "By considering sustainability as just another regulation and as an additional layer to the existing legal framework of their activity, developers have started the process of adherence (to environmental standards) out of obligation". The work of Guironnet et al. (2018) shows how the financial actors in commercial real estate in France, during the *Grenelle de l'Environnement*, have mobilized to limit the ambition of environmental policies. Under the pressure from these actors, environmental issues have remained subordinated to "financial sustainability" imperatives, referring to a "greening under the condition of maintaining and extending financialized accumulation practices" (Guironnet et al. 2018). Based on a case study conducted in Sweden, Storbjörk et al. (2018) also observe how developers oscillate between a constrained adaptation to the new rules and a resistance-negotiation of them. But developers are not only resisting or passively adapting to the growing importance of environmental standards and policies.

How developers reconcile business and environmental strategies is a major issue. The diversity of developers' profiles also influence the way they approach matters related to sustainable development (Beuschel and Rudel 2009). The development of practices that integrate an environmental dimension can make sense as a strategy to distinguish ourselves and build an image. According to Guy (2008), some developers in the United Kingdom have been developing environmental innovations since the 1990s with this in mind. From this perspective, the development of labels and certifications allows developers to pursue differentiation strategies that provide competitive advantages on the markets (Taburet 2012). Beyond certifications, the interpretation of the different dimensions of sustainable development opens up new profit perspectives for some developers, through the creation of new niches, or even new markets. Taburet (2012) gives the example of the Bi-Home label (a shared-housing concept) launched in France by the developer Icade in 2012, based on the combination of a main dwelling, associated with a living space dedicated to another person (dependent person, at-home childcare or student) or to working from home.

The **marketing dimension** of the integration of sustainable development criteria by developers is recurrent. Changes in regulations have led developers to put their sustainable development strategies into words in their communication materials and activity reports. The speeches made by developers abound on their desire to be cutting-edge players, seeking innovative solutions to combat climate change. Such statements may appear to be nothing more than *greenwashing*. The gap between this communicative showcase and the practices of the actors has been documented (Storbjörk et al. 2018)[13]. However, the changes at work cannot be reduced to this communicational dimension. The outcomes of these policies and strategies are difficult to document. The "measurement" of the greening of developers' projects is faced with the problem of defining indicators and monitoring instruments. (Beuschel and Rudel 2009). However, we observe that these concerns generate **other tangible effects**, for example, on the organizational structure of the developer companies or on the networks of actors with which the developers collaborate (Halpern and Pollard 2017). The creation of new jobs or departments in charge of sustainable development are part of this, although the fact that these positions are sometimes associated with few resources or attached to communications departments or services raises questions. The rise of new experts is also documented (Robin 2022).

The three lines of research presented above show the complex articulations between market dynamics and political regulation. Thus, the financialization of real estate development is largely dependent on political strategies that accompany or even anticipate the needs of investors, and political actors are themselves increasingly dependent on the financial markets. The intervention of developers in urban renewal districts or in the production of affordable housing is guided by national and local political actors aiming to encourage the involvement of developers in the implementation of public policies. However, for developers, these new activities also correspond to new markets with alternative ways of generating profit. In the same way, the taking into account of environmental standards is affected by both regulations and the expectations of investors.

2.3. References

Aalbers, M.B. (2017). The variegated financialization of housing. *International Journal of Urban and Regional Research*, 41(4), 542–554.

Aalbers, M.B. (2019). Financial geographies of real estate and the city. A literature review. *Financial Geography Working Paper Series*, no. 21.

Ball, M. (1998). Institutions in British property research: A review. *Urban Studies*, 35(9), 1501–1517.

---

13. Storbjörk et al. (2018) show, for example, through a case study of developers in a medium-sized city in Sweden, that the same actors show very contrasting positions when we focus on their writings and when we ask them about their practices during interviews. During the interviews, the cost of environmental innovations and the weakness of consumer demand justify much more reserved positions.

Ball, M. (2002). The organisation of property development professions and practices. In *Development and Developers: Perspectives on Property*, Guy, S. and Henneberry, J. (eds). Blackwell Science Ltd., Hoboken.

Ballard, R. and Butcher, S. (2020). Comparing the relational work of developers. *Environment and Planning A: Economy and Space*, 52(2), 266–276.

Beuschel, V. and Rudel, T.K. (2009). Can real-estate developers be "green"? Sprawl, environmental rhetoric, and land use planning in a New Jersey community. *Society & Natural Resources*, 23(2), 97–110.

Brill, F. (2022). Playing the game: A comparison of international actors in real estate development in Modderfontein, Johannesburg and London's Royal Docks. *Geoforum*, 134, 197–204.

Charney, I. (2007). Intra-metropolitan preferences of property developers in greater Toronto's office market. *Geoforum*, 38(6), 1179–1189.

Christophers, B. (2014). Wild dragons in the city: Urban political economy, affordable housing development and the performative world-making of economic models. UK case. *International Journal of Urban and Regional Research*, 38(1), 79–97.

Citron, P. (2017). Produire la ville grâce aux opérateurs immobiliers : quel modèle pour l'aménagement privé en zone dense ? *Métropoles*, 20 [Online]. Available at: http://journals.openedition.org/metropoles/5461.

Coiacetto, E. (2001). Diversity in real estate developer behaviour: A case for research. *Urban Policy and Research*, 19(1), 43–59.

Coiacetto, E. (2009). Industry structure in real estate development: Is city building competitive? *Urban Policy and Research*, 27(2), 117–135.

Coulondre, A. (2017). La création de profit par les promoteurs immobiliers : étude sur le travail entrepreneurial de qualification des biens. *Revue française de sociologie*, 58(1), 41.

David, L. and Halbert, L. (2014). Finance capital, actor-network theory and the struggle over calculative agencies in the business property markets of Mexico City metropolitan region. *Regional Studies*, 48(3), 516–529.

Domaradzka, A. (2022). The un-equal playground: Developers and urban activists struggling for the right to the city. *Geoforum*, 134, 178–186.

Drozdz, M., Guironnet, A., Halbert, L. (2020). Les villes à l'ère de la financiarisation. *Métropolitiques* [Online]. Available at: https://metropolitiques.eu/Les-villes-a-l-ere-de-la-financiarisation.html.

Elsmore, S. (2020). Strategies of responsibilization: Development contributions and the political role of property developers. *Urban Geography*, 41(3), 389–408.

Fainstein, S.S. (2001). *The City Builders: Property Development in New York and London, 1980–2000*, 2nd edition. University Press of Kansas, Lawrence.

Fields, D. and Uffer, S. (2016). The financialisation of rental housing: A comparative analysis of New York City and Berlin. *Urban Studies*, 53(7), 1486–1502.

Garboden, P. and Jan-Trettien, C. (2020). "There's money to be made in community": Real estate developers, community organizing, and profit-making in a shrinking city. *Journal of Urban Affairs*, 42(3), 414–434.

Geva, Y. and Rosen, G. (2018). The regeneration deal: Developers, homeowners and new competencies in the development process. *Geoforum*, 96, 10–20.

Gimat, M. and Pollard, J. (2016). Un tournant discret : la production de logements sociaux par les promoteurs immobiliers. *Géographie, économie, société*, 18(2), 257–282.

Gore, T. and Nicholson, D. (1991). Models of the land-development process: A critical review. *Environment and Planning A: Economy and Space*, 23(5), 705–730.

Guironnet, A. (2016). Une financiarisation si discrète ? La circulation des standards de la filière d'investissement en immobilier tertiaire dans les politiques de développement urbain du Grand Lyon. *Métropoles*, 19 [Online]. Available at: http://journals.openedition.org.

Guironnet, A., Halbert, L., Maisetti, N. (2018). Coproduire la régulation environnementale, reproduire l'accumulation financiarisée : experts et gestionnaires d'actifs immobiliers dans la fabrique d'une politique de réduction des consommations énergétiques en France (2007–2017). *Terrains & Travaux*, 33(2), 75.

Guy, S. (2008). Developing interests: Environmental innovation and the social organisation of the property business. In *Development and Developers: Perspectives on Property*, Guy, S. and Henneberry, J. (eds). Wiley-Blackwell, Hoboken.

Guy, S. and Henneberry, J. (2000). Understanding urban development processes: Integrating the economic and the social in property research. *Urban Studies*, 37(13), 2399–2416.

Guy, S. and Henneberry, J. (2008). *Development and Developers: Perspectives on Property*. John Wiley & Sons, Chichester.

Guy, S., Henneberry, J., Rowley, S. (2002). Development cultures and urban regeneration. *Urban Studies*, 39(7), 1181–1196.

Halbert, L. and Attuyer, K. (2016). Introduction: The financialisation of urban production: Conditions, mediations and transformations. *Urban Studies*, 53(7), 1347–1361.

Halpern, C. and Pollard, J. (2017). Les effets du Grenelle de l'environnement sur l'action publique. Analyse comparée entre deux secteurs : déchets et bâtiment. *Gouvernement et action publique*, 2(2), 107.

Healey, P. (1991). Models of the development process: A review. *Journal of Property Research*, 8(3), 219–238.

Henneberry, J. and Parris, S. (2013). The embedded developer: Using project ecologies to analyse local property development networks. *Town Planning Review*, 84(2), 227–250.

Hyde, Z. (2022). Giving back to get ahead: Altruism as a developer strategy of accumulation through affordable housing policy in Toronto and Vancouver. *Geoforum*, 134, 187–196

Leffers, D. (2018). Real estate developers' influence of land use legislation in the Toronto region: An institutionalist investigation of developers, land conflict and property law. *Urban Studies*, 55(14), 3059–3075.

Lorrain, D. (2011). La main discrète : la finance globale dans la ville. *Revue française de science politique*, 61(6), 1097–1122.

Nappi-Choulet, I. (2009). *Les mutations de l'immobilier. De la finance au développement durable*. Éditions Autrement, Paris.

Nappi-Choulet, I. (2012). Le logement, laissé pour compte de la financiarisation. *Esprit*, 1, 84–95.

Pollard, J. (2018). *L'état, le promoteur et le maire : la fabrication des politiques du logement*. Presses de Sciences Po, Paris.

Pollard, J. (2022). The political conditions of the rise of real-estate developers in French housing policies. *Environment and Planning C: Politics and Space, OnlineFirst*. doi: 10.1177/23996544221129125.

Raimbault, N. (2016). Ancrer le capital dans les flux logistiques : la financiarisation de l'immobilier logistique. *Revue d'économie régionale & urbaine, février*, (1), 131.

Robin, E. (2022). Performing real estate value(s): Real estate developers, systems of expertise and the production of space. *Geoforum*, 134, 205–215.

Romainville, A. (2017). The financialization of housing production in Brussels. *International Journal of Urban and Regional Research*, 41(4), 623–641.

Rosen, G. (2017). Toronto's condo-builders: Development approaches and spatial preferences. *Urban Geography*, 38(4), 606–625.

Rouanet, H. and Halbert, L. (2016). Leveraging finance capital: Urban change and self-empowerment of real estate developers in India. *Urban Studies*, 53(7), 1401–1423.

Ruming, K.J. (2010). Developer typologies in urban renewal in Sydney: Recognising the role of informal associations between developers and local government. *Urban Policy and Research*, 28(1), 65–83.

Searle, L.G. (2016). *Landscapes of Accumulation: Real Estate and the Neoliberal Imagination in Contemporary India*. The University of Chicago Press.

Shatkin, G. (2017). *Cities for Profit: The Real Estate Turn in Asia's Urban Politics*. Cornell University Press, New York.

Shimbo, L. (2019). An unprecedented alignment: State, finance, construction and housing production in Brazil since the 2000s. *International Journal of Housing Policy*, 19(3), 337–353.

Storbjörk, S., Hjerpe, M., Isaksson, K. (2018). "We cannot be at the forefront, changing society": Exploring how Swedish property developers respond to climate change in urban planning. *Journal of Environmental Policy & Planning*, 20(1), 81–95.

Taburet, A. (2012). Promoteurs immobiliers privés et problématiques de développement durable urbain. Thesis, Université du Maine.

Theurillat, T. (2011). La ville négociée : entre financiarisation et durabilité. *Géographie, économie, société*, 13(3), 225–254.

Theurillat, T. and Crevoisier, O. (2014). Sustainability and the anchoring of capital: Negotiations surrounding two major urban projects in Switzerland. *Regional Studies*, 48(3), 501–515.

Topalov, C. (1973). *Les promoteurs immobiliers. Contribution à l'analyse de la production capitaliste du logement en France*. Mouton, Paris.

Trouillard, E. (2014). La production de logements neufs par la promotion privée en Île-de-France (1984–2012) : marchés immobiliers et stratégies de localisation. Thesis, Université Paris 7.

Van Loon, J. (2016). Patient versus impatient capital: The (non-) financialization of real estate developers in the Low Countries. *Socio-Economic Review*, 14(4), 709–728.

Van Loon, J. and Aalbers, M.B. (2017). How real estate became "just another asset class": The financialization of the investment strategies of Dutch institutional investors. *European Planning Studies*, 25(2), 221–240.

Vergriete, P. (2013). La ville fiscalisée. Politique d'aide à l'investissement locatif, nouvelle filière de production du logement et recomposition de l'action publique locale en France (1985–2012). PhD Thesis, Université Paris-Est.

Weber, R. (2015). *From Boom to Bubble: How Finance Built the New Chicago*. The University of Chicago Press.

Wijburg, G. (2019). Reasserting state power by remaking markets? The introduction of real estate investment trusts in France and its implications for state-finance relations in the Greater Paris region. *Geoforum*, 100, 209–219.

3

Housing, Ownership, Assets and Debt: Geographical Approaches

Renaud LE GOIX[1,2]
[1] Université Paris Cité, France
[2] UMR Géographie-Cités, Campus Condorcet, Aubervilliers, France

3.1. Introduction: a renewed interest in housing finance and home ownership

Housing plays a key role in the reproduction of social inequality (Piketty 2013), while there is little empirical evidence on the spatial effects of housing market dynamics, and in particular home ownership, on inequality (Hochstenbach and Arundel 2020; Le Goix et al. 2022). However, housing affordability[1] is a major issue for social cohesion in countries where housing prices have increased faster than household incomes in many post-industrial cities and regions (Wetzstein 2017). The unprecedented house price inflation observed in many countries at the turn of the 1990s and 2000s (Kohl 2018) is leading to a renewed interest in home ownership by urban studies, across three main dimensions.

For a color version of all the figures in this chapter, see www.iste.co.uk/avelinedubach/globalization.zip.

1. This contribution was funded by the *Agence Nationale de la Recherche*, ANR, within the framework of the program ANR-18-CE41-0004 – Wealth Inequalities and the Dynamics of Housing Market. Interpreting real-estate market-based regime of spatial inequalities (WIsDHoM) – https://wisdhom.hypotheses.org.

The first dimension relates to the financialization of housing and home ownership. The *subprime* crisis of 2007–2008 and the global financial crisis that followed revealed the extent to which finance is related to home ownership, particularly in the ways in which the least creditworthy working-class groups and households were enrolled in the market. This crisis was caused by the massive devaluation of asset-backed securities issued on the international markets, related to variable-rate loans distributed massively in the 1990s and 2000s to the least creditworthy households in the United States (see, for example, Wyly et al. 2012; Aalbers 2016; Kutz and Lenhardt 2016). The crisis has been contextual in renewing the approaches in political economy (Aalbers 2012), with a greater focus on inequalities in access to housing, linking inflation and the expansion of housing debt. The contemporary situation, as described, for example, by Kohl (2018) for OECD countries, or Migozzi (2019) on the emerging South African market, confirms the hypothesis that the increase in real estate debt has more effect on prices and accumulation than on the increase in the rate of home ownership. Access to borrowing might have extended downwards, but the threshold of unaffordability for the working classes remains.

Housing affordability also constitutes a salient issue in defining access to ownership by income. The growing disconnect between the real cost of residential housing and buyers' incomes since 2000 follows trends also identified in other countries. Since the early 2000s, the gap has only widened. A recent study of 17 countries found that between 1985 and 2010, price-to-income ratios increased everywhere – up to +28 percent in France, +44 percent in the United Kingdom – except in Germany and Japan (Aalbers 2016). This dimension seems to be at odds with the orientations of housing policies, which, in advanced economies, are part of an ideology of home ownership and related government housing policy reforms (Malpass 2011; Ronald 2008). Such policies are supposed to contribute to the formation of an owner class. Asset inflation leads to alternative modes of ownership, decoupling ownership of the property from land ownership (Rowe et al. 2016; Le Rouzic 2019).

This chapter reviews the issues surrounding home ownership, household debt and wealth, and the social division of space, in the wake of the global housing and financial crisis of 2007–2008. Since Halbwachs' study (1913), theoretical works have sought to explain inequalities and segregation in terms of housing accessibility. Recent works re-evaluate the question of housing production, rent extraction and market regimes, partly theorized by Topalov (1984) in French, and by Harvey (1985) in English. In relation to this Marxist literature, neoliberal injunctions have reframed home ownership, along with the financialization of the productive and non-productive spheres of the economy, with housing playing an essential part.

Information technologies are allowing investors, households, financial institutions and market actors to optimize the value chain and rent extraction; post-industrial societies have gradually restructured around the way financial capital relies on a rentier logic, with property being a major asset (Ward and Swyngedouw 2018).

This literature review chapter starts from the issues of home ownership, as an essential and ideological element of housing policies in advanced economies, from which the economic geography of housing, from social rental to new development, is partly derived. A critical approach to the notion of financialization allows us first to show the coupling between the markets and regimes of financial asset valuation, from transnational to local scales, and national variations (see section 3.2). To do so, it is also necessary to discuss the classical and neoclassical theoretical and practical relationships of capital circuits linking household debt, the circulation of wealth, and real estate inflation in the construction of local market regimes and their dynamics (see section 3.3). In so doing, these factors are essential in the contemporary construction of social inequalities, and even define part of contemporary class relations, to which financing arrangements that include households in the residential and home ownership market respond in an unequal and filtered way (see section 3.4). The conclusion will outline some perspectives of contemporary research (see section 3.5).

3.2. Is residential real estate becoming a financialized asset?

Since the international financial crisis of 2007–2008, many studies have focused on what is generally referred to as the financialization of real estate and urban production (for a general summary, see Aveline-Dubach et al. 2020). There are several definitions of financialization. In different national contexts, financial capital has massively converged on cities and urban spaces, most visibly through large urban projects, associated with the increasing role of developers in urban planning (Guironnet et al. 2016). These investments are subject to the triptych risk, return, liquidity (Theurillat et al. 2015). In the context of the financialization of real estate, treated as an asset, this section analyzes the position that home ownership occupies, characterized by two main issues: inflation and insurance. Pro-home ownership housing policies jointly support these three mechanisms.

3.2.1. *Geographical approaches to the financialization of real estate*

Trends in the financialization of residential real estate are geographically uneven and vary across institutional and cultural contexts (Fernandez and Aalbers 2016; Aveline-Dubach 2020). Over the past decade, financialization has emerged as a term describing new forms of capital transfer whereby financial and non-financial firms are increasingly involved in financial markets (Aalbers 2016), evolving the functional integration of all economic sectors, and real estate in particular. This consolidation of economic power has contributed to an unprecedented accumulation of liquid assets around the world – also known as the "wall of money" (Fernandez and Aalbers 2016). In order to avoid the onset of a new financial crisis, institutional changes were made to facilitate the productive reinvestment of capital, and did so, which have affected real estate valuation and market stratification (French et al. 2011; Aalbers 2016). These innovations include, for example, the securitization of mortgages, rents, the privatization of public housing, the rent-capture strategies of institutional financial intermediaries, and the broader commodification of property, housing rights and urban planning itself.

Beyond these macroeconomic changes, financialization is also a cultural and socio-economic change in everyday life ("the financialization of everyday life", (French et al. 2011, p. 804)). Finance shapes everyday life in post-industrial economies, with an increasing importance of financial culture in the lives of households as the welfare state weakens in a post-Keynesian system (Martin 2002). For example, households make rental investments, take out loans using leverage, and anticipate asset appreciation in their residential investment strategy.

3.2.2. Property and inflationary mechanisms

Economists generally view house price inflation as the result of a shortage of housing supply relative to high demand, consistent with the underlying assumptions of market equilibrium. This refers to the frameworks of a home ownership ideology and associated government housing policy reforms (Ronald 2008; Malpass 2011). However, there is empirical evidence showing that inflation does not necessarily restrict the demand for residential real estate (Case and Shiller 1988; Goodman and Thibodeau 2008) and that an increased supply of housing does not depreciate market prices (Geniaux et al. 2015). Neoliberal economists nevertheless the support supply-side policies that seek to correct market imbalances by increasing the supply of housing and promoting the deregulation of market controls, when there is evidence that these measures are also likely to stimulate further price inflation by encouraging speculative investment (Aveline 2008).

Other inflationary effects are related to the massive influx of credit. The macroeconomic links between home ownership growth, housing or mortgage debt, and price inflation are well established (Kohl 2018). They have enabled the large-scale expansion of credit availability through government programs and tax incentives that promote home ownership in many OECD countries. In this respect, the real estate sector has been particularly helped by public policies for a long time. The links between this aid and inflation are fairly well established. The work of Aalbers (2016) on the financialization of real estate is essential in this respect.

There are several models of the relationship between the types of credit available and housing market regimes. Fernandez and Aalbers (2016) identify four broad types of national trajectories in one of the only comparative studies, based on data collected in the early 2010s. In the first group, most European Union countries and a few emerging countries (including Brazil, Mexico and Turkey) have high rates of home ownership (between 69% and 96%), with a large majority of owner-occupiers, and a low-financialized market, with a large share of household wealth mobilized in real estate, most of which is free from real estate debts (79% in Italy, 77% in Greece and 73% in Hungary). A second group is made up of the *usual suspects* of increased financialization of residential real estate investment: countries such as Iceland, Canada, Australia, the United Kingdom, the United States and Spain. They combine a high level of household debt in relation to GDP, intense international financial flows in the structure of the markets and a high level of complexity of financial products. Since the 2010s, monetary policies in the United States and the United Kingdom have made it possible to pursue this trajectory, combining strong monetary creation and low credit costs to support the markets. In Spain and Ireland, the markets have had to absorb the overcapacity of housing products, and investors have turned away from these domestic markets, shifting their investments (capital switching) to countries bordering them, for example, Morocco (Kutz and Lenhardt 2016). A third type of market regime would correspond to the situations developing in the Netherlands or Denmark. Its home ownership rate is modest, but the level of debt relative to GDP is high and very few households are debt-free. This group of countries has also seen a large increase in the proportion of homeowners in the OECD, through very large tax incentives. A final group of countries includes situations where the home ownership rate is structurally lower (France, Austria, Germany, Switzerland), and household wealth also consists of large bank deposits and not necessarily real estate. These countries have complex and deep financial systems. While Germany, remarkably, has not experienced a *price-to-income ratio* surge, this is not the case in France, which has seen a significant decoupling of prices and incomes since the 2000s. From this point of view, France seems to be sliding towards a regime that could progressively approach the first group, in terms of reforms of the welfare state and an increasingly assertive recourse to the construction of household wealth with an insurance value (Benites and Bonneval, 2022).

The role of credit is obviously essential in structuring these residential markets. Expanding access to credit (lower rates, longer repayment period) theoretically facilitates households' access to housing. Kohl (2018) reminds us that the evolution of the home ownership rate is relatively independent of the quantitative increase in real estate loans. But policies facilitating borrowing, particularly in OECD countries, actually fuel the rise in residential prices more than the access to home ownership of households that have long been excluded (see Figure 3.1). Since the 1970s, the liberalization of housing loan markets has contributed to an increase in household debt and house prices, for example in the United Kingdom, the United States and the Netherlands. The same effects materialize later in Canada, Spain, Sweden and France from the 2000s onwards. In Sweden, the deregulation of housing and the rise of home ownership have had tangible effects on inequalities in access to housing (Borg et al. 2022). The trend is not ubiquitous: Germany has long been an exception to this relationship, but deregulation of the rental sector has tipped it into inflation.

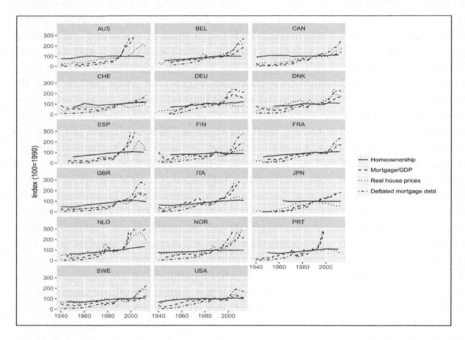

Figure 3.1. *Index of homeowner rates, real house prices, real mortgage debt and mortgage debt per GDP, base 1990 (source: Computer from Macrohistory Database (2018). Homeownership, Rent and Society. Kohl. See: http://www.macrohistory. net/data)*

3.2.3. *Asset-based welfare*

Topalov (1987) described the evolution of home ownership systems in France as a shift from a rentier system to massive credit-based home ownership, regulated by the convergence of public policies (to increase household creditworthiness and incentivize home ownership), the banking industry, the strategies of market actors (notably developers) and household asset preservation strategies (Bonneval and Robert 2013). This transformation is taking place in many advanced economies, under injunctions from the World Bank (Rolnik 2013), including the 1993 report *Housing: Enabling Markets to Work*, which promotes public policies to support housing markets. Scholarly works describe shifts in the organization of welfare states based on *asset-based welfare* models. This economic theory is based on a conception of the redistribution of the products of capital and accumulated wealth, and is underpinned by a growing ideology of home ownership in modern industrialized societies and a path dependence in housing policy reforms (Malpass 2011), favoring political support for market mechanisms (Ronald 2008) and accumulation regimes (Boyer 2000).

More specifically, theoretical work establishes a link between the high proportion of capital investment that housing represents for households and the modes of organization and reform of welfare states (Kemeny 2001). Homeownership is seen as a superior form of tenure, while public policies reduce the supply of social housing: a process known as the "residualization of social housing" (Van Gent 2010). Trajectories are highly dependent on national frameworks, but the state will usually allow households to act as investors, enrolling themselves in the markets with prospects of future gains, while exposing themselves to greater risks (price volatility, loss of property value, risks of bankruptcy and foreclosure, etc.). This raises the question of individual and systemic risks, and thus household vulnerabilities (Schwartz and Seabrooke 2009). In this context, housing has become a potential avenue for wealth accumulation. Home ownership rates have increased and state reforms have encouraged real estate investment in a context of reduced social protection (Driant 2010), promoting, for example, the insurance value of property for retirement.

This social insurance and wealth model actually leads to a form of "privatized Keynesianism" (Crouch 2009) as an asset-building model for households through debt-financed home ownership. Thus, since the early 1990s, the dramatic increase in investment in real estate (both household and institutional) and the associated growth of new financial products and services, which are aimed at increasing the purchasing power of buyers, have contributed to rising inflation and price volatility. In France, for example, although the housing market is often considered to be the domain of public policies that favor social housing, the market has nevertheless been thoroughly restructured to evolve according to this form of "privatized Keynesianism" characterized by tax incentives and subsidies to the homebuilding industry, borrowing (zero interest loans) and public policies in favor of home ownership. Wijburg (2019) demonstrates that the amount of subsidies for private investment in renting and home ownership exceeds that of subsidies in the social sector, an obvious inflection for the welfare state model. This has led to a very strong development of multiple property ownership: households owning at least five dwellings represent 3.5% of households, and hold 50% of the privately owned rental stock (André et al. 2021).

The question of protecting household real estate assets is therefore a remarkable economic, social and political issue, and is gradually being treated as an asset issue. In Florida, Taylor (2020) analyzes the role of securitization in the protection of real estate value by insurance companies against the devaluation of property because of rising waters and climate risk. Thus, despite the succession of hurricanes on the coast, the real estate market has remained particularly dynamic, with the construction of new condominiums (high-end residential buildings with services), particularly financed by investors. Florida residents spent $10.8 billion to protect 6 million properties ($1,600 per property), through products such as Catastrophe Bonds, which are securities issued on the financial markets by insurance companies to specifically cover natural hazards on the properties they insure. When real estate value is threatened, financial engineering can create insurance solutions that support vulnerable markets. This example shows the importance of the financial relations between the circuits of capital, those of intermediation and finally that of investment in residential property and housing, in short, the various circuits of capital in property and the forms of rent capture.

3.3. Geographical analysis of property market regimes

3.3.1. *The value of property in space, renewal of a critical analysis*

A geography of real estate markets relates to the broader theorization of the urban dynamic, the spatial structure of prices being indicative of "social morphology" (Halbwachs 1970 (originally published in 1946)), a question particularly invested in the French Marxist tradition (Halbwachs 1970; Lipietz 1974; Topalov 1984). Topalov (1974) goes beyond the structure of prices and inequalities, and analyzes the economic structures of the market, its institutions and financing circuits, and also its function of mobilizing investment capital. The fundamental hypotheses stems from the intrinsically limited nature of land on the earth's surface;

the soil and its appropriation are a central issue of capitalism (Lefebvre 1974). The hypothesis is that of fictitious capital: the entitlement to property is a right to future profits (the rent). We can, of course, present it in a simple way as a dialectic "between the law of value and the existence of rent on land" (Harvey 1982, p. 371): land seems to have value, and this value seems, in fact, to determine the amount of rent the owner receives for its use; but land is not the result of what produces value, i.e. work. Harvey therefore proposes to treat land as an asset, which as such is exchanged. Land and housing, and the level of rent derived from them, thus depend closely on the nature and location of investments made. This work by Harvey (1985, 2003) lays the foundations of the political economy of housing markets (Aalbers 2016). Housing and the land attached to it are thus both commodities and capital: "treating land in conceptual terms not as fictitious but as very much real – as real capital *and* as a real commodity" (Christophers 2016), which entails, for example, focusing on the set of power and promotion (Topalov 1974; Bonneval and Pollard 2017) and intermediation relations (Langley 2006; Aalbers 2016), market actors, and local structures for reproducing and anchoring capital in space (Theurillat et al. 2015).

3.3.2. *The limits of classical approaches to prices in the city*

In neo-classical approaches, the spatial structure, on the contrary, is only a container in a price–offer–demand relationship determined by a general equilibrium of optimal land allocation; prices are considered as an indicator of the value of utility distributed in space according to rent logic, summarized by a center-periphery model. The best-known models of utility and value distribution are those of Von Thünen and Alonso, in relation to the decrease in population density, land pressure, transport costs and utility from the center to the peripheries of cities. Such standard models (Bailly 1973) are based on auction mechanisms (Aveline-Dubach 2010) or competition for space between the housing function and the other functions of space, which are widely used in the work on segregation mechanisms aiming to understand a logic of spatial competition[2]. This is a descriptive approach, which gradually becomes an explanatory approach. This shift is the basis for modeling spatial price dynamics, the exercise of which in econometrics consists of analyzing, for example, changes in local equilibrium (Glaeser et al. 2014). These assumptions derive from the idea that:

---

2. For these notions, see in this collection *Cities at the Heart of Inequalities* in particular Cottineau and Pumain (2022) on the main models, Boulay (2022) on rent and Le Goix (2022) on segregation.

soil has value only because it provides a service [...], and thus consider that rent is no longer due to fertility or accessibility differentials in a context of private ownership of soil, but to the sole monetary expenditure that an individual makes to maintain his or her utility level (Boulay 2011, p. 57).

This formulation is probably the main criticism of a spatial approach to prices and markets, as envisaged by hedonic modeling, the standard procedure for estimating property prices as a function of location.

Indeed, spatial economics primarily approach the issue of price through the hegemonic framework of econometrics, reducing the issue to the control of dependent and independent variables in modeling housing market segments. The huge body of work on spatial econometrics and housing segmentation stems from neoclassical models, which tend to explain property valuation through the mixed effects of fixed characteristics and spatial attributes. This involves assigning a value to a typical property, based on the hedonic attributes of the property (willingness to pay for each attribute), under the assumption that sellers and buyers agree on a market price for the attributes. This is typically done using a regression model, explanatory variables derived from property's attributes, environmental characteristics (i.e. the social and natural environment), and information about the accessibility or characteristics of the local location or submarket, the neighborhood or street, for example (Rosen 1974). The aim is to explain prices in a structure of homogeneous sub-markets: the models therefore allow the definition of these sub-market segments (note the resulting tautology). These segments are described by typical goods, under the assumption of controlling for spatial autocorrelation problems (Cliff and Ord 1981) in price determination, for which many modeling implementations have been tested. The need for spatial analysis in hedonic price modeling to contextualize housing markets and their spatial interactions is often recognized as essential (Bowen et al. 2001), but there is no consensus on explanatory modalities. Some explore the multilevel interactions of property with price as a function of distance to better account for geographically nested effects and scalar interactions (Orford 2002; Chasco and Le Gallo 2012), to trams and light rail (Fritsch 2007), or to urban renewal districts (Beckerich 2000). This research has helped contextualize the effects of distance on real estate prices. Developing a theory of price and spatial interaction, however, requires a better and explicit understanding of how exogenous socio-spatial interactions interfere with many scalar effects in which real estate ownership is spatially *intertwined* (Le Goix et al. 2022), actor-arranged and socially *embedded* (Callon 1998) and politically *constructed* (Pollard 2018).

3.3.3. *Market regimes*

Dealing with the question of contemporary property markets entirely in one chapter would be a challenge, so this chapter will specifically offer our reading of it and a few supporting references. Let us remember that land–property relations highlight several fields, each with their own disciplinary anchorage and reference texts (orthodox economics and econometrics, heterodox economics; urban sociology, labor sociology, sociology of actors; geography and urban planning; political economy, etc.). Each of the explanatory theoretical frameworks, however, are not sufficient to analyze the structuring and evolution of urban systems, and in particular the great diversity of spatial configurations and their evolutions (Boulay 2012; Le Goix et al. 2022), which are difficult to reduce to a general model of cities (Cusin 2016) or to a singular spatial category (the peri-urban, for example, Le Goix et al. 2019). The synthesis by Aveline-Dubach et al. (2020) provides insights into the multiple evolutions of the relationship between property and land.

Le Corre (2019) offers a synthesis focused on the spatial structure of market regimes and their evolution. It analyzes the evolution between 1996 and 2012 of the Paris and Ile-de-France markets. This approach crosses property types and spatial arrangements, on the one hand (localized sub-markets), the characterization of the socio-economic profiles of buyers and sellers (who sells to whom), the purchase regimes, i.e. the financing modalities (reinvestment of assets/real estate loan) and the investment modalities. He distinguishes between the ordinary housing market; the investment market (assets intended for the rental market, either tax-free or furnished for tourism); the luxury market and second homes. He demonstrates that a property can move from one market regime to another during a sale, profoundly changing its nature and the valuation dynamics in which it is embedded. Using multivariate analysis, he distinguishes 11 types of market regimes in Ile-de-France (see Figure 3.2). The ordinary suburban housing market, characterized by a population of elderly homeowners and younger first-time buyers, occasionally describes the housing estates in the outer suburbs and in rural communities. It differs from a more mature market of a suburban family market where first-time homebuyers are only marginally involved, due to inflation. A suburban market regime in the upper-market western residential neighborhoods of the agglomeration stands out, characterized by second-home ownership in rather high-end suburban housing. It is an extension of all the neighborhoods in the western suburbs, which are fairly homogeneous in terms of concentration of affluence and assets, in neighborhoods with a high level of continuous real estate appreciation, and where purchasing strategies by owners are very local. These are enduring market regimes with a strong tendency for social reproduction in these very exclusive markets. This is a mixed regime of rental investment and occupancy. Finally, many peripheral areas, because of the structure of housing and prices, are rather affected by second-home-ownership logics, with a significant diversity of profiles. The remote secondary urban centers are thus attractive for purchases by retirees.

More specifically, the new real estate development market is structuring the outskirts of Paris. New start neighborhoods restructure the inner suburbs, with extensive urban renewal projects, especially in the vicinity of the new metro stations of the Greater Paris transit mega project. New developments also contribute to the densification of new towns in the outer suburbs (Marne-la-Vallée, Cergy-Pontoise). In the central zone of the Paris, the conurbation is characterized by very stable markets, benefiting from the situation rents for the western part of it, where investments in luxury goods, by corporate investors, by foreign buyers, often in large properties. Most of the central part of Paris, to the north, east and south, is characterized by rental investments (timeshares) and also by individual access for first-time buyers, more rarely by families, who are under-represented in owner-occupation. This is a mixed regime of rental investment and small home ownership, obviously affected by intense gentrification dynamics (Clerval 2013). Once the gentrification front affecting the communes close to Paris in the east has been crossed, this type is distinguished by a more commonplace market for first-time family home ownership, in apartments or small houses, in the dense areas of the conurbation, particularly in the eastern suburbs and in former industrial areas undergoing reconversion. The analysis also makes it possible to highlight the changes between the different periods analyzed, because of inflation dynamics, the devaluation of a neighborhood, gentrification, and the induced effects of aging and asset accumulation by households (see Figure 3.3).

These examples are to be related to the numerous works that analyze inequality and socio-spatial segregation as a function of the stratification of housing markets, urban cycles and housing affordability[3]. Work focuses on analyzing indices of inequality and segregation as a function of market regimes (Tammaru et al. 2016a, 2016b). Arbaci (2007), for example, demonstrates that cities characterized by a corporatist regime, which promotes social ownership or rental, have the lowest levels of segregation. On the contrary, regimes that promote individual ownership as the dominant model show the highest levels of segregation. This type of regime favors exclusionary processes induced by gentrification and urban renewal in inner-city neighborhoods, as well as by the dominant character of peri-urban ownership.

---

[3]. For questions of stratification, as analyzed in urban sociology, see the chapter by Le Goix (2022) in the book *Cities at the Heart of Inequalities*.

Housing, Ownership, Assets and Debt: Geographical Approaches 59

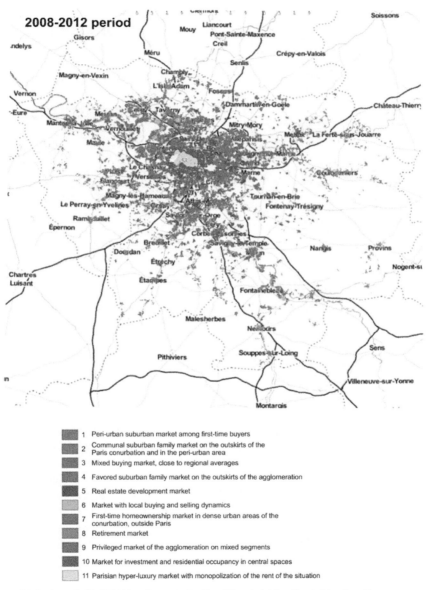

1	Peri-urban suburban market among first-time buyers
2	Communal suburban family market on the outskirts of the Paris conurbation and in the peri-urban area
3	Mixed buying market, close to regional averages
4	Favored suburban family market on the outskirts of the agglomeration
5	Real estate development market
6	Market with local buying and selling dynamics
7	First-time homeownership market in dense urban areas of the conurbation, outside Paris
8	Retirement market
9	Privileged market of the agglomeration on mixed segments
10	Market for investment and residential occupancy in central spaces
11	Parisian hyper-luxury market with monopolization of the rent of the situation

Sources: Data from the sample of the BIEN database after reconstruction of the variables and calculations of the potentials on the spatial units of the 200m2 grid of INSEE. Maps from the realization of the CAH under RStudio with the Cartography Package. OSM Basemap
Source: Thiboult Le Corre, 2018.

Figure 3.2. *Local market regimes in Ile-de-France, typology (2008–2012) (source: Le Corre (2019))*

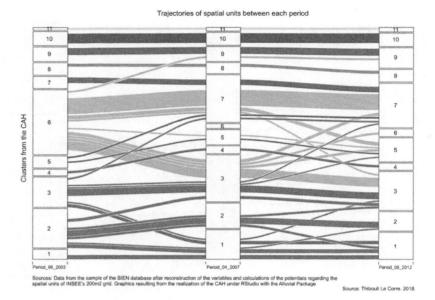

Figure 3.3. *Dynamics of local market regimes in Ile-de-France, typology (1996–2012) (source: Le Corre (2019))*

3.4. Property and socio-spatial segregation

To what extent is contemporary social inequality shaped by one's relationship to spatially stratified housing markets, particularly home ownership? The residential market and property ownership would be, in a regime of massification of access, a major system of wealth production and drivers of inequalities between social classes (Piketty 2013; Aalbers and Christophers 2014). In particular, household investments become an instrument of the dynamics of localized (anchored) capitalization of assets, and thus of socio-spatial inequality. This system is based on accumulation mechanisms, and also a strong institutional anchoring linked to credit intermediation and forms of reproduction of inequalities in space. However, solidarity-based mechanisms for decoupling land and property can help cushion the effects of these inequalities on housing affordability.

3.4.1. *The role of credit and intermediation in inequality and segregation*

Historically, home ownership markets have involved complex spatial sorting effects of buyers, based on credit and the role of banking intermediation in segregation. The most historically documented effects relate to redlining, a framework of racial discrimination in the allocation of housing loans, supported by the authorities (Federal Housing Authority) and prohibiting, depending on the neighborhood, the accession to property by a black African-American household. This practice, maintained until the Fair Housing Act of 1968, largely contributed to reinforcing the spatial segregation between the central black ghettos and the white suburbs, linked to white flight, the massive suburbanization movement of the white middle class from the 1930s to the 1980s. Since then, the devices for ranking household vulnerability to risky mortgages have been studied (Newman and Wyly 2004), as well as the impact of these market devices on stratification. While households in African American and Hispanic communities have been particularly targeted by subprime mortgages, these too are practices of market inclusion according to the formulas that proved discriminatory and particularly predatory for these households during the subprime boom (Immergluck 2012; Wyly et al. 2012).

Nevertheless, it is also possible to formulate the hypothesis that not only redlining but all market mechanisms play a role in the unequal accumulation of real estate wealth in space, with effects on socio-spatial inequalities. Thus, residential markets in France are structured by market mechanisms that influence locally unequal trajectories of real estate accumulation. For example, municipal zero-interest loans, affordable housing instruments, rental investment subsidies, tax incentives and local building legislation are among these (Pollard 2018). These local market dynamics depend heavily on national regulatory arrangements that allow households to act as investors seeking future gains, while exposing them to greater financial risks (price volatility, loss of property value, bankruptcy and foreclosure risks, etc.) and systemic shocks. But the housing policies and regulations that drive investment, as well as the interactions between public and private actors (developers, local governments, landlords, land holders…), play a key role in shaping and reinforcing inequality (Grandclement and Boulay 2016; Bonneval and Pollard 2017).

In advanced economies, home ownership is a major component of household wealth. The relationship of home ownership to credit structures how real estate is viewed as a commodity and as an investment. This has obviously been observed in the United States, in a suburban investment regime marked by a cyclicality of crises, of which the one in 2007–2008 left 12 million households evicted from their homes after foreclosure. An analysis conducted in Los Angeles shows how the development of planned subdivisions is the result of a series of relationships based on regimes of financial contracting and systematic indebtedness of several actors in urban production: developers, local governments, districts (water, sanitation, etc.), condominiums and ultimately buyers. All of these levels are financed by tax levies or fees indexed to property values. Buyers rely on the inflationary logic of prices in the hope of recouping their costs. However, although the general trend is for property values to rise, all households are far from benefiting from this because the value of properties differs greatly depending on the type of property and its location. This is particularly true for the most standard and low-end properties, and for the investments of modest households, which, in the long run, raises strategic questions about the viability of these neighborhoods, the fiscal balance of local governments and the sustainability of the investment for households (Le Goix 2016).

In this context, home ownership through credit, while seen by liberals as emancipatory, in an ideal of social ascension and patrimonial investment, nevertheless entails long-term financial dependence, which implies that households must have guarantees as to the durability of the value of the home. This also implies financial and moral discipline in what some interpret as a class of first-time buyers disciplined by financial logic (Langley 2006).

3.4.2. *The new market mechanisms, a strengthening of the relationship between property and inequality*

The spatial anchoring of property market regimes is determined by the modalities of financing (flows of capital into and out of local housing markets). Market regimes are influenced by the social division of space (or spatial stratification of urban inequalities). This stratification operates through the assembly of different housing policies, financial engineering and market devices (Callon et al. 2007) and also technologies (Porter et al. 2019; Fields and Rogers 2021). Such devices contribute to (re)stratifying the market, by constructing categories of buyers – based on databases, categories, and risk ratings determined automatically and algorithmically by market actors (Fourcade and Healy 2017). These devices correspond to an eminently performative logic: the categories constructed by the agents determine their vision and action (Callon et al. 2007). These effects are particularly powerful with real estate asset management platforms (Fields 2019) or the availability of numerous databases and market price references to professionals, buyers and sellers, which trivialize price information without making price references and markets less opaque (Boulay et al. 2020).

Among these market-restratifying devices, some works show that the estimation of the borrower's risk based on computerized systems, household classification indicators (e.g. based on wealth, assets, income) and credit histories, contribute to reinforcing the exclusion of social categories from the market (Fourcade and Healy 2017). This exclusion is often correlated with ethno-racial segregation in the characterization of buyers. Migozzi (2019) thus analyzes the emergence of a solvent middle class through the penetration of credit into black and *colored* populations in Cape Town, South Africa, based on the action of market actors (agencies, developers), who incorporate this new class of buyers through access to credit. The author demonstrates that the logics of segregation, in this Cape Town context, are no longer totally based on strategies or preferences, but, to a great extent, on assignments or filtering embedded (Callon 1998) in the systems of databases that allow for the provision of credit or the analysis of a tenant's creditworthiness (Migozzi 2019).

The massive devaluation of certain properties has contributed to the emergence of new strategies for rent extraction, a low-noise financialization (Fields 2019). The vacancy of many homes, and above all the foreclosures and auctions that took place after the crisis, were largely conducive to the massive purchase of properties by investors. In the United States, foreclosed and devalued properties are more likely to be sold to small individual or family investors, who intend the property for rental, than to an owner–occupier (Pfeiffer and Molina 2012). Nussbaum (2019) analyzes several categories of investors in Houston and Chicago deriving rent from these devalued properties in what she calls a "ruin economy", targeting dilapidated housing, sometimes degraded by long periods of vacancy. These investors are generally locally based and their portfolios are often modest. The less scrupulous are hidden behind post office boxes and phantom addresses. There are multiple strategies: in the short term, rapid resale (flipping); in the medium term, rehabilitation of the building, or demolition to allow for new construction; in the longer term, retention strategies, either for the constitution of land reserves or for renting out with the aim of eventual (future) gentrification of the neighborhood. The affordability crisis and housing shortage make these low-end properties highly profitable. For single-family homes, algorithmic valuation and risk assessment systems have allowed for the massive acquisition of properties by platforms linked to investment funds (Blackstone – Invitation Homes; American Homes 4 Rent; Waypoints etc.) that automate the valuation of the portfolio of primary residences – essentially devalued properties that had been foreclosed by banks, with a view to transforming them into investment properties. In turn, the tenant of these homes is also algorithmically screened by the platform (Fields 2019). What is remarkable about the cases discussed here is the crisis-induced transformation of housing built in owner-occupied market regimes into low-end rental housing restructured by the actions of investors (large and small), as part of the affordability crisis and a low-level financialization of residential markets.

3.4.3. *Sharing ownership*

In the context of the affordability crisis in metropolises, other market adjustments are taking place through actors, who reject the logics of monopolization and predation in order to promote logics of solidarity. Community land trusts are institutional land governance solutions that focus on the decoupling of property rights of land from those of building to limit capital gains and the effects of rent capture on land, and to favor the affordability of access to property and act on inequalities in access to property. These models were developed in particular in the 1980s in the United States (Attard 2013), and were carried by networks of activist expertise, embodied in particular by a personality such as Bernie Sanders in the United States (the Champlain Housing Trust) or the Caño Martín Peña Community Land Trust in Puerto Rico, both of which were awarded the World Habitat Prize by the NGO World Habitat recognized by the United Nations (Le Rouzic 2019). Beyond the simple decoupling of land from buildings, the form in which it is often presented (Thaden et al. 2013), these community land trust systems do in fact constitute a new common property regime (Le Rouzic 2019), in which the land rent is shared. They require heavy legislative work to adjust the property rights. Formalized as a cluster of rights, based in particular on the work of Ostrom and Hess (2008), residential appropriation regimes allow for a diversity of possible institutional arrangements. Le Rouzic (2021) analyzes this cluster of rights (see Table 3.1), with residential property being broken down into rights of use, and various forms of ownership in different contexts, with implications for collective management and governance, various forms of cooperatives, collective ownership and condominiums experimented within national contexts where decoupling of rights are common (Blandy et al. 2010) The results of the CLTs demonstrate the effectiveness of using land as a social asset, making it possible to implement mechanisms of solidarity in access to housing. The dissociation of land and buildings allows for the control of the resale price and the perpetual dissociation of land and real estate ownership via a mechanism of reloading the lease at each transfer.

Rights	Definition
Access/use	The right of access and use of the residential property
Collection	The right to draw an annuity
Management	The right to determine the internal rules of use and transformation of the residential property and to improve them
Exclusion	The right to determine who the other users of the residential property are and what their specific rights would be
Alienation	The right to sell one or more of the foregoing rights permanently (sale) or for a given period (including short- or long-term leases)
Transformation	The right to build, renovate, destroy or enlarge existing constructions
Preemption	The right to redeem certain rights previously disposed of

Table 3.1. *The cluster of rights associated with home ownership (source: Le Rouzic 2021)*

3.5. Conclusion

The gap between housing prices and incomes is a key problem in the affordability crisis that has been affecting OECD metropolises for the past two decades, as most have become owner-occupied societies. A market equilibrium is not working: supply-side policies do not regulate prices, but fuel inflationary mechanisms. Housing price inflation is then essentially fueled by the debt of low-cost buyers. The swelling of household debt is supported by public policies, through tax incentives. A second mechanism must also be considered: the insurance value of goods, in a context of erosion of welfare state systems. The accumulation of value in housing (as a household financial asset) contributes to widening inequalities and reinforcing the stratification of the markets. In urban areas, these structures are profoundly unequal, depending on the market regime and the type of housing. For households, entering, staying in or moving through the various housing market regimes are subject to a whole series of filters, selection and unequal valuation of property and assets according to the areas of investment and living space. These are all elements that link social inequalities to the real estate debt regime and to the patrimonial value of housing, in societies of owners.

In a number of countries, issues emerging with the health crisis of 2020–2021 are affecting real estate markets and residential real estate investment, especially as the home has also become, in some cases, a remote workplace. This is seen as both a slowdown and a reversal after a historic 25-year phase of real estate inflation, with demand shifting to homes, large suburban areas of metropolitan areas, and small- and medium-sized cities. There are many indications that the social and political construction of the property markets is changing in this context. Although the flows seem modest, the effects will be tangible (Popsu Territoires 2022). Each of these elements contributes to the profound restructuring of what constitutes the value of a property, beyond the classic land rent and *rent gap*, redistributing the methods of valuation, and changing the winners and losers of the markets.

3.6. References

Aalbers, M.B. (ed.) (2012). *Subprime Cities: The Political Economy of Mortgage Markets*. Wiley-Blackwell, Oxford.

Aalbers, M.B. (2016). *The Financialization of Housing: A Political Economy Approach*. Routledge, London and Taylor & Francis Group, New York.

Aalbers, M.B. and Christophers, B. (2014). Centring housing in political economy. *Housing, Theory and Society*, 31(4), 373–394.

André, M., Arnold, C., Meslin, O. (2021). 24 % des ménages détiennent 68 % des logements possédés par des particuliers. *INSEE, France, portrait social, édition 2021* [Online]. Available at: https://www.insee.fr/fr/statistiques/5432517?sommaire=5435421.

Arbaci, S. (2007). Ethnic segregation, housing systems and welfare regimes in Europe. *European Journal of Housing Policy*, 7(4), 401–433.

Attard, J.-P. (2013). Un logement foncièrement solidaire : le modèle des *community land trusts*. *Mouvements*, 74(2), 143–153.

Aveline, N. (2008). *Immobilier, la mondialisation, l'Asie, la bulle*. CNRS-Éditions, Paris.

Aveline-Dubach, N. (2010). Les marchés fonciers à l'épreuve de la mondialisation : nouveaux enjeux pour la théorie économique et pour les politiques publiques. Thesis, Éditions Universitaires Européennes, Riga.

Aveline-Dubach, N. (2020). The financialization of real estate in megacities and its variegated trajectories in East Asia. In *Handbook of Megacities and Megacity-Regions*, Sorensen, A. and Labbe, D. (eds). Edward Elgar Publishing, Northampton.

Aveline-Dubach, N., Le Corre, T., Denis, E., Napoleone, C. (2020). Les futurs du foncier : modes d'accumulation du capital, droit de propriété et production de la ville. *Pour la recherche urbaine*, 312–335.

Bailly, A.-S. (1973). Les théories de l'organisation de l'espace urbain. *L'Espace géographique*, 81–93 [Online]. Available at: https://www.persee.fr/doc/spgeo_0046-2497_1973_num_2_2_1384.

Beckerich, C. (2000). Biens publics et valorisation immobilière. Thesis, Université Lumière Lyon 2 [Online]. Available at: http://demeter.univ-lyon2.fr/sdx/theses/lyon2/2000/beckerich_c.

Benites-Gambirazio, E. and Bonneval, L. (2022). Housing as asset-based welfare. The case of France. *Housing Studies*, 1–15. DOI: 10.1080/02673037.2022.2141205.

Blandy, S., Dupuis, A., Dixon, J.E. (2010). *Multi-owned Housing: Law, Power and Practice*. Ashgate, Abingdon.

Bonneval, L. and Pollard, J. (2017). Promoteurs immobiliers, bailleurs sociaux, collectivités locales : des acteurs aux frontières des marchés du logement. *Métropoles*, 20(5423) [Online]. Available at: http://metropoles.revues.org/5423.

Bonneval, L. and Robert, F. (2013). *L'immeuble de rapport, l'immobilier entre gestion et spéculation (Lyon 1860–1990)*. Presses Universitaires de Rennes.

Borg, I., Kawalerowicz, J., Andersson, E.K. (2022). Socio-spatial stratification of housing tenure trajectories in Sweden – A longitudinal cohort study. *Advances in Life Course Research*, 52, 100467.

Boulay, G. (2011). Le prix de la ville. Le marché immobilier à usage résidentiel dans l'aire urbaine de Marseille-Aix-en-Provence (1990–2010). Thesis, Université de Provence Aix-Marseille 1 [Online]. Available at: https://tel.archives-ouvertes.fr/tel-01121417.

Boulay, G. (2012). Real estate market and urban transformations: Spatio-temporal analysis of house price increase in the centre of Marseille (1996–2010). *Articulo – Journal of Urban Research*, 9, 1–21. DOI: 10.4000/articulo.2152.

Boulay, G. (2022). Gentrification and the real estate market: What can we learn from the rent gap theory? In *Cities at the Heart of Inequalities*, Cottineau, C. and Pumain, D. (eds). ISTE Ltd, London, and John Wiley & Sons, New York.

Boulay, G., Blanke, D., Casanova Enault, L., Granié, A. (2020). Moving from market opacity to methodological opacity: Are web data good enough for French property market monitoring? *The Professional Geographer*, 73(1), 115–130.

Bowen, W.M., Mikelbank, B.A., Prestegaard, D.M. (2001). Theoretical and empirical considerations regarding space in hedonic housing price model applications. *Growth and Change*, 32(4), 466–490.

Boyer, R. (2000). Is a finance-led growth regime a viable alternative to Fordism? A preliminary analysis. *Economy and Society*, 29(1), 111–145.

Callon, M. (1998). Introduction: The embeddedness of economic markets in economics. *The Sociological Review*, 46(1_suppl), 1–57.

Callon, M., Millo, Y., Muniesa, F. (2007). *Market Devices*. Blackwell, Oxford.

Case, K.E. and Shiller, R.J. (1988). The behavior of home buyers in boom and post-boom markets. NBER Working Paper (2748).

Chasco, C. and Le Gallo, J. (2012). Hierarchy and spatial autocorrelation effects in hedonic models. *Economics Bulletin*, 32(2), 1474–1480.

Christophers, B. (2016). For real: Land as capital and commodity. *Transactions of the Institute of British Geographers*, 41(2), 134–148.

Clerval, A. (2013). *Paris sans le peuple*. La Découverte, Paris.

Cliff, A.D. and Ord, J.K. (1981). *Spatial Processes: Models and Applications*. Pion, London.

Cottineau, C. and Pumain, D. (2022). Major models of the spatial organization of urban societies. In *Cities at the Heart of Inequalities*, Cottineau, C. and Pumain, D. (eds). ISTE Ltd, London, and John Wiley & Sons, New York.

Crouch, C. (2009). Privatised keynesianism: An unacknowledged policy regime. *The British Journal of Politics & International Relations*, 11(3), 382–399.

Cusin, F. (2016). Y a-t-il un modèle de la ville française ? Structures urbaines et marchés immobiliers. *Revue française de sociologie*, 57(1), 97–129.

Driant, J.-C. (2010). Vertus et vices du développement de l'accession à la propriété. *Métropolitiques*, November 25, 2010 [Online]. Available at: https://www.metropolitiques.eu/Vertus-et-vices-du-developpement.html.

Fernandez, R. and Aalbers, M.B. (2016). Financialization and housing: Between globalization and varieties of capitalism. *Competition and Change*, 20(2), 71–88.

Fields, D. (2019). Automated landlord: Digital technologies and post-crisis financial accumulation. *Environment and Planning A: Economy and Space*, 0308518X19846514.

Fields, D. and Rogers, D. (2021). Towards a critical housing studies research agenda on platform real estate. *Housing, Theory and Society*, 38(1), 72–94.

Fourcade, M. and Healy, K. (2017). Seeing like a market. *Socio-Economic Review*, 15(1), 9–29.

French, S., Leyshon, A., Wainwright, T. (2011). Financializing space, spacing financialization. *Progress in Human Geography*, 35(6), 798–819.

Fritsch, B. (2007). Tramway et prix des logements à Nantes. *Espace géographique*, 36(2007/2), 97–113 [Online]. Available at: http://www.cairn.info/resume.php?ID_ARTICLE=EG_362_0097.

Geniaux, G., Napoléone, C., Leroux, B. (2015). Les effets prix de l'offre foncière. *Revue d'économie régionale et urbaine*, (1–2 (May)), 273–320.

Glaeser, E.L., Gyourko, J., Morales, E., Nathanson, C.G. (2014). Housing dynamics: An urban approach. *Journal of Urban Economics*, 81, 45–56.

Goodman, A.C. and Thibodeau, T.G. (2008). Where are the speculative bubbles in US housing markets? *Journal of Housing Economics*, 17(2), 117–137.

Grandclement, A. and Boulay, G. (2016). Residential function and local fiscal resources on the French Mediterranean coastal areas. *Espace géographique*, 44(1) [Online]. Available at: https://hal.archives-ouvertes.fr/hal-01331407.

Guironnet, A., Attuyer, K., Halbert, L. (2016). Building cities on financial assets: The financialisation of property markets and its implications for city governments in the Paris city-region. *Urban Studies*, 53(7), 1442–1464.

Halbwachs, M. (1913). *La classe ouvrière et les niveaux de vie. Recherches sur la hiérarchie des besoins dans les sociétés industrielles contemporaines*. Félix Alcan, Paris.

Halbwachs, M. (1970). *Morphologie sociale*. A. Colin, Paris.

Harvey, D. (1982). *The Limits to Capital*. Blackwell, Oxford.

Harvey, D. (1985). *The Urbanization of Capital: Studies in the History and Theory of Capitalist Urbanization*. Johns Hopkins University Press, Baltimore.

Harvey, D. (2003). *Paris, Capital of Modernity*. Routledge, New York.

Hochstenbach, C. and Arundel, R. (2020). Spatial housing market polarisation: National and urban dynamics of diverging house values. *Transactions of the Institute of British Geographers*, 45(2), 464–482.

Immergluck, D. (2012). Distressed and dumped: Market dynamics of low-value, foreclosed properties during the advent of the federal neighborhood stabilization program. *Journal of Planning Education and Research*, 32(1), 48–61.

Kemeny, J. (2001). Comparative housing and welfare: Theorising the relationship. *Journal of Housing and the Built Environment*, 16(1), 53–70.

Kohl, S. (2018). More mortgages, more homes? The effect of housing financialization on homeownership in historical perspective. *Politics and Society*, 46(2), 177–203.

Kutz, W. and Lenhardt, J. (2016). Where to put the spare cash? Subprime urbanization and the geographies of the financial crisis in the Global South. *Urban Geography*, 37(6), 926–948.

Langley, P. (2006). Securitising suburbia: The transformation of Anglo-American mortgage finance. *Competition & Change*, 10(3), 283–299.

Le Corre, T. (2019). Paris à tous prix. Analyse des inégalités par une géographie de l'investissement sur le marché immobilier résidentiel en Île-de-France. PhD Thesis, Université Paris 1 Panthéon-Sorbonne [Online]. Available at: https://tel.archives-ouvertes.fr/tel-02298354.

Le Goix, R. (2016). L'immobilier résidentiel suburbain en régime financiarisé de production dans la région de Los Angeles. *Revue d'économie régionale et urbaine*, 1, 101–129.

Le Goix, R. (2022). Socio-spatial segregation in cities. In *Cities at the Heart of Inequalities*, Cottineau, C. and Pumain, D. (eds). ISTE Ltd, London, and John Wiley & Sons, New York.

Le Goix, R., Giraud, T., Cura, R., Le Corre, T., Migozzi, J. (2019). Who sells to whom in the suburbs? Home price inflation and the dynamics of sellers and buyers in the metropolitan region of Paris, 1996–2012. *PLoS ONE*, 14(3), e0213169.

Le Goix, R., Casanova Enault, L., Bonneval, L., Le Corre, T., Benites, E., Boulay, G., Kutz, W., Aveline-Dubach, N., Migozzi, J., Ysebaert, R. (2021). Housing (in)equity and the spatial dynamics of homeownership in France: A research agenda. *Tijdschrift voor economische en sociale geografie*, 112(1), 62–80.

Le Rouzic, V. (2019). Essais sur la post-propriété : les organismes de foncier solidaire face au défi du logement abordable. PhD Thesis, Université Paris 1 Panthéon Sorbonne [Online]. Available at: http://www.theses.fr/2019PA01H075.

Le Rouzic, V. (2021). Cooper Square is here to stay. Une relecture institutionnaliste du droit à la ville. *Métropoles*, 27, 2020(7477).

Lefebvre, H. (1974). *La production de l'espace*. Éditions Anthropos, Paris.

Lipietz, A. (1974). *Le tribu foncier urbain : circulation du capital et propriété foncière dans la production du cadre bâti*. François Maspero, Paris.

Malpass, P. (2011). Path dependence and the measurement of change in housing policy. *Housing, Theory and Society*, 28(4), 305–319.

Martin, R. (2002). *Financialization of Daily Life*. Temple University Press, Philadelphia.

Migozzi, J. (2019). Selecting spaces, classifying people: The financialization of housing in the South African city. *Housing Policy Debate*, 30(4), 640–660.

Newman, K. and Wyly, E. (2004). Geographies of mortgage market segmentation: The case of Essex county, New Jersey. *Housing Studies*, 19(1), 53–83.

Nussbaum, F. (2019). Le pavillon et le bulldozer. Les suburbs en crise face à la vacance résidentielle aux États-Unis. *Géographie, Economie, Société*, 21(1), 89–116.

Orford, S. (2002). Valuing locational externalities: A GIS and multilevel modelling approach. *Environment and Planning B: Planning and Design*, 29(1), 105–127.

Ostrom, E. and Hess, C. (2008). Private and common property rights. School of Public & Environmental Affairs Research Paper, No. 2008-11-01 (November 29, 2007).

Pfeiffer, D. and Molina, E.T. (2012). The trajectory of REOs in Southern California Latino neighborhoods: An uneven geography of recovery. *Housing Policy Debate*, 23(1), 81–109.

Piketty, T. (2013). *Le capital au XXIe siècle*. Le Seuil, Paris.

Pollard, J. (2018). *L'État, le promoteur et le maire. La fabrication des politiques du logement*. Presses de la Fondation nationale des sciences politiques, Paris.

Popsu, T. (2022). Exode urbain ? Petits flux, grands effets. Les mobilités résidentielles à l'ère (post-) Covid. Plan Urbanisme Construction Architecture (PUCA) [Online]. Available at: http://www.urbanisme-puca.gouv.fr/exode-urbain-realisation-d-une-etude-sur-les-a2388.html.

Porter, L., Fields, D., Landau-Ward, A., Rogers, D., Sadowski, J., Maalsen, S., Kitchin, R., Dawkins, O., Young, G., Bates, L.K. (2019). Planning, land and housing in the digital data revolution. *Planning Theory & Practice*, 20(4), 575–603.

Rolnik, R. (2013). Late neoliberalism: The financialization of homeownership and housing rights. *International Journal of Urban and Regional Research*, 37(3), 1058–1066.

Ronald, R. (2008). *The Ideology of Home Ownership: Homeowner Societies and the Role of Housing*. Palgrave Macmillan, Basingstoke, New York.

Rosen, S. (1974). Hedonic prices and implicit markets: Product differentiation in pure competitions. *Journal of Political Economy*, 72, 34–55.

Rowe, M., Engelsman, U., Southern, A. (2016). Community land trusts – A radical or reformist response to the housing question today? *Journal for Critical Geographies*, 15(3), 26 [Online]. Available at: http://ojs.unbc.ca/index.php/acme/article/view/1348/1204.

Schwartz, H.M. and Seabrooke, L. (2009). *The Politics of Housing Booms and Busts*. Palgrave Macmillan, Basingstoke, New York.

Tammaru, T., Musterd, S., Van Ham, M., Marcińczak, S. (2016a). A multi-factor approach to understanding socio-economic segregation in European capital cities. In *Socio-Economic Segregation in European Capital Cities: East Meets West*, Tammaru, T., Van Ham, M., Marcińczak, S., Musterd, S. (eds). Taylor & Francis, London.

Tammaru, T., Van Ham, M., MarcińCzak, S., Musterd, S. (2016b). *Socio-Economic Segregation in European Capital Cities: East Meets West*. Routledge, Abingdon.

Taylor, Z.J. (2020). The real estate risk fix: Residential insurance-linked securitization in the Florida metropolis. *Environment and Planning A: Economy and Space*, 0(0), 0308518X19896579.

Thaden, E., Greer, A., Saegert, S. (2013). Shared equity homeownership: A welcomed tenure alternative among lower income households. *Housing Studies*, 28(8), 1175–1196.

Theurillat, T., Rérat, P., Crevoisier, O. (2015). The real estate markets: Players, institutions and territories. *Urban Studies*, 52(8), 1414–1433.

Topalov, C. (1974). *Les Promoteurs immobiliers : contribution à l'analyse de la production capitaliste du logement en France*. Mouton, Paris and The Hague.

Topalov, C. (1984). *Le Profit, la rente et la ville*. Economica, Paris.

Topalov, C. (1987). *Le logement en France. Histoire d'une marchandise impossible*. Presses de la Fondation nationale des sciences politiques, Paris.

Van Gent, W.P.C. (2010). Housing policy as a lever for change? The politics of welfare, assets and tenure. *Housing Studies*, 25(5), 735–753.

Ward, C. and Swyngedouw, E. (2018). Neoliberalisation from the ground up: Insurgent capital, regional struggle, and the assetisation of land. *Antipode*, 50(4), 1077–1097.

Wetzstein, S. (2017). The global urban housing affordability crisis. *Urban Studies*, 54(14), 3159–3177.

Wijburg, G. (2019). Privatised Keynesianism and the state-enhanced diversification of credit: The case of the French housing market. *International Journal of Housing Policy*, 19(2), 143–164.

Wyly, E., Moos, M., Hammel, D. (2012). Race, class, and rent in America's subprime cities. In *Subprime Cities*, Aalbers, M. (ed.). Blackwell Publishing, Oxford.

4

Logistics Urbanization, Between Real Estate Financialization and the Rise of Logistics Urban Planning

Nicolas RAIMBAULT[1,2] and Adeline HEITZ[3]
[1] Nantes University, France
[2] UMR Espace et société, France
[3] LIRSA, Conservatoire National des Arts et Métiers (CNAM), Paris, France

4.1. Introduction

For about half a century, changes in capitalism have led to the globalization, fragmentation and flexibilization of value chains. These are based on a just-in-time organization of production and distribution and, more recently, are being transformed by the explosion of e-commerce. All these dynamics are leading to a marked development of logistics activities (Coe 2014).

Logistics activities organize and manage the flow of goods between the various links in the economic system, from production sites to consumption sites, with the aim of optimizing lead times and costs. Logistics include both concrete and physical operations, such as transport and warehousing (the preparation of orders and loads in

---

For a color version of all the figures in this chapter, see www.iste.co.uk/avelinedubach/globalization.zip.

Globalization and Dynamics of Urban Production,
coordinated by Natacha AVELINE-DUBACH. © ISTE Ltd 2023.

logistics facilities), and more organizational operations of flow management, which are part of "supply chain management"[1].

The origins of these flows, and even more so their destinations, correspond to the major metropolitan areas. Indeed, these are the main consumption areas for goods produced on a global scale. Logistics activities are therefore becoming essential services for daily urban life, as the SARS-CoV-2 pandemic and the various containment episodes in 2020 and 2021 have clearly shown (Benvegnù et al. 2020).

In order to organize these flows, logistics activities rely on specific sites where goods are unloaded, sorted, grouped into containers, pallets or parcels and reloaded into new vehicles. These places correspond, on the one hand, to large infrastructures emblematic of economic globalization: seaports and airports. On the other hand, it is the warehouses that are the most numerous logistics sites. Some of these logistics facilities can be called "logistics platforms" or "distribution centers", "hubs", "fulfillment centers" or "sorting centers". We will use the term "warehouses" here to refer to all these logistics buildings and logistics facilities. These buildings are essential for the organization of flows on different scales. Mostly used to supply metropolitan areas, warehouses are concentrated in and around major cities. They are part of the ordinary landscape of urban peripheries. The development of logistics activities has thus resulted in the intense production of urban and (outer) suburban areas.

The objective of this chapter is to present the contemporary dynamics of logistics urbanization corresponding to the different activities and logistics sites in urban and suburban areas. Indeed, the supply chain relies on very different logistics spaces: from warehouses of more than 100,000 m² in remote logistics parks to sites for organizing the last mile[2] with decarbonized vehicles (i.e. Cargo cycles or electric vehicles), via small logistics facilities nestled in former commercial premises, old industrial areas and even parking lots. These urbanization dynamics will be analyzed as different modalities of articulation between urban planning, economic development policies and real estate market interventions, in relation to the demands of companies in the logistics sector.

---

1. *Supply chain management* is the management, through and within a network of upstream and downstream organizations, of both relationships and flows of materials, information and resources.
2. The last mile is the set of logistic and transport operations that constitute the last link of the logistic chain, materialized by the last journey of the vehicle to deliver the goods from the last warehouse where it was processed to the final customer (company or individual).

Based on the case of the Ile-de-France region, this chapter highlights a phenomenon of dualization in the production of metropolitan logistics spaces (Heitz 2021) and gathers evidence indicating the generalization of this phenomenon in many urban regions. An experimental urban logistics urban planning, supported by public actors, contrasts with the private logics of the development of peripheral business parks where the majority of logistics facilities are located (Raimbault 2017). Between these two poles, an "intermediate logistics" (Heitz 2021) maintains itself at a low level, often in old industrial zones. In this way, we propose a reflection on the issues of public regulation, in terms of development, urban and regional planning tools and economic development policies, corresponding to the different dynamics of logistics urbanization. These distinctions are necessary in order to consider the contemporary ecological and social issues of logistics activities in urban spaces.

The Île-de-France region has been a prolific field for studies devoted to logistics dynamics (Dablanc and Frémont 2015; Heitz 2017; Raimbault 2017). Consequently, this region is a privileged source of analysis and examples in this chapter. Often, evidence gathered in other areas helps to put the Ile-de-France results into perspective. We therefore propose elements of comparison with other northern metropolitan areas and, to a lesser extent, with southern metropolitan areas (for a work dedicated to southern logistics dynamics, see Mareï and Savy (2021)).

Based on a review and perspective of the growing body of work on logistics urbanization, this chapter successively examines the logistics development of (outer-) suburbs, that of urban logistics in the centers and, finally, the persistence of intermediate logistics in the former industrial suburbs.

4.2. Logistics development in the outer-suburbs: a dynamic of sprawl and financialization of logistics real estate

The logistics development of major metropolitan areas on a global scale has mainly involved the massive construction of warehouses on the outskirts of metropolitan areas since the 1980s. These logistics facilities serve the supply of consumer basins, i.e. large metropolises, and the organization of flows of goods on an international and regional scale. Their construction is part of the movement of urban sprawl and suburbanization, which has continued to grow. The multiplication of outer-suburban logistics zones is directly fueled by the financialization of logistics real estate. The issues arising from the urbanization of logistics on the outskirts of cities are those of diffuse urbanization: land take and difficult access to jobs.

4.2.1. *An increase in the number of warehouses to supply major cities*

The development of logistics activities on a global scale is closely linked to the transition from Fordism to post-Fordism, i.e. the emergence of globalized, flexible and increasingly financialized production systems (Coe 2014). The efficiency of these production systems, which are split up into numerous suppliers and controlled downstream by the principals (make to order), is based on the use of just-in-time production. However, this organization leads to a multiplication of shipments of goods of ever-smaller sizes to be processed (Bonacich and Wilson 2008). This organization increases the logistics services required, both operational (transport and especially good handling) and strategic (supply chain management), tenfold. Moreover, the generalization of this production system on a global scale has led to an increase in the travelled distances and fragmentation of supply chains (Hesse 2008; Cowen 2014; Danyluk 2018). Downstream, retail and e-commerce industries are expanding their empire in the commercial realm with a business model also based on efficient logistics systems with ever-shorter delivery times. The goal is to sell a product before paying the supplier, which means that trade logistics must be highly responsive to get suppliers' product onto store shelves or customers' packages quickly (Bonacich and Wilson 2008). In this way, logistical efficiency becomes crucial for the entire production and distribution system and makes it possible to control the latter from downstream (Hesse 2008).

The construction of several generations of logistics facilities has made this "logistics revolution" possible (Bonacich and Wilson 2008). Warehouses are multiplying in and around metropolises around the world. A first generation of warehouses was built by manufacturers to optimize supplies and shipments around their production lines. At the same time, mass retail groups are developing logistics facilities to support the growth of their activities. These groups, like Walmart in the United States, are building giant warehouses of several tens of thousands of square meters, and even more than 100,000 square meters for the largest (Bonacich and Wilson 2008). These facilities are often referred to by these groups as "distribution centers" or "hubs". In the latter, four basic operations can be carried out: collection and sorting of goods, packing and unpacking operations, cross-docking (switching from one mode of transport or type of vehicle to another) and storage. In contrast to traditional warehouses, the objective of mass retail establishments is to limit the storage of goods in order to deliver to final customers quickly (Cidell 2015).

These shippers[3] from manufacturing or retail do not necessarily manage the warehouses they use directly. Indeed, many of them decide to outsource all or part of their logistics activities to a third-party logistics or logistics service provider (LSP). The latter then manages the shipper's flows and stocks in its own logistics facility. Shippers can also entrust an LSP with the operation of only part of their logistics facilities, while keeping control of their overall supply chain. The meteoric growth of logistics service providers from the 1980s onwards, the best-known being Géodis, DHL, XPO logistics, STEF and Kuehne+Nagel, has led to a wave of new logistics facility construction.

Finally, during the last two decades, the growth of logistics activities has accelerated further with the explosion of e-commerce globally. According to the United Nations Conference of Trade and Development (UNCTAD), e-commerce grew by 16% between 2017 and 2018 (UNCTAD 2020). 87% of British people, 80% of Americans and 73% of Chinese people made purchases on the Internet in 2018 (UNCTAD 2020). In France, according to the Federation of E-Commerce and Distance Selling (FEVAD), e-commerce will represent 13.4% of retail trade in 2020, compared to 9.8% in 2019[4]. This growth is due both to companies specializing in e-commerce alone, known as "pure players", and to mass retail groups that are developing an online shopping offer in response. As they develop their activities, pure player e-merchants are building many new logistics facilities. In fact, according to a Prologis study on the United States, pure players need three times more warehouse space than traditional retailers[5]. Their logistics organizations are based on three types of site. First, the parcels sent to their customers are prepared in very large logistics facilities. Second, the loading of delivery vehicles to homes and outlets is organized in smaller sites. Finally, the third type of site are small logistics facilities set up in the heart of cities for so-called "instant" deliveries and quick commerce.

Amazon's logistics facilities are emblematic of the case for pure players (Blanquart et al. 2019). The company calls its largest logistics facilities "fulfillment

---

3. The shippers are the owners of the goods. They are mainly industrialists, large-scale distribution companies and e-commerce companies.
4. Source: Fevad (2021): https://www.fevad.com/bilan-du-e-commerce-en-2020-les-ventes-sur-internet-atteignent-112-milliards-deuros-grace-a-la-digitalisation-acceleree-du-commerce-de-detail/.
5. Source: Prologis, "COVID-19 Special report #6: Accelerated retail evolution could bolster demand for well-located logistics space" (2020): https://www.prologis.com/logistics-industry-research/covid-19-special-report-6-accelerated-retail-evolution-could-bolster.

centers". In these, goods from suppliers arrive. Several thousands of workers prepare the packages ordered by Amazon's customers. The organization is industrial; these places can be described as "parcel factories" (Gaborieau 2016). These warehouses are very large, often over 100,000 square meters. The parcels are then shipped by road to two types of sites: mostly to the logistics facilities of courier companies[6] specialized in parcel delivery (such as the Post Office in France) and, sometimes, to Amazon's sites, from which the company itself organizes some of its urban deliveries. Courier companies have a network of relatively small warehouses, known as "sorting centers" or "parcel delivery agencies", located near the heart of urban areas. The explosion of e-commerce has been a boon to these LSP, who have therefore expanded the networks of their facilities. Amazon's other parcels are delivered directly by the group's logistics subsidiary, Amazon Logistics. To organize these deliveries and offer products with fast delivery, the company develops smaller facilities than suburban fulfillment centers. The company calls them "sortation centers", "delivery stations" or "fast delivery hubs", mostly located in dense urban areas close to consumers. Whether they are operated by couriers or by the logistics subsidiaries of e-retailers, these logistics facilities, which also rely on the work of dozens or even hundreds of workers, make it possible to organize home deliveries or pick-up point deliveries by light vehicles.

4.2.2. *The logistics sprawl of metropolitan areas on a global scale*

The development of logistics activities is one facet of the broader dynamics of metropolization. On the one hand, metropolitan areas, as the main economic hubs, concentrate logistics facility construction. On the other hand, within metropolitan areas, these warehouses are spreading further and further from the centers and thus contributing to the expansion of these areas. This phenomenon is referred to as "logistics sprawl" (Dablanc and Frémont 2015). Indeed, these activities require large buildings located within or near large urban areas. In order to establish a facility, the challenge for the companies concerned is to find large, inexpensive land on which it is possible to construct a large building on the ground floor, with truck access and parking facilities. These lands must offer good accessibility to the heart of the urban area: they must be well connected to freeways, ring roads and, to a lesser extent, to rail, port and airport infrastructures.

---

6. Courier service is the transport activity that handles small shipments (less than three tons), as opposed to full truck loads. The transport of parcels is emblematic of the shipments managed by courier companies.

The geography of logistics sites therefore follows a relatively similar evolution in most urban regions around the world (Dablanc and Browne 2020), in two distinct phases. In the first phase, from the 1970s to the early 1990s, warehouses were mainly built in the industrial and working-class suburbs inherited from the Fordist period, where large plots of land were available that were relatively well connected to road, rail and even waterway transport networks. Logistics facilities thus complement existing industrial zones when they do not directly replace manufacturing sites that are closing. The case of the former industrial suburbs of the inner belt of Paris is emblematic[7]. In North America, suburban industrial zones are hosting more and more warehouses, as shown by the work conducted in Atlanta (Dablanc and Ross 2012) or in Los Angeles (De Lara 2018). This first stage of logistical urbanization goes largely unnoticed insofar as the construction of a warehouse in an existing industrial zone rarely raises significant political issues. These logistics facilities are now partly obsolete. However, they are still used for industrial and wholesale logistics activities, as in Brussels (Strale 2020) or Berlin (2008), which brings us back to the issues of intermediate logistics (see section 4.3).

Starting in the 1990s, a new generation of larger, more modern warehouses was built in new areas beyond the historically industrial suburbs. We are witnessing a true phenomenon of logistics sprawl in many urban regions on a global scale (Dablanc and Browne 2020). Case studies are numerous in Europe–Paris (Raimbault and Bahoken 2014), The Randstad (Heitz et al. 2017a), Gothenburg (Heitz et al. 2020), as well as in North America – Chicago (Cidell 2011), San Francisco (Hesse 2008), Atlanta (Dablanc and Ross 2012), Los Angeles (Dablanc 2014), Toronto, Vancouver and Calgary (Woudsma et al. 2016). A growing body of work reports logistical sprawl in Latin America – Belo Horizonte (Guerin et al. 2021) and East Asia – Tokyo (Sakai et al. 2015), Shanghai and the Yangtze River Delta (He et al. 2019) and Wuhan (Yuan and Zhu 2019). This sprawl is also documented within emerging countries' metropolises, such as Casablanca (Debrie and Mareï 2019) or Delhi (Gupta 2017). Indeed, the growing demand for logistics space is driving the dynamics of logistics location further and further out to the periphery. New warehouses are being set up in business parks (see Figure 4.1), developed in outer-suburbia, at the urbanization front, or even in the ex-urban fringes, where larger plots of land are available and cheap, and close to highway infrastructures, which makes it possible to compensate for the distance from the delivery centers by

---

7. In particular in the municipalities of Gennevilliers, Ivry-sur-Seine, Vitry-sur-Seine, Nanterre and Saint-Denis.

excellent road accessibility. In this sense, this logistics urbanization contributes directly to urban sprawl. The transformation of former agricultural land into logistics zones within the outer-suburbia clearly contributes to land artificialization. The term "logistics sprawl" also emphasizes the similarities between the logistics of residential and outer-suburban development in these areas, combining the search for cheap land and road accessibility. In the case of the Paris region, outer-suburban logistics facilities represent more than 75% of the surface area of logistics real estate (Heitz 2017). The price of land for logistics activities is approximately €8,000/m² in the city of Paris, €5,500/m² in the inner suburbs and €1,350/m² in the outer suburbs[8].

Figure 4.1. *Landscape of a logistics zone (Parc de l'A5 in Réau, 77) (source: Raimbault (2022))*

---

8. Source: OfficeLocations (2020).

Logistics Urbanization 81

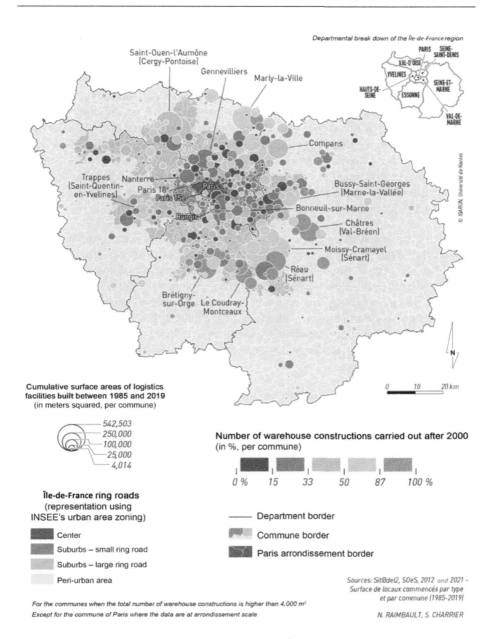

Figure 4.2. *Logistics sprawl in the Île-de-France region*

The case of Île-de-France shows that logistics sprawl does not uniformly affect the entire urbanization front, but rather specific large sectors (see Figure 4.2). Indeed, a broad northern, eastern and southern crescent is emerging, which to some extent extends the historical industrial suburbs (Heitz et al. 2018). This geography can be explained, on the one hand, by the configuration of transport networks, which are more suitable in this eastern part (A104 outer ring road) and, on the other hand, by the social division of space: the very upmarket western suburbs do not offer space for logistics activities, as land is too expensive and the employment areas are not very suitable (logistics facilities depend on a working-class workforce). A similar configuration can be found in Los Angeles, where a vast logistics sector has emerged on the eastern edge of the metropolis, the "Inland Empire", with a concentration of logistics facilities and workers of Latin American origin (De Lara 2018).

Finally, this suburban logistics geography reflects the structuring of a specific urbanization dynamic. This mode of production of logistics spaces articulates two modalities of action. First, these logistics zones are the result of strategies of specialized real estate developers and investors (Raimbault 2022). Second, these strategies are supported by the planning and economic development policies and choices of outer-suburban local authorities (Raimbault 2017). This mode of urban production was gradually structured during the 1990s and has proven to be particularly attractive to the demand of companies in the logistics sector.

4.2.3. *Financialized production of outer-suburban logistics zones*

Today, logistics real estate is a type of financial investment sought after by major institutional investors such as banks, insurance companies, pension funds and sovereign wealth funds, in the same way as investment in commercial real estate or in shares/bonds. Investment products involving logistics facilities are therefore offered on the financial markets, within specialized or diversified real estate funds. Logistics real estate is therefore financialized. The key players in this financialization are international real estate developers and investors, who specialize in the logistics real estate market (Raimbault 2022). This financialization is a crucial dimension of the mode of urban production specific to the dynamics of logistics sprawl.

Since the 1990s, the logistics real estate market has been structured around large international firms specializing in the management of logistics real estate assets[9].

---

9. A financial asset is a title or a contract that can be traded (e.g. on a financial market). An asset is included in its owner's assets and is likely to produce income or a capital gain for its holder.

The leaders in the sector, Prologis, Global Logistic Properties, Goodman and Segro (from the United States, Singapore, Australia and the United Kingdom, respectively) have developed a business model that consists of acting as developers, fund managers[10] and even land developers. Their main income comes from the rent of the logistics facilities they own and rent out. Their goal is therefore to build up vast holdings of logistics real estate on a global scale. As developers, they build numerous logistics facilities around major cities (Hesse 2004, 2008), partly with the capital raised via funds, and then embed them within investment funds, whether listed or not. Where possible, these real estate companies develop private logistics parks. Indeed, rather than building and renting out logistics facilities spread across different industrial zones, the leaders of this market prefer to develop closed complexes of several logistics facilities of which they are the sole owners and managers (see Figure 4.3). These private developments therefore entail the integration of the entire real estate chain: the construction of buildings, and also the development of the zone and its daily management, instead of the intermunicipal government that traditionally develops and markets industrial lands and then manages the public spaces of these lands, notably the roads (Raimbault 2022).

Indeed, in outer-suburbia, many small local governments do not have the administrative, operational and financial resources to conduct the large-scale development projects required to create logistics parks. The supply of private logistics parks has therefore met with the interest of these local governments in search of economic development, particularly to increase their tax revenues. Many local governments have welcomed private logistics park projects presented to them by international real estate companies. Such firms offer to finance and manage all of these operations, from the modification of planning documents to the marketing of buildings and the long-term maintenance of the parks (Raimbault 2022). The principle of these logistics parks thus leads to the privatization of part of the local development policies: the design, maintenance and even access to the logistics zone are the exclusive responsibility of the manager. It also privatizes economic development policies – the choice of companies renting the park depending solely on its manager (Raimbault 2017).

This kind of logistics parks has thus multiplied on the urbanization front in many metropolitan areas around the world: Paris (Raimbault 2022), Berlin (Hesse 2008), Frankfurt (Barbier et al. 2019), the Bay Area (Hesse 2008), Atlanta (Dablanc and

---

10. Investment funds are investment vehicles in which several investors join together, each contributing a share of the capital, in order to acquire a portfolio of properties and earn income from them both by leasing and by reselling (arbitrage). These funds are managed by third-party companies whose role is to select the assets to be acquired and resold: the fund manager.

Ross 2012), and also, for example, Mexico City (David and Halbert 2014) and Sao Paulo (Magnani and Sanfelici 2021; Yassu 2021).

Figure 4.3. *Entrance to the Prologis "Moissy 2 Les Chevrons" logistics park in Moissy Cramayel (77) (source: Raimbault (2022))*

At the same time, some logistics real estate projects have been made possible by the strategies of local governments in these outer-suburban areas. In order to increase their tax revenues and, to a lesser extent, increase the number of jobs, some local authorities are launching policies to develop vast industrial lands designed to accommodate logistics facilities. The availability of these plots is a godsend for real estate developers-investors. In the Île-de-France region, the case of "New Towns"[11] shows how public land developers in charge of urbanizing these areas have collaborated with developers to concentrate logistics facilities (Raimbault 2017). Similar entrepreneurial approaches have occurred in the Frankfurt metropolitan area (Barbier et al. 2019) or around Atlanta (Dablanc and Ross 2012).

The financialization of logistics real estate finally brings a capacity to produce logistics parks in areas where the local authorities concerned do not have the capacity to carry out such projects alone. The offer made by major logistics real estate firms in these remote outskirts is therefore a powerful vector for logistics sprawl. It offers cheap space for logistics activities and relative economic

---

11. New Towns were planned by the French government in the 1970s in order to regulate the urbanization of the Paris region.

development, in terms of local taxation and jobs, to areas in the outer-suburbs that are often unable to attract companies on their own.

4.2.4. The challenges of regulating the diffuse urbanization of economic activities

The dynamics of logistics sprawl are in direct opposition to the very principle of a regional development policy for logistics spaces, which could be justified by these environmental and social issues. With this mode of production, it is the real estate industry that plans its investments: local governments simply negotiate their landing.

Logistics sprawl raises two main ecological issues. First, it contributes, like residential and commercial urbanization, to land take, and thus to the reduction of land available for agriculture. Second, it increases the distances traveled by delivery vehicles and, consequently, greenhouse gas emissions and local pollution from freight transport (Coulombel et al. 2018; Perez-Martinez et al. 2020). In addition, the distance of these logistics parks from river ports and rail infrastructures limits the possibilities of modal shift, while road transport represents 90% of freight transport in France. These logistics facilities are also often far from the places of residence of logistics workers, who are still mostly concentrated in the historical industrial suburbs (Raimbault 2020). The distance complicates the daily commute of these workers. In addition, logistics zones are often located in municipalities that are poorly served by public transportation. These elements make this workforce dependent on the automobile, which again raises ecological and also social issues. Indeed, access to jobs is complicated for these low-skilled workers, who are finding it increasingly difficult to afford a car (Korsu and Wenglenski 2010).

Finally, logistical sprawl exacerbates the challenges posed by diffuse urbanization, which also concerns economic activities. While the outer-suburbs still largely escape binding planning and rarely receive the attention of governments operating on a metropolitan scale, the financialization of real estate, with the resulting forms of privatization, raises crucial issues of public regulation of the urbanization of these peripheries, both in terms of planning and of public tools for urban development.

4.3. Logistics development in urban centers: urban logistics

In contrast to (outer-)suburban logistics development, public policies seek to encourage a "return of logistics activities to the city center" (Diziain et al. 2012), which is consistent with sustainable urban policies (e.g. promoting urban densification and mix-used development). The conceptual framework of urban logistics, which appeared in the 2000s, proposes to integrate the development of these activities in dense urban areas with architectural and urban innovations to ensure their integration into the urban fabric. This model challenges a functionalist and spread out vision of the city (Reigner et al. 2013) by giving the logistics function, mostly developed in the suburban areas, the opportunity to develop in dense and central urban areas. Urban logistics make it possible to achieve the objectives of functional mix by keeping the productive activities of storage and handling of goods in the city.

4.3.1. *The rise of logistics real estate in urban centers: urban logistics facilities*

Urban logistics aims to optimize the flow of goods in cities in order to limit their negative effects (pollution, congestion) by regulating traffic and parking, on the one hand, and by developing urban logistics real estate, on the other hand. Several typologies of urban logistics facilities coexist in the literature. Onstein et al. (2021) describe the typology of facilities that has emerged as a result of going from "XXL" to "XXS". This typology focuses on a range of existing sizes among logistics facilities. XS or XXS facilities are dedicated to urban logistics. Buldeo-Rai et al. (2022) propose a typology of facilities dedicated to proximity logistics based on three criteria (size, service, area and activity). Here, we choose to rely on a simple typology that distinguished two types of logistics functions: cross-docking, on the one hand, and storage and fulfillment, on the other hand (Heitz 2021). First, urban logistics facilities dedicated to cross-docking operations to organize the modal shift of goods to clean vehicles (electric, natural gas, hydrogen) or demotorized vehicles (bicycles) were designed to organize the "last mile" (i.e. the final delivery to shops, offices, public services or inhabitants). They are also known as Urban Consolidation Centers (UCCs).

Then, a second type of urban logistics facility corresponds to the rise of e-commerce (Rodrigue 2020; Heitz 2021). The strong growth of fast deliveries is driving demand for urban logistics real estate development in all metropolitan areas (Dablanc 2018), not only for cross-docking facilities, but also for facilities that host storage functions for products (fresh or with a high turnover) ordered and delivered in a few hours. These logistics facilities of several tens of thousands of square meters, are part of the logistics organization of e-retailers, whether they are mass retailers or pure players (i.e. Amazon), but above all of the carriers and logistics service providers to whom shippers subcontract urban distribution. Among them, we find traditional last mile players (i.e. La Poste, DHL, UPS) and also increasing startups that offer delivery services from these urban logistics facilities (Buldeo-Rai et al. 2022). For mass retailers, these small logistics facilities are generally back-up bases near their stores, allowing them to increase their storage space for proximity logistics services. The development of these urban logistics does not concern all logistics sectors. E-commerce, and also to a lesser extent, mass distribution and last-mile carriers are the main users. Recently, several digital platforms (restaurants, food, consumer goods) offering instant delivery services, known as "quick commerce", have appeared on the market (Dablanc et al. 2017) (i.e. Amazon Prime Now). Proximity to the consumer is essential for these services, as they need to be able to deliver within a few hours. The rise of dark stores is a good example of this quick commerce development. Dark stores are retail facilities that resemble conventional supermarkets, but are not open to the public, housing goods used to fulfill orders placed online. So, they can be classified as warehouses. They are developed by startups (i.e. Gorillas, Getir), which offer instant deliveries (less than 20 minutes) to their consumers, relying on gig economy workers. These dark stores are controversial because they tend to develop in the place of former stores, becoming the symbol of a physical trade in competition with e-commerce, arousing debates on the impact of the digital economy on the city. E-commerce and quick commerce increase demand for logistics facilities in the heart of cities.

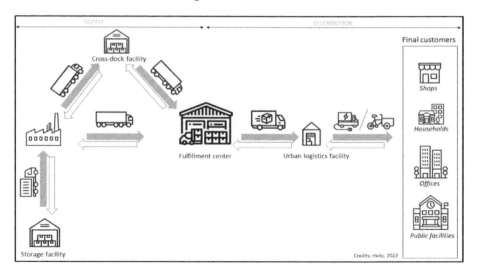

Figure 4.4. *Illustration of an urban logistics facility (source: Heitz (2022))*

Unlike (outer-)suburban logistics real estate, urban logistics is characterized by small surfaces, integrated into existing buildings (former industrial or logistics buildings, former parking lots, railway halls) or "hollow spaces", i.e. abandoned spaces that are not the subject of any urban project (e.g. under infrastructure, such as the Paris ring road: see Figure 4.5). In Japan, Takuybin, an express parcel service specializing, in particular, in home deliveries, has long been developing platforms in the heart of cities (Dablanc 2009). Inspired by this model, urban logistics facilities vary in size (between 100 m² and 1000 m²) and can also be integrated into buildings with other functions (housing, offices, shops), following the example of logistics hotels, such as the one at Chapelle International in the 18th arrondissement of Paris (see Figure 4.6). The urban logistics facilities thus make it possible to densify and diversify land uses, and also to reappropriate spaces formerly dedicated to the automobile in a context of decreasing car use in the city. These logistics facilities can also reinvest, by renewing them, former sites dedicated to the transport of goods, such as railway or river spaces, making this activity part of the long history of cities.

Figure 4.5. ULS "P4 Pantin Logistique" (Paris 19th arrondissement) under the ring road (a) goods grouping/deconsolidation area, (b) external view of the building (source: Heitz (2021))

Today, urban logistics real estate in the Paris region represents about 5% of the region's total logistics real estate market. The recent enthusiasm for urban logistics does not make it a dominant trend in the logistics real estate market, which is still mainly located on the outskirts (Heitz 2021). The price of land, and therefore the high rent in dense areas, is an obstacle to the development of real estate for urban logistics, compared to the low rent offered in outer-suburban logistics parks. In addition to the cost of land, the production costs of urban logistics facilities, which are not standardized buildings like (outer-)suburban warehouses, but "tailor-made" to fit into a dense urban fabric, are higher. This may explain the reluctance of real estate developers and private investors to invest in urban centers until very recently. In the absence of private investment, public actors tried to develop an initial real estate offer at the end of the 1990s. For nearly 30 years, urban logistics was the subject of public experimentation (Debrie and Heitz 2017). It was not until the recent period that a logistics urban planning and a nascent real estate market emerged from these experiments.

4.3.2. Towards a logistics urban planning

For a long time, the implementation of public policies in favor of the development of urban logistics remained a matter of local transport regulations (traffic, parking) and urban experimentation in terms of logistics real estate. This also explains the low volume of urban logistics facilities and UCC built in cities since the 1990s. The role of public authorities has been to encourage their development through experimentation.

UCCs were the first form of urban logistics facilities experimented with in European city centers (i.e. Monaco, La Rochelle (France), Bristol (UK), Vicenza (Italy)) in the 2000s (Browne and Ryan 2011), and as early as the late 1990s. Similar to small cross-docking logistics facilities, they are mainly used by carriers specializing in parcel delivery that can make the last mile with cargo bikes or electric vehicles. While Paris has been a highly invested field, other European cities have also been the subject of UCC experiments (Gonzalez-Feliu 2018) carried out by local public actors or public companies in partnership with certain carriers (Browne et al. 2018). In Île-de-France, the public company Sogaris, which specializes in the development and investment of logistics spaces[12], has developed several real estate projects dedicated to urban logistics such as the Beaugrenelle (15th arrondissement of Paris) UCC.

These UCCs quickly became a controversial issue with respect to their funding, feasibility and effectiveness (Leonardi et al. 2012). Indeed, the main problem with these experiments has been their financial return. In many cases, regardless of the public funding provided, these projects were not economically viable (Kin et al. 2015). Some of them even ceased activity (i.e. La Rochelle). The cost of land in the city center was a major obstacle to the profitability per square meter of logistics activities and the possibility of setting up in less dense areas for less money. In addition, there was less need for e-commerce at the time, and there were far fewer carriers or logistics operators interested in these projects. In 2014, in France, the

---

12. Sogaris is a public developer and real estate investor specializing in logistics spaces. It was created in the 1970s to manage the Rungis National Interest Market. Then, it gradually evolved to specialize in logistics real estate. Its majority shareholders are the departments of Paris and the inner suburbs of the Île-de-France region.

number of parcels delivered was about 462 million, compared to 1 billion in 2020[13]. The local governments, who defended these projects with the aim of optimizing the circulation of goods flows in cities, often found themselves confronted with modest effects, leaving these projects to appear as "urban logistics utopias that did not materialize" (Dablanc 2018).

More recently, other forms of urban logistics facilities have been experimented with, such as logistics hotels. Mainly developed in France, although still few in number, these logistics hotels allow for financial equalization between office, retail, service and housing activities and logistics activities. The diversity of activities helps to alleviate the financial problems of urban logistics facilities by offering a better return on the land acquired. These hotels are designed in particular to accommodate logistics activities related to e-commerce and parcel's delivery. Other projects are being carried out by public or semi-institutions in the Paris region or elsewhere. This is the case, for example, with the logistics hotel project in the Port of Lyon, which is being carried out by the Compagnie Nationale du Rhône and the Lyon metropolitan government. Whether it is a question of UCC or logistics hotels, the transition from urban experimentation to a model that can be generalized to all urban areas, which would make it possible to systematize urban logistics, takes time and relies, in terms of planning, on public action. In addition, the change in attitude of private sector actors (carriers, logistics service providers, retailers, e-retailers and real estate developers) with regard to urban logistics in recent years has contributed to the evolution of the role of the public authorities. From a public policy that pushes these experiments to improve the circulation of goods in the city in a context of tightening regulations (i.e. low emission zones), we are moving towards a public policy that tries to improve the land use regulation. Indeed, the rise of the quick commerce logistics facilities that are more or less compatible with the sustainability objectives set by planning (e.g. dark stores and dark kitchens) questioned the role of the public authorities in this development.

Long neglected by urban planning, the logistics issue is gradually making its way onto the public agenda, particularly in European metropolitan areas, in the context of the fight against pollution (by identifying pollutant emissions from road freight transport) and against urban sprawl (by identifying the contribution of logistics to land take) in metropolises. Faced with these new challenges, some local authorities are integrating logistics issues into the objectives of their local urban planning documents and the organization of urban mobility.

---

13. Evolution of the e-commerce delivery services market since 2015, Colissimo study, 2021.

Figure 4.6. *Chapelle International (Paris 18th arrondissement) (a) entrance to the railway hall and (b) entrance to the "Metro" warehouse (source: Heitz (2018))*

Today, the impact of public policies on urban logistics is significant, whether direct, through dedicated policies (i.e. subsidies for urban logistics facilities projects, reserved land, dedicated parking), or indirect, through environmental, social or organizational regulations designed to restrict the accessibility of freight vehicles to cities and limit flows. Beyond the urban experiments conducted, local authorities are rethinking their urban planning tools to integrate this issue into city planning. The case of Paris illustrates the means developed in terms of urban planning to promote the development of urban logistics.

In terms of planning, the city of Paris has, since 2013, integrated urban logistics development objectives into its documents with the aim of reducing the flow of goods and associated pollutants, and of framing the effects of the growing demand of residents for e-commerce (Debrie and Heitz 2017). The City of Paris had also initiated "goods" charters, an instrument of coordination between transport and logistics operators, shopkeepers and even residents since 2006.

In terms of urban design, they can impose the creation of urban logistics facilities, as is the case with "location perimeters" in Paris. These are perimeters within which project designers are obliged to integrate a logistics facility in order to serve the future neighborhood and district (Buldeo-Rai et al. 2022).

In terms of regulations, the Paris municipality has created dedicated areas in its Local Urban Plan (*Plan Local d'Urbanisme* (PLU)) for logistics activities. This is the meaning of the "Major Urban Services" (*Grands Services Urbains* (UGSU)) zoning, which is often located at the gates of Paris, along the railway lines and the Seine (Raimbault et al. 2018).

Box 4.1. *Urban planning in Paris*

Public policies through regulations can encourage companies to change their behavior. The development of low emission zones (LEZ) in European cities (Browne et al. 2005) or night-time deliveries in the United States (Holguin-Veras et al. 2014) are all regulations that are pushing companies to rethink the organization of their last mile and the vehicles they use. The new objectives regarding ecological transition strongly reinforce the attention paid to urban logistics.

For the past 10 years, major cities have been working to better integrate logistics activities, particularly urban logistics, into urban planning and design. Examples from the Netherlands, Sweden (Citylab 2018) and New York show this shift in focus by public authorities (Raimbault et al. 2018). More recently, the European Commission has included the issue of urban logistics in the "mobility" package and produced a best practice guide for collaboration and public policy (European Commission 2018).

Thus, urban logistics is gradually moving from being politically unthinkable to a lever for urban development, and a means of implementing environmental objectives to regulate the urban mobility of goods. Urban logistics also serves new forms of collaboration between transport and logistics operators, which until now have been little involved in dialogue with public actors. While this logistics issue is still dealt with unevenly from one city to another (Heitz and Dablanc 2019), we can observe, in the major metropolises, the rise of urban logistics planning policies, i.e. a way of thinking about space and tools that make it possible to develop and organize logistics activities and the flows associated with them. Beyond urban experiments, it seems that we have entered a new era for urban logistics planning. This observation should not overshadow the fact that we are witnessing a duality in logistics urbanization, between poorly regulated suburban areas and the consolidation of public actions dedicated to urban logistics with regard to proximity logistics. The Île-de-France region offers a good example of this configuration.

4.3.3. *The rise of a logistics real estate market in urban centers*

Since the late 2010s, the behavior of developers and investors has changed. This has been driven, additionally, by the Covid-19 crisis, which increased demand for e-commerce, and also a context where the ecological transition is encouraging stricter access conditions for polluting vehicles, such that local governments have gradually changed their view of urban logistics. While they have long neglected this sector in the absence of strong demand from carriers and shippers commensurate with development costs, they now perceive an urgent need to develop urban logistics real estate.

In Paris and the inner suburbs, demand for land and logistics real estate has increased considerably in recent years, leading to higher rent. The emergence of "XXS" urban logistics facilities, which are neither planned nor financed by public policies, unlike the case of the logistics hotels presented above, marks a turning point in the development of urban logistics. Since 2017, small logistics facilities supported by real estate investors have emerged in the dense Paris area to meet this new demand from service providers and shippers. For example, in the Parisian dense urban area, real estate developer Segro has built a warehouse in Gennevilliers for Ikea and Leroy Merlin (for their e-commerce channel) to organize their last mile, and developer CBRE has rehabilitated a hall in Pantin for the Saint Gobain group (a distributor of construction materials).

Finally, it appears that two modes of production of urban logistics spaces coexist today. On the one hand, urban experiments led by public actors have made it possible to stimulate a real estate dynamic. These still account for the majority of urban logistics development. On the other hand, an emerging, semi-autonomous, market is emerging, in which traditional logistics real estate developers and investors are beginning to position themselves, as are shippers and logistics service providers themselves. While public authorities initially provided the impetus for urban logistics real estate, they are now seeking to support this emerging private market through planning, urban programming and land regulations. The challenge for the urban logistics sector is to enter a phase of generalization and standardization of a real estate model in order to limit the additional costs of production in an urban environment, and thus be more competitive in relation to suburban areas.

4.4. Logistics spaces in the inner suburbs: the case of intermediate logistics as a blind spot in logistics urban planning

This dual interpretation of outer-suburban logistics, on the one hand, and urban logistics, on the other hand, must be qualified. The observation of logistics activities in the suburbs of metropolises, dense but non-central areas, which do not offer the land availability of outer-suburban or exurban areas, shows the existence of a third category, constituting a blind spot for research and public policies. Intermediate logistics, constituting a fabric of diverse logistics activities that can be applied to urban distribution, as well as on a national or international scale, is distinct from the urban and outer suburban logistics mentioned above.

4.4.1. *Permanence and mutations of intermediate logistics activities in the suburbs*

While transport and logistics operators and public authorities are currently working on the development of urban logistics in dense areas of metropolises, particularly in the hypercenters, there is already a logistics real estate stock in dense areas, in the inner suburbs. Similar to urban logistics in that it is integrated into a dense urban fabric, intermediate logistics brings together activities that are not often present in the central cities. These include logistics facilities in the industrial or wholesale trade sector, often held by small owners (SMEs, VSEs), as Strale (2020) in Brussels, Hesse (2008) in Berlin or Heitz (2021) in Île-de-France have shown. These logistics facilities can be used both for urban distribution and for regional, national and continental trade. These former industrial suburbs, often affected by deindustrialization, have thus retained a fabric of logistics activities that continue to provide low-skilled labor jobs.

Logistics facilities belonging to the intermediate logistics sector, which are often old, are not subject to specific development projects. In Île-de-France, these logistics activities represent about 20% of the real estate stock in the region, and correspond to non-standardized logistics facilities (pointed roofs, wooden frames, height of less than 10 m, no dock doors or maneuvering area for heavy goods vehicles, etc.). The nature of the buildings can sometimes be misleading and make us think of trade, retail or manufacturing activities (see Figure 4.7). However, these buildings do have a logistics function. Large logistics providers, retail or e-commerce are less represented there than in outer-suburban logistics zones (Heitz et al. 2017).

These suburbs, because of their proximity to the central cities, are subject to strong urban pressure. They are very attractive for the development of new services, businesses and residential projects (Albecker 2015). Given the pressure on land, competition with other sectors of activity and urban renewal policies, intermediate logistics is declining and being redeployed to outer-suburban logistics zones. The latter are attracting transport, logistics and retail operators, previously located in the suburbs, in search of a larger, more modern and less expensive warehouses. The municipalities in the inner suburbs rely on the development of new activities to accelerate their economic and urban transition. Faced with a housing project, the installation of a new metro station, intermediate logistics activities often find themselves pre-emptively replaced, without another logistics activity being integrated into the new urban program of the neighborhood (Debrie and Heitz 2017).

Figure 4.7. *Intermediate logistics facilities in the Paris inner suburbs (a) Saint Germain warehouse in Romainville and (b) Warehouse being destroyed in Bagnolet (source: Apau et al. (2020)[14])*

Paradoxically, certain specific areas within these suburbs are relatively protective of logistics activities, such as economic activity zones (EAZs). Developed in the 1970s and 1980s, these EAZs are home to numerous industrial, commercial, trade and logistics activities. These zones, preserved by urban planning documents, without being well integrated into the urban fabric, allow logistics to be maintained. However, as they are identified as going against the grain of a city model based on functional diversity, these zones tend to be the subject of requalification policies. The difficult identification of logistics activities in these areas (Heitz 2021) contribute to the invisibility of these intermediate logistics.

In addition, new activities related to the emergence of digital platforms are also appearing in these areas. There are more and more "quick commerce" and "rapid delivery" facilities, such as "dark kitchens[15]" (Aguiléra et al. 2018). These new logistics activities contrast with the characteristics of intermediate logistics marked by wholesale trade and industrial logistics. It is, in fact, an urban logistics intended for last-mile delivery. The players in the logistics real estate market are therefore

---

14. Apau, S., Baro, A., Carraud, V., Coq, C., Gabilan, S., Haladjian, T.-O., Jäis, J., Le Bihan, J., Marion, C., Pallon, E. (2020). L'immobilier logistique intermédiaire dans la petite couronne. Le cas du territoire d'Est Ensemble. Compte rendu de l'atelier encadré par Madame Adeline Heitz et Monsieur Elvan Arik, École d'Urbanisme de Paris.

15. Kitchens of restaurants that only offer delivery (i.e. Frichti).

interested in these areas and start to invest in them to develop urban logistics dedicated to e-commerce and parcel delivery. For example, real estate developers can buy land occupied by an intermediate logistics activity and renovate the building, then replace the activity with an e-commerce or delivery logistics activity. The development of urban logistics in the suburbs therefore also entails the renewal of logistics activities.

The port and airport areas, managed as transport infrastructures, are also privileged areas for logistics redevelopment. They are also mainly located in these inner suburbs. In the Paris region, the port of Gennevilliers, the port of Bonneuil sur Marne and Orly airport are preserved logistics zones that continue to develop. In these areas, as in business parks, there is a new interest on the part of logistics players to develop and densify logistics activities. Amazon has built a warehouse in the port of Bonneuil, and Ikea and Leroy Merlin share another in the port of Gennevilliers. While the objective is not necessarily to use the river to make their deliveries, these spaces guarantee their users proximity to Paris and a lower land price than in the city center. The role of public infrastructure managers is essential in the redevelopment of these business parks. Following the example of the large maritime ports (Magnan 2014), they develop these areas to make them attractive to logistics companies (Raimbault 2019). These activity zones thus constitute land opportunities in dense urban areas for the redevelopment of logistics, particularly concerning urban logistics.

4.4.2. Intermediate logistics, a blind spot in public policy

Despite these recent developments in business parks, intermediate logistics remains a blind spot in local public policies. The French case illustrates the absence of urban planning for this type of activity. Often poorly identified, these activities are rarely the subject of public policy attention, and are even pushed out of new urban projects that focus on other activities. In the absence of strong public policies insisting on the preservation of land for productive activities (industrial or logistics), we are witnessing a gradual mutation of intermediate logistics facilities to the benefit of other urban projects focused on office activities or residential development, or other forms of urban logistics dedicated instead to e-commerce activities.

Finally, the resilience of intermediate logistics depends on two main factors. First, the degree of public policy involvement and planning to preserve or develop logistics activities. Second, the interests and strategies of logistics real estate developers, who follow the demand of carriers and shippers, and who are increasingly inclined to invest in land located in dense areas, given the needs of e-commerce. The future of intermediate logistics is linked to the development of urban logistics beyond the walls of central cities.

Combined with urban renewal, the decline of this intermediate logistics in the dense zone sheds light on the process of logistics dualization, i.e. the existence of two concomitant real estate markets, (outer-) suburban and urban, which do not meet the same demand from logistics operators.

At the same time, the identification of a declining intermediate logistics sector highlights the heterogeneity of logistics, composed of both recent logistics facilities located in city centers and older warehouses, which may also be used for last-mile distribution, also located in dense urban areas, but mostly in the inner suburbs. Above all, the observation of intermediate logistics illustrates the major changes in production and consumption systems, and the changes in historically industrial suburbs. From the manufacturing industry to e-commerce logistics, the inner suburbs of large metropolises remain, albeit to a lesser extent, productive areas providing low-skilled jobs, especially blue-collar jobs (Raimbault 2020). The absence of public policies on logistics in these suburbs reflects the difficulty these areas have in seizing the tools of logistics urban planning to support this change, and also the problems of governance within metropolitan areas. Municipalities hosting logistics activities refuse to be the "servants" of others and gather negative externalities. They also tend to limit logistics projects. The absence of a coordinated logistics policy at the regional or metropolitan level also puts them in difficulty when faced with the arrival of "giants" like Amazon or Alibaba.

4.5. Conclusion

This chapter highlights the existence of three concomitant dynamics of logistics urbanization. They explain the contemporary landscape of logistics spaces within metropolitan areas. On the one hand, the strategies of international real estate investors are causing logistics sprawl that is poorly regulated by planning policies. On the other hand, public actors in the metropolitan cores are promoting the development of urban logistics facilities and gradually developing urban planning expertise for urban logistics. Between these two poles, an intermediate logistics sector is maintained at a low level or is asserting itself, for the real estate market, as a new front for the development of urban logistics, partly renewing the productive function of inner suburbs.

These three dynamics indicate the importance, for public regulation tools, of going beyond the urban/(outer-)suburban, center/periphery dichotomy to evolve towards an urban planning apparatus, on the scale of metropolitan areas, that can respond to the various economic, social and ecological challenges of the metropolitan logistics development of metropolitan areas (Heitz 2021).

Reflections on the production of logistics spaces are still very recent and many aspects remain unexplored. Beyond the academic world, these issues are gradually being highlighted by new dynamics. On the one hand, certain local authorities are questioning the place of productive functions in urban fabrics and are grasping the current importance of logistics activities, particularly because they continue to employ workers in the city and in the former industrial suburbs (PUCA 2021). On the other hand, social movements are gradually emerging around logistics spaces. Strikes and struggles led by logistics workers are increasingly numerous and highlight the social stakes of this development (Benvegnù and Gaborieau 2017). Large demonstrations, bringing together environmental and labor activists, are expressed in particular against Amazon's new warehouse projects. Beyond the sole case of Amazon, these movements highlight the problems raised by large, outer-suburban and exurban logistics facilities: land take, increased flows of goods at different scales, poor quality of jobs and difficulties in accessing them.

4.6. References

Aguiléra, A., Dablanc, L., Rallet, A. (2018). L'envers et l'endroit des plateformes de livraison instantanée. Enquête sur les livreurs micro-entrepreneurs parisiens. *Réseaux*, 212(6), 23–49.

Albecker, M.-F. (2015) Banlieues françaises/La banlieue parisienne, périphérie réinvestie ? *Urbanités* [Online]. Available at: http://www.revue-urbanites.fr/la-banlieue-parisienne-peripherie-reinvestie/.

Barbier, C., Cuny, C., Raimbault, N. (2019). The production of logistics places in France and Germany: A comparison between Paris, Frankfurt-am-Main and Kassel. *Work Organisation, Labour & Globalisation*, 13(1), 30–46.

Benvegnù, C. and Gaborieau, D. (2017). Produire le flux. *Savoir/Agir*, 1(39), 66–72.

Benvegnù, C., Gaborieau, D., Rivoal, H., Tranchant, L (2020). Les enjeux sanitaires de la pandémie dans le secteur logistique. *La Revue des conditions de travail*, 10, 54–60.

Blanquart, C., Liu, Z., Maudhuit, N., Zéroual, T. (2019). Les entrepôts du e-commerce : quelles spécificités ? Une étude du cas Amazon. *Logistique & Management*, 27(1), 44–54.

Bonacich, E. and Wilson, J.B. (2008). *Getting the Goods: Ports, Labor, and the Logistics Revolution*. Cornell University Press, Ithaca.

Browne, M. and Ryan, L. (2011). Comparative analysis of evaluation techniques for transport policies. *Environmental Impact Assessment Review*, 31(3), 226–233.

Browne, M., Allen, J., Anderson, S. (2005) Low emission zones: The likely effects on the freight transport sector. *International Journal of Logistics Research and Applications*, 8(4), 269–281

Browne, M., Bettmo, A., Lindholm, M. (2018). Stakeholders engagement and partnerships for improved urban logistics. In *Urban Logistics: Management, Policy and Innovation in a Rapidly Changing Environment*, Browne, M., Behrends, S., Woxenius, J., Giuliano, G., Holguin-Veras, J. (eds). Kogan Page, London.

Buldeo-Rai, H., Kang, S., Sakai, T., Tejada, C., Yuan, Q., Conway, A., Dablanc, L. (2022) "Proximity logistics": Characterizing the development of logistics facilities in dense, mixed-use urban areas around the world. *Transportation Research Part A*, 166(2022), 41–61.

Cidell, J. (2011). Distribution centers among the rooftops: The global logistics network meets the suburban spatial imaginary. *International Journal of Urban and Regional Research*, 35(4), 832–851.

Cidell, J. (2015). Distribution centers as distributed places. In *Cargomobilities: Moving Materials in a Global Age*, Birtchnell, T., Savitzky, S., Urry, J. (eds). Routledge, New York.

CITYLAB (2018). City logistics living lab: A way forward with city logistics innovation [Online]. Available at: https://www.citylab.soton.ac.uk/brochure/LL.pdf.

Coe, N.M. (2014). Missing links: Logistics, governance and upgrading in a shifting global economy. *Review of International Political Economy*, 21(1), 224–256.

Coulombel, N., Dablanc, L., Gardrat, M., Koning, M. (2018). The environmental social cost of urban road freight: Evidence from the Paris region. *Transportation Research Part D: Transport and Environment*, 63, 514–532.

Cowen, D. (2014). *The Deadly Life of Logistics: Mapping Violence in Global Trade*. University of Minnesota Press.

Dablanc, L. (2009). Le territoire urbain des konbinis et des takkyubins au Japon. *Flux – Cahiers scientifiques internationaux*, Réseaux et territoires, Metropolis/Université Paris-Est Marne la Vallée, 68–70.

Dablanc, L. (2014). Logistics sprawl and urban freight planning issues in a major gateway city. In *Sustainable Urban Logistics: Concepts, Methods and Information Systems*, Gonzalez-Feliu, J., Semet, F., Routhier, J.-L. (eds). Springer, Berlin and Heidelberg.

Dablanc, L. (2018). E-commerce trends and implications for urban logistics. In *Urban Logistics, Management Policy and Innovation in Rapidly Changing Environment*, Browne M., Berhends, S., Holguin-Veras, J., Giuliano, G., Woxenius, J. (eds). Kogan Page, London.

Dablanc, L. and Browne, M. (2020). Introduction to special section on logistics sprawl. *Journal of Transport Geography*, 88, 102390.

Dablanc, L. and Frémont, A. (eds) (2015). *La Métropole logistique*. Armand Colin, Paris.

Dablanc, L. and Ross, C. (2012). Atlanta: A mega logistics center in the Piedmont Atlantic Megaregion (PAM). *Journal of Transport Geography*, 24, 432–442.

Dablanc, L., Morganti, E., Arvidsson, N., Woxenius, J., Browne, M., Saidi, N. (2017). The rise of on-demand "Instant Deliveries" in European cities. *Supply Chain Forum: An International Journal*, 18(4), 203–217.

Danyluk, M. (2018). Capital's logistical fix: Accumulation, globalization, and the survival of capitalism. *Environment and Planning D: Society and Space*, 36(4), 630–647.

David, L. and Halbert, L. (2014). Finance capital, actor-network theory and the struggle over calculative agencies in the business property markets of Mexico City Metropolitan Region. *Regional Studies*, 48(3), 516–529.

De Lara, J. (2018). *Inland Shift: Race, Space, and Capital in Southern California*. University of California Press, Oakland.

Debrie, J. and Heitz, A. (2017). La question logistique dans l'aménagement de l'Ile-de-France : formulation d'un enjeu métropolitain versus absence de concrétisation dans les projets urbains ? *Géographie, économie, société*, 19(1), 55–73.

Debrie, J. and Mareï, N. (2019). Politiques territoriales et évolution des registres d'action de l'Etat au Maroc : une entrée par la logistique. *L'Espace Politique*, 36.

Dizain, D., Dablanc, L., Ripert, C. (2012). How can we bring logistics back into cities? The case of Paris metropolitan area. *Procedia – Social and Behavioral Sciences*, 39, 267–281.

European Commission (2018). Engagement of stakeholders when implementing urban freight logistics policies. Non-binding guidance documents on urban logistics, N°3/6, 35.

Gaborieau, D. (2016). Des usines à colis : trajectoire ouvrière des entrepôts de la grande distribution. PhD Thesis, Paris 1.

Gonzalez-Feliu, J. (2018). Where are we after 20 years of urban logistics? In *Sustainable Urban Logistics, Planning and Evaluation*. ISTE Ltd, London, and John Wiley & Sons, New York.

Guerin, L., Vieira, J.G.V., de Oliveira, R.L.M., de Oliveira, L.K., de Miranda Vieira, H.E., Dablanc, L. (2021). The geography of warehouses in the São Paulo metropolitan region and contributing factors to this spatial distribution. *Journal of Transport Geography*, 91, 102976.

Gupta, S. (2017). Logistics sprawl in timber markets and its impact on freight distribution patterns in metropolitan city of Delhi, India. *Transportation Research Procedia*, 25, 965–977.

He, M., Zeng, L., Wu, X., Luo, J. (2019). The spatial and temporal evolution of logistics enterprises in the Yangtze River Delta. *Sustainability*, 11, 5318.

Heitz, A. (2017). La Métropole Logistique : structure urbaine et enjeux d'aménagement. La dualisation des espaces logistiques métropolitains. PhD Thesis, Université de Paris Est.

Heitz, A. (2021). The logistics dualization in question: Evidence from the Paris metropolitan area. *Cities*, 119(3), 103407.

Heitz, A. and Dablanc, L. (2019). *Mobilité des marchandises dans la ville durable : les nouveaux enjeux de l'action publique locale*. Editions CGF, Paris.

Heitz, A., Dablanc, L., Tavasszy, L. (2017a). Logistics sprawl in monocentric and polycentric metropolitan areas: The cases of Paris, France, and the Randstad, the Netherlands. *Region: The Journal of ERSA*, 4(1), 93–107.

Heitz, A., Launay, P., Beziat, A. (2017b). Rethinking data collection on logistics facilities: New approach for measuring the location of warehouses and terminals in metropolitan areas. *Transportation Research Record: Journal of the Transportation Research Board*, 2609, 1.

Heitz, A., Raimbault, N., Beziat, A., Bounie, N. (2018). Can logistics compensate for the local effects of deindustrialisation? The situation in the Ile-de-France region between 1982 and 2012 [Online]. Available at: https://www.cget.gouv.fr/sites/cget.gouv.fr/files/atoms/files/ah.pdf.

Heitz, A., Dablanc, L., Olsson, J., Sanchez-Diaz, I., Woxenius, J. (2020). Spatial patterns of logistics facilities in Gothenburg, Sweden. *Journal of Transport Geography*, 88, 102191.

Hesse, M. (2004). Land for logistics: Locational dynamics, real estate markets and political regulation of regional distribution complexes. *Tijdschrift voor economische en sociale geografie*, 95(2), 162–173.

Hesse, M. (2008). *The City as a Terminal. The Urban Context of Logistics and Freight Transport*. Ashgate, Aldershot.

Holguin-Veras J., Wang, C., Browne, M., Darville Hodge, S., Wojtowicz, J. (2014). The New York City off-hour delivery project: Lessons for City Logistics. *Procedia – Social and Behavioral Sciences*, 125, 36–48.

Kin, B., Verlinde, S., van Lier, T., Macharis, C. (2015). Is there life after subsidy for an urban consolidation centre? An investigation of the total costs and benefits of a privately-initiated concept. *Transportation Research Procedia*, 12(2016), 357–369.

Korsu, E. and Wenglenski, S. (2010). Job accessibility, residential segregation and risk of long-term unemployment in the Paris region. *Urban Studies*, 47(11), 2279–2324.

Leonardi, J., Browne, M., Allen, J. (2012). Before-after assessment of a logistics trial with clean urban freight vehicles: A case study in London. *Procedia – Social and Behavioral Sciences*, 39, 146–157.

Magnan, M. (2014). La gestion foncière dans les grands ports maritimes français entre mission d'utilité publique et activité commerciale : un modèle en transition. HAL ID: hal-01070346.

Magnani, M. and Sanfelici, D. (2021). O e-commerce e os fundos imobiliários logísticos: Estratégias de captura de rendas imobiliárias. *Cadernos Metrópole*, 24, 173–198.

Mareï, N. and Savy, M. (2021). Global south countries: The dark side of city logistics. Dualisation vs bipolarisation. *Transport Policy*, 100, 150–160.

Onstein, A.T.C., Bharadwaj, I., Tavasszy, L.A., Van Damme, D.A., El Makhloufi, A. (2021). From XXS to XXL: Towards a typology of distribution centre facilities. *Journal of Transport Geography*, 94, 103128.

Pérez-Martínez, P.J., Miranda, R.M., Andrade, M.F. (2020). Freight road transport analysis in the metro São Paulo: Logistical activities and CO_2 emissions. *Transportation Research Part A: Policy and Practice*, 137, 16–33.

PUCA (2021). Quelle place pour quel travail en ville ? Les conditions économiques, sociales et environnementales de la ville productive. Document, Éditions PUCA.

Raimbault, N. (2017). Le développement logistique des grandes périphéries métropolitaines : régimes (péri-)urbains et privatisation silencieuse de la production des espaces logistiques. *Métropoles*, 21 [Online]. Available at: http://journals.openedition.org/metropoles/5564.

Raimbault, N. (2019). From regional planning to port regionalization and urban logistics. The inland port and the governance of logistics development in the Paris region. *Journal of Transport Geography*, 78, 205–213.

Raimbault, N. (2020), Nouveaux emplois ouvriers, nouveaux territoires ouvriers ? Une comparaison des géographies professionnelles et résidentielles des ouvriers de l'industrie et des ouvriers de la logistique en Île-de-France. *Travail et emploi*, 162, 71–102.

Raimbault, N. (2022). Outer-suburban politics and the financialisation of the logistics real estate industry: The emergence of financialised coalitions in the Paris region. *Urban Studies*, 59(7), 1481–1498.

Raimbault, N. and Bahoken, F. (2014). Quelles places pour les activités logistiques dans la métropole parisienne ? *Territoire en mouvement. Revue de géographie et aménagement*, 23–24, 53–74.

Raimbault, N., Heitz, A., Dablanc, L. (2018). Urban planning policies for logistics facilities. A comparison between US metropolitan areas and the Paris region. *Urban Logistics*, Kogan, London, 82–107.

Reigner, H., Brenac, T., Hernandez, F. (2013). *Nouvelles idéologies urbaines. Dictionnaire critique de la ville mobile, verte et sûre*. Presses universitaires de Rennes.

Rodrigue, J.P. (2020). The distribution network of Amazon and the footprint of freight digitalization. *Journal of Transport Geography*, 88, 102825.

Sakai, T., Kawamura, K., Hyodo, T. (2015). Locational dynamics of logistics facilities: Evidence from Tokyo. *Journal of Transport Geography*, 46, 10–19.

Strale, M. (2020). Logistics sprawl in the Brussels metropolitan area: Toward a socio-geographic typology. *Journal of Transport Geography*, 88, 102372.

UNCTAD (2020). UNCTAD estimates of global e-commerce 2018: UNCTAD technical notes on ICT for Development N°15 [Online]. Available at: https://unctad.org/en/PublicationsLibrary/tn_unctad_ict4d12_en.pdf.

Woudsma, C., Jakubicek, P., Dablanc, L. (2016). Logistics sprawl in North America: Methodological issues and a case study in Toronto. *Transportation Research Procedia*, 12, 474–488.

Yassu, A.M.D.S. (2021). O galpão logístico e a financeirização urbana: Da flexibilidade produtiva ao imobiliário. *Cadernos Metrópole*, 24, 257–282.

Yuan, Q. and Zhu, J. (2019). Logistics sprawl in Chinese metropolises: Evidence from Wuhan. *Journal of Transport Geography*, 74, 242–252.

5

The City–Port Relationship in the Metropolitan Fabric

Jean DEBRIE
[1] Université Paris 1 Panthéon-Sorbonne, France
[2] UMR Géographie-Cités, Campus Condorcet, Aubervilliers, France

5.1. The shift in city-port relations and the reconfiguration of intra-urban scales

The development of international trade in goods since the 1950s has been structured around the logic of specialization (of port terminals) and massification (the growth of trade). These logics have led to a significant evolution of the city–port relationship in coastal and river metropolises (Hoyle and Pinder 1992; Ducruet 2008; Hall 2008). This evolution is characterized by a modification of the original link between port and urban areas. The displacement of industrial-port activities from the urban core is thus the corollary of the logic of massification and specialization of port facilities in a globalized economy. From the 1960s onwards, this resulted in the multiplication of port wastelands in the urban heartland. These land reserves were to be the subject of sometimes conflicting negotiations between the managers of port areas and public actors in urban areas to discuss their requalification. This reconversion of derelict land has played an important role in the renewal of the urban fabric in most of the world's major metropolises, in North America (Brown 2009) and Europe (Hoyle 1989), but more recently has been

---

For a color version of all the figures in this chapter, see www.iste.co.uk/avelinedubach/globalization.zip.

generalized to all port fronts in the world (Boquet 2014). The notion of "docklandization" (Charlier 1990) defines this reconversion of historical industrial areas into recreational and residential uses, and this requalification of port buildings (the docks in particular), which have been given a heritage status, to serve new uses. This notion addresses the movement initiated in the 1960s in the cities of the North American East Coast (Boston, Baltimore, etc.) then from the 1970s and 1980s in English cities (London, Liverpool, etc.) and progressively in the rest of Northern Europe (Hamburg, Rotterdam, etc.) and the South (Genoa, Barcelona, etc.). This reconversion of historic port areas is now widespread. It is based on large-scale urban projects capable of modifying the very image of the city. This movement has been widely studied by researchers from different disciplines and backgrounds (Chaline and Rodriguez-Malta 1994; Brown and Hall 2014), who have highlighted the trajectory and characteristics of this reconversion of port spaces.

This chapter aims to address the evolution of the city–port relationship, drawing on a number of illustrations, in order to trace the new geography of its interfaces (the urban scales of the port management), associated planning issues and actors' strategies (actors of the urban fabric). This relationship is marked by a change of scales, comprising an evolution of the very interfaces between port and city, an evolution that was already pointed out a long time ago in the academic literature (Hayut 1982; Hoyle 1989). Port authorities and local authorities are currently engaged in a strategy of completing this dissociation between port spaces in the heart of cities (docklandization) and the development of port activity outside central cities on a metropolitan and regional scale. This chapter will address this new geography and how it translates into the making of the city. It will be based on a literature review of current academic work supplemented by examples from various urban contexts (London, Montreal, Le Havre, New York). First, we will briefly approach the new geography of this city–port relationship by explaining an evolution between terminalization and docklandization. The second part of this chapter will address the major urban projects related to this evolution of city–port interplay (between standardization and differentiation) and to the associated actors' strategies (who governs the port metropolis?).

5.2. The levels of the port metropolis

5.2.1. *The terminalization movement*

The development of industrial-port zones and the specialization of port terminals in different port ranges have resulted in the removal of port infrastructures from their original urban sites. This movement has established a form of city–port disconnection. According to Hall (2010), this disconnection is threefold, characterized by a physical dimension (the "out-of-town" extension of port facilities), an institutional dimension (the autonomy of port authorities) and an economic dimension (the reduction of port value added (jobs, taxes) in the port city). The connection between city and port is being challenged with varying degrees of intensity depending on the profiles of the ports, thus reflecting a form of rupture amplified by the distance of port land from the urban core. In more recent work with Jacobs, Hall also noted that it is a change of scale rather than a divorce that needs to be addressed in this city-port relationship. (Hall and Wouter 2012). In an article with an evocative title (*"Why are maritime ports (still) urban* and *why should policy-makers care?"*), these authors demonstrate that ports are not "despatialized" but are still part of urban systems at different scales (labor market, economic network, training, infrastructure, etc.). This work echoes the typological approach to city–port relations proposed by Ducruet (2008), which states, beyond regional specificities, the "functional interdependence" between city and port at a metropolitan level, despite the spatial dissociation between port and urban spaces at a local level. This evolution is reflected in a change in the scales of ports.

The academic literature has finely described this modification of port scales through the networking of port terminals on a global scale. The literature on the impact of containerization (transport of general cargo in standard boxes/containers) – the "World in a Box", to use Frémont's expression (2008) – focuses on the strategies of the major operators of this containerization (shipowners and port terminal operators), on the one hand, and the consequences of these strategies on the evolution of the port hierarchy on a global scale, on the other hand. This research agenda (ports and globalization) is discussed in various disciplinary fields (geography, economics, management, history). Two important epistemological steps proposed in 1993 and 2005 by Slack illustrate the terms of this agenda. First, he indicated that ports integrated into intermodal networks, and authorized by containerization, are no more than "pawns in the game", to quote the title of an article cited in the latest academic papers on the port question (Slack 1993). The ports would thus be no more than connection points in a network run by global operators. Later, Olivier and Slack (2006) pointed out the need for an epistemological break in order to rethink the role of the object within a geographical perspective (transport geography, economic geography) and an economic perspective (the analysis of firm networks). The theoretical model proposed is then that of *terminalization* (Slack 2005), an important theoretical reference point that indicates that the port no longer exists as an explanatory geographical category. Ports are then sets of terminals linked on a global scale by the strategies of network operators (shipowners and port terminal operators; Box 5.1), and it is this "terminal" category that should be understood in order to fully grasp port dynamics. This epistemological break, which has been widely discussed in the literature, will thus renew research questions to address the spatial and functional fragmentation of the port (Lavaud-Letilleul 2005).

> The "terminalization" movement is the result of a worldwide concentration of port traffic under the aegis of a few large network firms. It was made possible from the 1970s onwards by the transition, in a context of liberalization of port services, and the opening up of port terminals to competition, from a "public" port model (a public port authority in charge of the ownership, management and operation of ports) to a model in which this same authority refocused on a function of managing port land and contracting with operators, equipping and operating these terminals. This shift towards port concessions (for concession periods of more than 20 years) is gradually becoming widespread on the various port fronts and is currently the classic model for large ports throughout the world (a port authority that owns the land, concession contracts and operation by operators). Shipowners and port terminal operators are developing global networks by multiplying the number of terminals operated under concession. These strategies are complex and have been analyzed in numerous studies (global network but regional specialization of operators, cooperation vs. competition between terminal operators and amateurs, shipowners developing a terminal operator function, etc.). They attest to the consolidation of worldwide terminal networks operated by a handful of operators, who have become essential players in globalization (Dubai Ports, Hutchinson, PSA, AP Moller-Terminal, CMA-CGM, MSC, etc.).

Box 5.1. *The "terminalized" port: the generalized port concession model*

It is important to note that most of the work carried out on this port renewal focuses on container transport (admittedly an overwhelming share of the value transported in the world) and a heuristic observation point for the logics of globalization (actors/networks). This logic of terminalization therefore mainly concerns a part of port traffic, a part composed of what statistics call *general cargo* (clothing, computer equipment, electronics, various processed products, etc.) transported in containers. The transport of solid bulk (coal, cereals, etc.) or liquid bulk (oil, gas, etc.) follows other network logics. Various studies that take a more general view of port traffic (Dubreuil 2005) or of bulk traffic (Lacoste 2004), point to different network logics (more regionalized, on the one hand, operated by other specialized operators, on the other hand), without calling into question this movement towards internationalization and specialization of port terminals. Beyond the globalization of maritime networks, Rodrigue and Notteboom (2009) also extend and complete the discussion by highlighting a process of port regionalization. The logic of global maritime networks is expressed on a regional scale, linking maritime port terminals with inland ports serving the hinterland as part of a strategy of integrating transport chains (intermodal services). This movement of terminalization (of port areas) and internationalization (of the actors operating the networks) is therefore being driven at different scales by operators who have become essential actors in the urban fabric of the port city. This fabric is reflected in a new fragmentation of port areas and a modification of the strategies of the associated actors.

5.2.2. *The docklandization movement*

The consequence of this port evolution is therefore a rupture of the original link between city and port, a link defined by the permeability of port and urban functions. The title of the collective work directed by Chaline and Rodriguez-Malta (1994) – "*Ces ports qui créèrent des villes*" – illustrates this initial permeability between the spaces dedicated to the port function and urban spaces. Numerous historical photographs of the port of New York (the Chelsea docks) or of Le Havre (the southern districts), for example, make it possible to grasp a sense of port activity within urban space. Different works showcase this trajectory. In the urban core, it was characterized, from the 1960s onwards, by a gradual multiplication of vacant or underused spaces defined by the term "port wastelands". If these spaces in the urban heart are rarely wastelands in the literal sense of the term (as they are often used for storage activities), the displacement of the main port activity to large specialized terminals outside the historical heart of the cities (relocation) introduces a negotiation between port actors and local public actors on the requalification of these lands in a context of urban growth and scarcity of available land. The question of city–port interfaces thus becomes a metropolitan agenda (Hoyle and Pinder 1992) around the objective of requalification of port waterfronts. It characterizes public policies specific to port cities, marked by negotiation between port infrastructure managers and urban public actors.

5.2.2.1. *From Baltimore to Baltimore*

The requalification of these port waterfronts in the 1960s in North America initiated this process. The Baltimore model, examined in academic literature and also explicitly mentioned in the requalification strategies of other port cities, allows us to identify the main elements. Initiated in the 1960s with the aim of requalifying the city center and relocating port activity to the south of the city, this project, centered on the CBD and the historic port basins (inner harbor), validates the logic of the *Festival Market Place* described by Gravari-Barbas (1998), i.e. the "*transformation of former industrial-port wastelands of American cities into tourist, leisure and commercial hotspots*". This requalification project is supported by a coalition associating the municipality and a group of entrepreneurs (*Greater Baltimore Committee*). It is based on the mobilization of these port fronts to develop recreational uses (the Baltimore Aquarium, a totem of the requalification if ever there was one, widely reproduced throughout the world, restaurants and event venues in the former port infrastructures such as the former thermal power plant, commercial (the Harborplace commercial complex) and tertiary (World Trade Center)). These uses are structured by public spaces staging a commodified relationship to the port past. The relaunch of a new project in 2003 (Inner Harbor 2.0), currently underway, renews this requalification by integrating new objectives (active mobility, new promenade, accessibility, new areas for commercial, sports and cultural activities). It extends for Baltimore, "a 'port saga'" (Baffico 2014) exemplary of the terms of this progressively generalized docklandization.

> The revitalization of waterfronts, lakes and rivers from the 1960s onwards around this strategy of "waterfront tourism" and the logic of the Festival Market Place in American cities has been finely described by Gravari-Barbas (1998). According to this author, port revitalization is one of the "most important and exciting chapters in the urban history of American cities". Gravari-Barbas traces the initial production (Boston and then Baltimore) by the developer Rouse and the architect Thompson, who defined this model with strict specifications, which was then declined in different cities by the Rouse company (New York, Miami, Jacksonville, etc.) and other developers (Portland, Seattle, San-Francisco, Denver, etc.). Gravari-Barbas explains the terms of this *"Rousification"* of American cities (taking up a formula of Peter Hall), namely, the production of a standardized urban environment staging a port architecture and heritage in the service of a commercial and cultural offer, in a controlled and secured space attracting a large tourist population. The product conceived by the *Rouse Co* (conceiving the commercial space and cultural practices in detail) is thus declined in most of the waterfronts in North America acting on these former industrial spaces in the heart of the city a requalification structured around commercial and cultural facilities, which are finally standardized (aquariums, maritime museums, commercial docks, marinas, old ships, hotel complexes, food markets).

Box 5.2. *The Market Place Festival or the "Rousification" of the port waterfronts*

5.2.2.2. *The requalification of port waterfronts: a generalized (post-modern?) turning point*

This port requalification is part of a cyclical dimension of urban economies (Hall 2010), a cycle in which these historic port fronts become specific spaces of urban promotion around a model of requalification in support of a "showcase economy" (Rodrigues-Malta 2001). The port waterfronts thus become the development ground for large tourist and recreational facilities. This requalification is characterized by what Norcliffe et al. (1996) will identify as the emergence of postmodernism *on the urban waterfront* (to use the title of this article), namely, the passage from a Fordist logic (the port as a place of production) to a post-Fordist logic (the port front as a place of consumption). This post-modernist turn is defined by the characteristics of jobs, housing, uses and heritage in accordance with the terms of this requalification (recreation, patrimonialization, commercialization). The terms of this requalification can be found today in most port metropolises. The special issue proposed by journal Revue Urbanités (see: https://www.revue-urbanites.fr/4-edito/) in 2014, entitled "Repenser la Ville Portuaire" gives an illustrated reading of it in various contexts. Albeit to varying degrees, this trajectory (exit of the commercial port from the historical city/docklandization of the former port fronts) is found in most of the configurations studied: in Baltimore (Baffico 2014), New York (Gras 2014), Toronto (Poiret 2014), Saint-Nazaire (Le Gallou 2014) or in the Asian cities of Kobe, Singapore, Shanghai (Boquet 2014). We could add to the examples here, especially with those of Mediterranean cities (Rodrigues-Malta 2004), in particular that of the port front of Barcelona requalified for the 1992 Olympic Games, or that of Genoa and its requalification piloted by Renzo Piano on the occasion of the 1992 festivities (500 since the discovery of America), or the more recent example of Tangier (a new Mediterranean port in Tangier, a conversion of the old port of Tangier) to illustrate the generalization of a movement of docklandization. Rereading the evolution of city–port interfaces is therefore a matter of grasping this general trajectory and the different ways in which it manifests, according to the local and regional contexts of each port metropolis.

5.3. The city–port interfaces, support for major urban projects

5.3.1. *Standardization versus differentiation (forms/functions)*

This requalification of port wastelands is thus an important element of standardization of urban production methods in port and river metropolises – most metropolises, in other words. On the one hand, the "waterfront" supports large urban projects in the same way as projects developed on large railway wastelands in the urban heartland. On the other hand, it is a model that can be "duplicated" in many contexts. Upon reflection on the circulation of models (Leducq et al. 2018), it represents a strong example of this duplication (Gras 2019). The main characteristics of this model have been noted: public space in the service of a recreational turn of these port lands, the commodification of these port lands around different tourist economic activities (catering, stores, exhibition, sports, etc.), the patrimonialization of historical infrastructures (docks, cranes, railroad) and the mobilization of former warehouses and docks in the service of a functional mix objective (offices, co-working spaces, convention centers). The patrimonialized port crane and the Aquarium constitute two totems of a generalized standardization of these lands at the heart of the development projects of post-industrial cities. While this is a standard model, the characteristics of this port requalification are transposed and differentiated according to the institutional, economic and morphological contexts of each port. Between standardization and differentiation, therefore, four examples (the London docks, the port wastelands of Queens in New York, the Old Port in Montreal and the southern districts of Le Havre) illustrate the terms of this requalification.

5.3.1.1. *The London Docklands*

The requalification of the London docklands, initiated in the 1980s, is a model widely commented on. Michon's (2008a, 2008b) work allows for a detailed description of the interplay between actors, and the characteristics of these formerly industrial spaces and how they have been repurposed into their form and uses. This requalification involves considerable land areas (2,200 ha), gradually freed up after the closure of the West India Docks (1967) in a trajectory of deindustrialization (leading to a loss of 150,000 jobs in the docklands area between 1965 and 1975) and a marked decrease in the number of inhabitants (of 41% of the population between 1976 and 1981). The creation of the London Docklands Development Corporation in 1981 by the new Conservative government was part of the deregulation of urban planning implemented in the former industrial cities by the development of these Urban Development Corporations. The requalification of the London Docks is thus identified by Michon (2008a) as the *"urbanistic quintessence of Thatcherism"*. This deregulation is marked by the absence of a master plan and urban planning regulations (a project-by-project negotiation with private developers) and a refocusing of public action on the preparation of land for these private developers (demolition, depollution, new transport infrastructures). These former port areas are gradually giving way to a new financial center (Canada Tower inaugurated in 1990) and the accompanying skyscrapers, office and retail complexes, new or renovated luxury housing in the former warehouses also used by certain creative activities (studios, advertising agencies, etc.). An itinerary from Tower Bridge to Canary Wharf (see Figure 5.1) shows the characteristics of this specific urbanity, between the patrimonialization of the former docks, commercialization, tertiary centralities, privatization and commodification of public space in the service of the gentrification of East London (Michon 2008b).

Figure 5.1. *The London Docklands (source: Jean Debrie, Université Paris 1 (2015))*

5.3.1.2. *The Queens West Project*

The requalification of the Queens port waterfront in New York offers a second illustration of this marked city–port trajectory. On the one hand, by the relocation of port infrastructures and terminals in the State of New Jersey and, on the other hand, by a repurposing of former port land (docks in Chelsea, Brooklyn and Queens). In the west of Queens, the development of a new district on the site of Hunter Point on nearly 30 hectares of wasteland is a powerful indicator of the mobilization of city–port interfaces authorizing the production of housing buildings, commercial spaces and public facilities (school, park, promenade). Orchestrated by the Queens West Development Corporation (created in 1992, associating the Port Authority of New York-New Jersey, the City and the State of New York) in charge of the development function (acquisition of the land, design guide, contractualization with private promoters), the project is delineated by four phases authorizing a progressive densification of the site. The work of Saillard (2014) allows us to reconstruct the trajectory between opposition to projects (the Hunter Point Community Coalition militating against density, gentrification and environmental impact), aborted projects (UNICEF headquarters, Olympic village as part of the bid for the 2012 Olympics) and finally, the emergence of a mixed project (housing, economic activities, parks), assuming a verticality that responds to the Manhattan skyline. Figure 5.2 shows this historical trajectory of the port city.

Figure 5.2. *The Queens West Project (source: Saillard (2014))*

The quays of the Old Port of Montreal provide a third illustration of the terms of the repurposing of these historic port properties. These wharves are being redeveloped on 52 hectares in the heart of Montreal, following the relocation of the port terminals to the east of the Island, which took effect in the 1970s. The creation of a federal corporation (the Old Port of Montréal Corporation) in 1981, in charge of this reconversion, marked the beginning of a project that was discussed in two public debate procedures. One debated the initial tone of the project, which, like the projects carried out by other corporations of this type (Toronto, Vancouver), was marked by a real estate dimension. This dimension was challenged by the citizens' and politicians' consultation, who demanded free access, complementarity with the downtown area, and, above all, the idea of a public space and an urban park. The *Société du Vieux-Port* then orchestrated a repurposing around a pedestrian line and various recreational amenities (Science Center, entertainment venues, small restaurants, games, aquatic equipment) around a double seasonality (winter/summer). The merger of the *Société du Vieux-Port* with the *Société Immobilière du Canada* in 2012 led to a second project (Master Plan delivered in 2015), which, following a new consultation, validated the creation of a new recreational and cultural activity pole and, above all, the development of a new mixed-use district (hotel, housing, public facilities, economic activities) to the west of the Pointe du Moulin, densifying an initially recreational project (Plessy 2019).

Figure 5.3. *The docks of the Old Port of Montreal (source: Jean Debrie, Université Paris 1 (2018))*

5.3.1.3. *The southern districts of Le Havre*

The southern districts of Le Havre-city provide a fourth illustration of this double movement of exit of the industrial port from the city center (towards the east of the city and also in the estuary of the Seine around new container terminals) and of repurposing the lands freed by this displacement. The southern districts correspond to an 800 hectare area at the interface of the urban domain and the port domain, which has been redeveloped within the framework of a planning exercise involving the Agglomeration Community, the City, the Port Authority and the Chamber of Commerce and Industry (steering committee and Master Plan initiated in 2013). This repurposing – supported by a European program (PIC Urban) – is based on a land hierarchy carried out according to proximity to the port domain: a zone dedicated to the development of mixed urban functions, a zone for the development of added value economic functions and a zone for long-term development to be defined. The effective repurposing of the first zone, based on an urban reappropriation of the historic docks and warehouses, allows for the development of a new urban district (new luxury housing, sports and cultural facilities, commercial spaces, new university facilities). It is an indicator of an effective docklandization, assumed in the very toponymy of the new commercial and recreational spaces realized in the former docks (Dock océane, Docks cafés, Dock Vauban) and is a symbolic reminder of port culture (university container city, river garden). This requalification, resulting from the displacement of the city–port interfaces, is reflected in the emergence of a new centrality of Le Havre and participates in a form of gentrification noted and analyzed in the work of Boquet (2009).

Figure 5.4. *The docklandization of the southern districts, Le Havre (source: Magistère Aménagement, Université Paris 1 (2016))*

5.3.1.4. Requalification models

These four illustrations exemplify an evolution of city–port interfaces and the associated requalification projects. This movement of requalification is generalized and shows that urbanism is in some ways standard in the general terms of requalification, but projects are part of a territorial trajectory specific to each port site marked by distinct institutional, economic, land and cultural characteristics (Debrie et al. 2013). The deregulated urbanism characterized by an absence of consultation present in London is, of course, different in nature from the plan urbanism discussed in a political steering committee in Le Havre or by the importance of citizen consultation granted in different requalification projects, as in Montreal. The very nature of the evolution of economic fabric (a total tertiarization in London, the maintenance of port production facilities in Le Havre or Montreal) also contributes to disparities in the ways in which requalification unfolds, as does land composition and whether it is marked by more or less important free resources. Culture, understood here in its relationship to urbanity and public space (and whether or not it is commodified), is another factor to be taken into account in discussing the manifestation of a general model (docklandization) in urban spaces (Michon 2008b). An exhaustive analysis of the differences apparent within processes of requalification remains to be carried out. The fact remains that this relation between standardization (of the requalification model) and differentiation (e.g. economic, political and cultural factors specific to each city) shapes the project urbanism associated with the requalification of the port waterfront and the relational dynamics of actors.

5.4. Who governs the port metropolis?

This evolution of the levels of the city–port relationship is a transposition of a specific set of actors underlying a metropolitan governance specific to port cities. The role of large public and private infrastructure managers in metropolitan governance has been discussed in numerous works, notably those of Lorrain (2009), who defines these large infrastructure managers in charge of managing technical networks (transport, electricity, energy, etc.) as "hard" actors in the governance of metropolises, as opposed to the "soft" institutions of metropolitan government. In port cities, port infrastructure managers are thus at the heart of this dual process of terminalization (contractualization with private operators) and docklandization (negotiation with local public actors). Numerous works refer to the importance of these port land developments on policy and the metropolitan form itself (Raimbault 2014; Heitz 2017). The already cited example of the New York–New Jersey Port Authority (in charge of the port and also the tunnel and subway airports) is a well-known example of this technical metropolitan management. The status of these "managers" is diverse (public establishment, mixed company, private law company), but marked by a context of common deregulation of port activity on most of the port fronts. This deregulation has led to a new dissociation between infrastructure managers (port authorities in charge of land management of the port domain) and the major operators developing terminal networks on a regional and global scale (see Box 5.1), a dissociation at the heart of the terminalization movement and the change in scale of the port metropolis.

These port authorities, beyond their management of the industrial and logistical domain (in charge of the contractual terms of use of this domain), are also important actors in the docklandization movement. The requalification of historic port land shapes a specific policy associating the actors of the port sector (port authorities, port operators, users) and territorial actors (local public actors, and actors on regional, national, European levels). Observing the terms of this negotiation between the port sector and territories enables us to understand the interplay of actors in a port and its translation into this new geography of city–port interfaces (Debrie and Raimbault 2016). Of course, the status of port authorities differs according to national contexts. The vast majority are public, but these authorities are nevertheless marked by strong differences in supervisory authority (national, regional, municipal) and varying statuses of commercial and financial autonomy in relation to these supervisory authorities. These variations obviously say a lot about the terms of negotiation specific to each port. Observing different requalifications (Queens, Montreal's Old Port, Le Havre's southern district, Liverpool's docks, Vancouver's Coal Harbour, etc.) enables us to analyze these variations (from the corporation to the mixed union), without examining the intermediary role of the port authorities, which have become important players in urban production. Moreover, the new powers of planners will be manifested in numerous recruitments within port authorities (urban planners, lawyers, architects, politicians), capable of assuming this new function. In fact, in this urbanism of major projects and new associated policies (Pinson 2009), most of the major metropolitan operations concern either port land or railway land, making the managers of these lands central actors in this urban production from the 1980s onwards. The planning function of these major managers has become more complex, ranging from the management of an industrial tool (a port or a railway station) to the development of territorial and urban projects, a diversification that has been studied in detail in recent works on port authorities (Magnan 2016) and railway authorities (Adisson 2016; Aveline-Dubach and Blandeau 2019). These major infrastructure managers (port, rail, and also airport) are thus often unrecognized leaders of metropolitan restructuring because they shape its new levels.

5.5. Conclusion: "Creating the city with the port?" The agenda of the port metropolis

The trajectory of the port metropolis is thus characterized by a double movement of delocalization of port land (outside the urban core, but integrated into the metropolitan system) and requalification of historical land (support for major urban projects). Through various illustrations, this chapter has aimed to restore the terms of this trajectory. Although the examples mentioned relate mainly to North American and European ports, it is important to point out that this dual movement (a new geography) is found, to varying degrees on different port waterfronts all over the world, to which the works mentioned in this review attest. Admittedly, the movement of terminalization is more recent on the port fronts of the "South" as a corollary of a progressive generalization of containerization initiated on the North American, European and Asian fronts, then progressively on the other port fronts (South American and African). The evolution of city–port interfaces is thus more recent, particularly in African port cities, but it is underway and reflects a similar movement of requalification of historic port spaces and a development of port terminals outside the historic city. The example of Tangier, a symbolic port city, the last illustration used in this chapter, can summarize this trajectory. The evolution of this geography is driven by a set of actors specific to port cities, characterized by negotiations between sectoral (port) actors and public (territorial) actors. The terms of this negotiation, between standardization and differentiation, are part of the urban fabric.

> Like the North American and European examples used in this chapter, the example of the evolution of the interfaces between city and port in Tangier bears witness to this new geography of the port city in another context. The creation of a new Tangier Med port complex 40 km from the historic city, piloted by the Tangier Med Special (Public) Agency (TMSA), authorizes the development of three container terminals operated by major global operators (AP Moller Terminal, CMA-CGM, Eurogate, MSC), complemented by industrial and logistics platforms hosting industrial players (Renault) and players in international trade and distribution (Adidas, Decathlon, Bosch, etc.). The Tangier Med complex, the first container port in Africa, evidences this terminalization and port exit from the original city, modifying the metropolitan trajectory of Tangier (Marei and Wippel 2020). This exit allows for a reconversion project for the historic port of Tangier City led by the *Société d'aménagement pour la reconversion de la zone portuaire de Tanger* (SATP) with the explicit objective of positioning Tangier as a tourist and cultural city. The rehabilitation of the old port (new cruise terminal, Marina) is based on "urban-compatible" activities in a context of requalification of the corniche and the entrances to the Medina, as well as a development of real estate (residences, shops, business centers) piloted by the developer Eagle Hills. This rehabilitation thus attests to the mobilization of the former port waterfronts in the service of a post-industrial trajectory of urban centers.

Box 5.3. *Tangier, new geography of the port city*

While this trajectory has been widely documented by works from a variety of disciplinary fields, it is important in the end to point out a few prospective elements of the ongoing evolution of these negotiations. The 2030 Agenda of the International Association of Port Cities (AIVP) – a structure bringing together port authorities and local public actors from the world's major port centers – is one of the witnesses of a new reflection on the terms of this evolution. This agenda, signed by 100 port cities, is a transposition of the objectives of Sustainable Development of the UN (Habitat) to the context of city–port relations. It sets out ten or so commitments in conformity with the sustainability benchmark fixed by the UN. This benchmark is, of course, debatable (and discussed), but it allows us to grasp the themes debated in the port cities on this issue of sustainability. Without going into a precise description of the commitments and objectives of sustainability (see: www.aivp.org), it is interesting to note that attention is paid to issues of adaptation to climate change, the energy transition and the potential contribution of ports to the circular economy, mobility, quality of life, biodiversity, implying renewed policy, the mobilization of human capital and a cultural identity specific to port cities. More than these general objectives (a non-prescriptive agenda), it is the various case studies, illustrating these objectives, proposed by the AIVP that allow us to point out a new reflection on this relationship between city and port. It translates into an objective of cohabitation ("to make the city with the port") defined by a referential framework of sustainability. Some works allow us to observe these new negotiations reintroducing the potential permeability of port activities (urban-compatible) and urban activities (Mazy 2014). These issues of functional mix (the port as an element of urban distribution and productive activity in cities) are reflected in new experiments (the urban insertion of ports, the maintenance of port activities in the city), participating in a modification of the terms of the urban project on these city–port interfaces. Admittedly, these experiments are still scarce, but depending on the intensity of their generalization, they could constitute a third movement (a new city–port permeability) in this geographical trajectory of port metropolises.

5.6. References

Adisson, F. (2016). Analysing state and urban restructuring through public landownership. The case of the urban projects of railway sites in France and Italy. LATTS Working Paper, no. 16–08.

Aveline-Dubach, N. and Blandeau, G. (2019). The political economy of transit value capture: The changing business model of the MTRC in Hong Kong. *Urban Studies*, 56(16), 3415–3431

Baffico, S. (2014). Baltimore, une saga portuaire. *Urbanités*, #4 – Repenser la ville portuaire [Online]. Available at: https://www.revue-urbanites.fr/4-baltimore-une-saga-portuaire/.

Beyer, A. and Debrie, J. (2014). *Les métropoles fluviales. Concilier aménagement et logistique pour un développement urbain durable*. L'Oeil d'Or, Paris.

Bird, J. (1963). *The Major Seaports of the United Kingdom*. Hutchinson, London.

Boquet, M. (2009). Ségrégation et transformation urbaine : quelle évolution de l'espace havrais ? *Mappemonde*, 95(3) [Online]. Available at: http://mappemonde.mgm.fr/num23/articles/art09304.pdf.

Boquet, Y. (2014). La relation ville-port dans la ville asiatique. *Urbanités*, #4 – Repenser la ville portuaire [Online]. Available at: https://www.revue-urbanites.fr/4-la-relation-ville-port-dans-la-ville-asiatique/.

Brown, P. (2009) *America's Waterfront Revival*. University of Pennsylvania Press, Philadelphia.

Brown, P. and Hall, P. (2014) Ports and waterfronts. In *Infrastructure Planning and Finance: A Smart and Sustainable Guide*, Elmer, V. and Leigland, A. (eds). Routledge, Abingdon.

Chaline, C. and Rodrigues-Malta, R. (1994). *Ces ports qui créèrent des villes*. L'Harmattan, Paris.

Charlier, J. (1990). A port-oriented strategy of dockland redevelopment: Examples from Ghent and Antwerp. In *Port Cities in Context: The Impact of Waterfront Regeneration*, Hoyle, B.S. (ed.). Transport Geography Study Group.

Daamen, T. and Vries, I. (2013). Governing the European port-city interface: Institutionnal impacts on spatial projects between city and port. *Journal of Transport Geography*, 27, 4–13.

Debrie, J. and Raimbault, N. (2016). The port-city relationships in two European inland ports: A geographical perspective on urban governance. *Cities – International Journal of Urban Policy and Planning*, 50, 180–187.

Debrie, J., Lavaud-Letilleul, V., Parola, F. (2013). Shaping port governance: The territorial trajectories of reform. *Journal of Transport Geography*, 27, 56–65.

Dubreuil, D. (2005). Le triptyque portuaire est-il toujours pertinent ? L'exemple des services maritimes de cabotage. *Flux*, 59("Flux portuaires" Edition), 46–58.

Ducruet, C. (2007). A metageography of port-city relationships. In *Ports, Cities, and Global Supply Chain*, Wang, J.J., Olivier, D., Notteboom, T., Slack, B. (eds). Routledge, Milton Park.

Ducruet, C. (2008). Typologie mondiale des relations ville-port. *Cybergeo: European Journal of Geography*, Espace, Société, Territoire, Document 417 [Online]. Available at: http://journals.openedition.org/cybergeo/17332 [Accessed 3 February 2021].

Fremont, A. (2007). *Le monde en boîte : conteneurisation et mondialisation*. INRETS, Bron.

Gras, P. (2014). La recomposition du waterfront new-yorkais, entre patrimoine, gentrification et mobilisation sociale. *Urbanités*, #4 – Repenser la ville portuaire [Online]. Available at: https://www.revue-urbanites.fr/4-la-recomposition-du-waterfront-new-yorkais-entre-patrimoine-gentrification-et-mobilisation-sociale/.

Gras, P. (2019). Mondialisation et standardisation. Le cas des Métropoles portuaires. *Annales Recherche Urbaine*, 113 [Online]. Available at: http://www.annalesdelarechercheurbaine.fr/IMG/pdf/aru113-pgras.pdf.

Gravari-Barbas, M. (1998). La "festival market place" ou le tourisme sur le front d'eau. Un modèle urbain américain à exporter. *Norois*, 178, 261–278.

Hall, P.V. (2010). Maritime ports and the politics of reconnection. In *Transforming Urban Waterfronts: Fixity and Flow*, Desfor, G., Laidley, J., Stevens, Q., Schubert, D. (eds). Routledge, Abingdon.

Hall, P.V. and Wouter, J. (2012). Why are maritime ports (still) urban and why should policy-makers care? *Maritime Policy & Management*, 39(2), 189–206.

Hayut, Y. (1982). The port-urban interface: An area in transition. *Area*, 14(3), 219–224.

Heitz, A. (2017). La métropole logistique : structure métropolitaine et enjeux d'aménagement. PhD Thesis, Université Paris Est.

Hoyle, B.S. (1989). The port-city interface: Trends, problems and examples. *Geoforum Perspektiv*, 20(4), 429–435.

Hoyle, B.S. and Pinder, D. (1992). *European Port Cities in Transition*. Belhaven Press, London.

Lacoste, R. (2004). Les opérateurs maritimes et portuaires européens dans la mutation de la chaîne de transport de marchandises en vrac, essai de géographie économique. PhD Thesis, Institut de Géographie et d'Aménagement Régional de l'Université de Nantes.

Lavaud-Letilleul, V. (2005). L'aménagement de nouveaux terminaux à conteneurs et le renouvellement de la problématique flux-territoires dans les ports de la Rangée Nord. *Flux*, 59, 33–45.

Leducq, D., Bourdin, A., Demaziere, C., Orillard, C. (2018). Circulation des modèles, méthodes et références en urbanisme : pistes pour un débat. *Riurba*, 6 [Online]. Available at: http://www.riurba.review/Revue/circulation-des-modeles-methodes-et-references-en-urbanisme-pistes-pour-un-debat/?pdf=2490.

Lorrain, D. (2003). Gouverner "dur-mou" : neuf très grandes métropoles. *Revue française d'administration publique*, 107, 447–454.

Magnan, M. (2016). La production et la gestion de l'espace portuaire à vocation industrielle et logistique. Les grands ports maritimes français : gestionnaires d'espaces infrastructurels. PhD Thesis, École doctorale de Géographie de Paris, Université Paris 1.

Marei, N. and Wippel, S. (2020). Une perspective urbaine de la régionalisation du monde : Tanger, métropole (eu)africaine. *Belgéo*, 4. doi: 10.4000/belgeo.43518.

Mazy, K. (2014). Villes et ports fluviaux : le projet comme dispositif de reconnexion ? Regards croisés sur Bruxelles et Lille. PhD Thesis, Art of Building and Town Planning, Université Libre de Bruxelles-Université Lille I, Brussels.

Michon, P. (2008a). L'opération de régénération des Docklands : entre patrimonialisation et invention d'un nouveau paysage urbain. *Revue Géographique de l'Est*, 48, 1–2.

Michon, P. (2008b). Le partenariat public-privé et la régénération urbaine. L'exemple des Docklands. *Géocarrefour*, 83(2). doi:10.4000/geocarrefour.5702 [Online]. Available at: http://geocarrefour.revues.org/5702 [Accessed 9 October 2014].

Norcliffe, G., Bassett, K., Hoare, T. (1996). The emergence of postmodernism on the urban waterfront: Geographical perspectives on changing relationships. *Journal of Transport Geography*, 4(2), 123–134.

Notteboom, T.E. and Rodrigue, J.P. (2005). Port regionalization: Toward a new phase in port development. *Maritime Policy Managment*, 32(3), 297–313.

Oakley, S. (2011). Re-imagining city waterfronts: A comparative analysis of governing renewal in Adelaide, Darwin and Melbourne. *Urban Policy and Research*, 29(3), 221–238.

Olivier, D. and Slack, B. (2006). Rethinking the port. *Environment and Planning*, 38, 1409–1427.

Pinson, G. (2009). *Gouverner la ville par projet. Urbanisme et gouvernance des villes européennes*. Presses de Sciences Po, Paris.

Plessy, M. (2019). La requalification des fronts d'eau portuaires : les cas de Montréal et Toronto. Master's Research Thesis, Town Planning and Construction, Université Paris 1.

Poiret, S. (2014). Une requalification portuaire inaboutie : le cas de Toronto. *Urbanités*, #4 – Repenser la ville portuaire [Online]. Available at: https://www.revue-urbanites.fr/4-une-requalification-portuaire-inaboutie-le-cas-de-toronto-canada/.

Raimbault, N. (2014). Gouverner le développement logistique de la métropole : périurbanisation, planification et compétition métropolitaine, le cas du bassin parisien et éclairages étrangers. PhD Thesis, Université Paris Est.

Rodrigue, J.-P. and Notteboom, T. (2009). The terminalization of supply chains: Reassessing the role of terminals in port/hinterland logistical relationships. *Maritime Policy & Management*, 36(2), 165–183.

Rodrigues-Malta, R. (2004). Une vitrine métropolitaine sur les quais. Villes portuaires au sud de l'Europe. *Les Annales de la recherche urbaine*, 97, 93–101.

Saillard, S. (2014). Gouverner par les réseaux. Le rôle de l'autorité portuaire de New-York-New-Jersey dans la gouvernance métropolitaine. Master's Thesis, Université Paris 1 Panthéon-Sorbonne.

Slack, B. (1993). Pawns in the game: Ports in a global transportation system. *Growth & Change*, 24(4), 579–588.

Slack, B. (2005). Terminalisation of ports: An academic question? *International Workshop on New Generation Port Cities and Global Supply Chains*, December, University of Hong Kong.

Wiegmans, B. and Louw, E. (2011). Changing port city relationships at Amsterdam: A new phase in the interface. *Journal of Transport Geography*, 19, 575–583.

PART 2

Regional Dynamics of Capital Accumulation in East Asian, Middle Eastern and West African Real Estate Markets

Part 2

6

Land Value Capture and Its Large-Scale Application in Northeast Asia

Natacha AVELINE-DUBACH[1,2]
[1] UMR Géographie-cités, CNRS,
Aubervilliers, France
[2] CNRS@CREATE, Singapore

6.1. Introduction

Over the past two decades, the practice of "land value capture" (LVC) has gained traction as an effective way to finance urbanization. According to the definition proposed by Martim Smolka (2013, p. 2),

> the notion of value capture is to mobilize for the benefit of the community at large some or all of the land value increments (unearned income or plusvalias) by actions other than the landowner's, such as public investments in infrastructure or administrative changes in land use norms and regulations.

Some authors see ordinary fiscal instruments, such as property taxes or capital gain taxes, as value capture mechanisms. Smolka's definition adopted here is more restrictive. It includes only value capture strategies applied, upstream or

---

For a color version of all the figures in this chapter, see www.iste.co.uk/avelinedubach/globalization.zip.

downstream, to urbanization and/or infrastructure projects, which often entail a significant change in the land use and constructability rules[1] (see Figure 6.1).

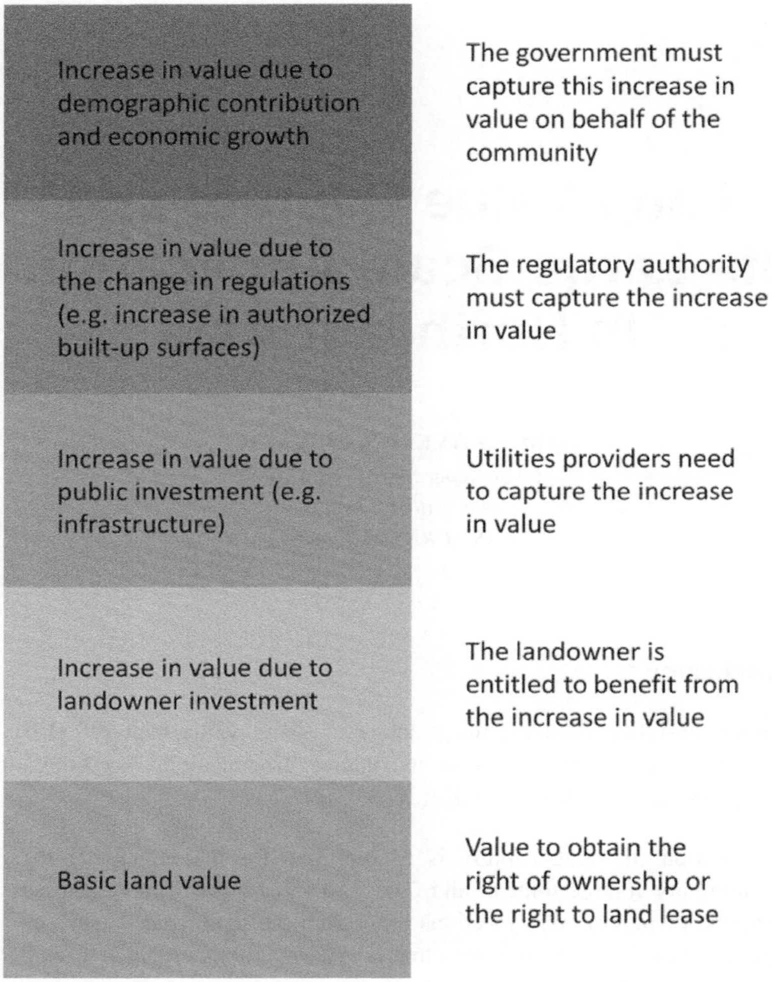

Increase in value due to demographic contribution and economic growth	The government must capture this increase in value on behalf of the community
Increase in value due to the change in regulations (e.g. increase in authorized built-up surfaces)	The regulatory authority must capture the increase in value
Increase in value due to public investment (e.g. infrastructure)	Utilities providers need to capture the increase in value
Increase in value due to landowner investment	The landowner is entitled to benefit from the increase in value
Basic land value	Value to obtain the right of ownership or the right to land lease

Figure 6.1. *Conceptualization of land value using the LVC approach (source: author's elaboration based on Suzuki et al. (2015))*

---

1. While ordinary property taxes are also inherited from the Ricardian–Georgian rent paradigm presented in this chapter, they are a simple levy on the resources of individuals and corporations and as such cannot be considered instruments of public action.

While LVC is becoming increasingly widespread, particularly in developing countries under the active promotion of the World Bank, large-scale forms of land value capture have long been observed in East Asia. This is especially the case in Japan and Hong Kong, where these practices date back to the 19th century. As China adopted a land tenure system similar to the Hong Kong model during its economic transition, LVC was deployed through various instruments, also becoming a preferred means of financing urbanization.

How can we characterize these forms of LVC on a scale unprecedented in the West? Rachel Alterman (2012) has formulated the notion of "macro-value capture"[2] to refer to practices of meta-capture of land rent considered more virtuous than a market regime. Alterman distinguishes four categories of macro value capture, according to a decreasing degree of state interference with private property rights: 1) public land ownership regimes; 2) regimes dominated by long-term public leases; 3) regimes with large land reserves (land banks); and 4) land readjustment (land donation by private owners to finance public infrastructure and public spaces; see Box 6.1). The public land tenure systems of Hong Kong and mainland China fall into the first category, while Japan is at the other end of the spectrum with its widespread practice of land readjustment. However, Japan's approaches to LVC go well beyond land readjustment in the strict sense. In the Tokyo and Osaka metropolitan areas, private railways serving the suburbs have been developing rail-related activities for more than a century to monetize the gains in accessibility capitalized along their networks. Their value capture strategies thus extend over large geographic areas and across sectors, well beyond the operational perimeters of land readjustment. Similarly, in Hong Kong and China, the state practice of LVC is far from uniform. It presents different configurations depending on its objectives and territorial scope.

This chapter examines the complex forms and geometries of large-scale value capture in Northeast Asia. It first traces the origins of LVC, noting an initial circulation of its instruments from the West to Asia, and then a reverse movement driven by the success of Asian approaches. The second part examines in more detail the contemporary uses of LVC in Japan, Hong Kong and China. It shows that while macro value-capture makes the quest for profit compatible with the provision of

---

[2] "Macro value capture instruments are not freestanding. They are embedded in some overarching land policy regime, motivated by some broader rationale and ideology. These regimes are assumed to provide a better land and development policy than a market regime" (Alterman 2012, p. 8).

quality public services, its success must be qualified by undesirable socio-economic effects, and its long-term sustainability must be questioned in a context of demographic decline.

6.2. Origins and contemporary forms of LVC

6.2.1. *Circulation of LVC models between the West and the East*

The idea of having beneficiaries co-fund infrastructure is not new. Even as early as in ancient Roman times, landowners were required to contribute to the construction of aqueducts (Smolka 2013) and the 19th century has plenty of examples of private entrepreneurs, such as Baron Hausmann, who cofinanced the construction of public roads through real estate projects. However, these were ad hoc techniques that were not thought of as regulatory or fiscal instruments with routinized uses.

The origins of LVC as urban planning tools instead lie with an approach to the recovery of capital gains from land, based on the theorization of ground rent. At the beginning of the 19th century, the economist David Ricardo had revisited in depth the representations of land ownership by showing that the British aristocratic class, made up of large absentee landlords, benefited from a surplus of production provided by the farmers of their land. Inspired by this thesis, John Stuart Mill advocated taxing any increase in land rent from landlords who "grow richer, as it were in their sleep, without working, risking, or economizing" (Mill 2001 [1848], p. 941). But it was Henry George who popularized the idea of recovering capital gains from land in urban areas in his famous book, *Progress and Poverty*, published in 1879 in the United States. George argued that the wealth created by urban growth and infrastructure investment was being captured by landowners. He advocated the abolition of all taxes in favor of a single tax on land, considering that such an instrument for the socialization of ground rent had the power to abolish poverty and solve a large part of the social ills.

Georgism was popular in East Asia but did not find a foothold there. In Japan, many prominent intellectuals such as Fukuzawa Yukichi expressed support for the redistributive goals of this project, but they did not think it was acceptable to deprive landowners of the benefits of their land, and did not believe in abolishing poverty through a simple tax (Yamazaki 1996).

China, on the other hand, found a powerful proselytizer of Georgism in Sun Yat Sen. The father of the Chinese republic included the "Equalization of Land Rights" (ELR) as one of his three main principles for reforming the Chinese system. The

ELR provided for the appropriation by the state of any future increase in land value through taxation (Schiffrin 1957). The project was mainly aimed at capturing land rent in urban areas to finance public infrastructure, but was very badly perceived in the countryside where peasants aspired to a more radical reform of land ownership (Trescott 1994). Eventually, land nationalization prevailed with the communist revolution, but the ELR principle was experimented with in Taiwan, where the Nationalist government led by Chiang Kai-shek found refuge and asserted its dominance in 1949. The ELR is still taxed under the Taiwanese constitution, but on much reduced tax bases, so that it is now similar to an ordinary tax (Lam 2000).

While the LVC tax-based approach did not flourish in East Asia, other techniques for capturing land rent were developed there, based on a more pragmatic approach centered on the land development projects. Japan played a major role in the elaboration and dissemination of these alternative models to the tax-based approach. These instruments were based on the appropriation by Japan of several techniques and urban models of Western origin.

A decisive inspiration was the land readjustment technique originating in Germany (*Umlegung*). Introduced in Japan in 1899 to improve the productivity of agricultural land, it was adapted to the Japanese urban context in 1919, to become a structuring tool for planning policies (Sorensen 2000). Named *tochi kukaku seiri*, its principle consists of reshaping the parcel of land in an agricultural area destined for urban expansion without public appropriation of the land. The landowners keep their property but contribute to the financing of the land readjustment project by giving up about 30% of the surface area of their plot. The land plots collected through this mecanism are used for the development of infrastructure and public spaces (roads, parks, plazas, etc.) as well as to the creation of reserve land, the sale of which makes it possible to recover most of the development cost (see Box 6.1). This LVC technique is advantageous for the land rightholders, as their land contribution is largely offset by the higher value of a fully serviced land. It also avoids the political and financial cost to the public authorities of expropriation procedures. The Japanese land readjustment system is thus different from its European counterparts, which are based on the expropriation and reallocation of the land. It was widely used in Taiwan and Korea during the Japanese colonial period (Aveline 1997), and then in major cities in South and Southeast Asia via Japanese development aid (Home 2007).

Another European LVC model based on a land development project comes from Ebenezer Howard's vision of a garden city. The 1903 implementation of Howard's project in the city of Letchworth appealed to the father of Japanese capitalism, Eichi Shibusawa, who in the 1920s built an urban entity called *Den'en chôfu* ("city in the countryside") in the western suburbs of Tokyo. This Japanese version of the garden city shared with its British model was grafted onto the then expanding urban transit network, making the railway station the functional and symbolic central node of the city (Oshima 1996). However, the Japanese approach differed from the Howardian vision in two decisive aspects: it was not based on the socialization of rent through common ownership of land, and it did not claim to be a self-sufficient anti-urban model, integrating employment and residential functions. It was rather conceived as a suburban development project for middle class households commuting to Tokyo (Watanabe 1980). With its elegant semicircular arteries radiating around the station, the *Den'en chôfu* district could not be replicated elsewhere because it required land control that was very difficult to maintain in the Japanese context. However, as an urban project centered on railway stations and offering a diversity of commercial and leisure functions, the garden city planned on a larger scale (*Den'en toshi* developed by the same Tokyu group) was to become a common reference for new town projects developed by private railway groups in the suburbs of Tokyo (Aveline 2003).

At the same time, in Osaka, the CEO of the Hankyu Railway company, Ichizo Kobayashi, had laid the foundations for diversification beyond railway operations through the concept of a "general private operation" (*sôgôtekina minkan eigyô*). As early as the 1920s, he had been building residential areas along his railway networks, hotel and leisure facilities at the peripheral ends, and a department store at his Umeda terminal station in central Osaka. This business model was not inspired by the garden city – although the residential operations were borrowed heavily from the rural narrative – but was more akin to that of private streetcar companies in European and North American cities that developed suburban housing in the mid-19th century[3] (Knowles et al. 2020). Whatever their original frame of reference, the private railways operating in the suburbs of Tokyo and Osaka quickly converged in their strategies of business diversification focused on railway transport. They were not allowed to cross-subsidize their transport operations with their extra-rail activities, but the business diversification enabled the railway groups to recoup the uplift in the value generated by their investment in infrastructure and provision of multifaceted services (Shoji 2001).

This business model could not be transposed to other national contexts as it was, having contributed to tremendous urban sprawl in the two major Japanese urban regions (Aveline 2003). It was therefore not the suburban development strategy of these operators that inspired other initiatives, but the treatment of their terminal stations as real estate complexes associated with multimodal platforms, offering a wide range of services to the "customer passenger". The idea then arose to finance

---

3. It is possible that Kobayashi was aware of these initiatives, although this has not been established to the author's knowledge.

the construction of rail infrastructure, especially stations, using the the revenues generated by real estate projects and transport-related services. This has had a strong impact in Europe, as the stations which had been kept away from urban cores have become economic centers with the development of high-speed rail networks and the spatial reconfiguration of the logistics sector (Van der Krabben and Needham 2008; Bertolini et al. 2012).

6.2.2. Contemporary approaches to LVC

Contemporary LVC systems, largely inherited from these two-way circulations between the East and the West, are today very diverse. Several authors have sought to categorize LVC tools by their underlying rationales.

A first categorization distinguishes between direct and indirect instruments (Alterman 2012). The former are derived directly from the Ricardian–Georgian concept of land rent. They consist of various taxes (betterment levy, capital gain tax, etc.) intended to recover all or part of the uplift in the value generated by a new public facility or development project. This levy is based on the principle that landowners have a moral obligation to return to the community a portion of the unearned increment from which they benefit. A levy is often exercised within special perimeters whose configuration is set by the local administration according to rather uniform norms, often in the form of a circle with a radius of 500 meters around a railway station. Indirect instruments, on the other hand, do not aim to redistribute profits, but to create revenues in order to cofinance an infrastructure or public service provision. They follow a more pragmatic approach, aiming to make property owners and/or developers bear a share of the cost of the new development project. They are easy to implement at all stages of the urban planning process, and take much more variable forms than direct instruments due to their dependence on the local context. According to Alterman, these instruments most often take the form of a contribution imposed on the developer, the *developer obligation*, whether in monetary form or in kind (donation of land, development of public space or affordable housing). Muñoz Gielen et al. (2017) distinguish between non-negotiable and negotiable developer obligations, drawing on European and North American examples. In the first case (e.g. *taxe d'aménagement* in France, *impact fees* in the United States, *community infrastructure levy* in Great Britain) a legislative framework is generally necessary, whereas in the second case (*participations* in France, *exactions* in the United States, *development charges* in Canada, *planning obligations* in Great Britain), the contributions are negotiated on a case-by-case basis between the local authority and the private operator (see Table 6.1).

Category	Type of instrument	Principles	Example(s)
Tax and fee-based instruments	*Betterment levy* or *special assessment* Contribution to the financing of an infrastructure or public service improvement in a given area.	A fee charged to property owners to defray all or part of the cost of improvements to infrastructure or public services that will benefit them.	In the United States, a *special assessment* is used in most states, particularly for the construction of transport infrastructure. The *betterment levy* has also been common in South American countries since the 1920s, particularly in Colombia where it contributes to the development of the road network.
	Tax increment financing (TIF) An additional tax imposed on owners in an area where a public investment project is planned.	In a municipally defined TIF area where a public investment project is planned, the tax revenues resulting from the increase in property values are paid to the municipality or an economic development authority operating on its behalf, and are used to repay the cost of the investment.	Introduced in California in 1952, TIF has become the primary economic development financing tool for cities in the United States. It is implemented in 49 states.
	Impact fees or *contributions* One-time contribution paid by developers to cofinance the cost of a city's infrastructure and public facilities.	These contributions are collected by local governments on new real estate developments. They are calculated according to a fixed formula for impact fees, while developer contributions are negotiated. In both cases, these contributions may relate to public investments outside the development perimeters.	In Orange County, Florida, impact fees are used to generate funds for parks and public safety investments.
Development-based instruments	*Joint development* Formal arrangement between the public sector and one or more private companies to share the cost of building or improving infrastructure.	The increased land/real estate value generated by the infrastructure improvement is partially recovered through specific joint development agreements to finance the initial cost of the improvement.	This approach is mainly used for the financing of transport infrastructure (high-speed trains and urban subways). It is common in the United States as well as in Asia. It mobilizes a wide range of business models.

Development-based instruments (cont'd)	*Rail+Property model* Transfer of land by the local government to a rail company, which builds lines and finances the cost of construction through real estate transactions with private developers.	The railway operator buys the land ceded by the government at "pre-rail" value. It builds the lines and sells the land to the developers at the serviced price. It may also receive physical assets (buildings or shares of buildings) from developers to supplement its income through asset management (see below).	This model has been specific to Hong Kong for a long time, where it covered the whole cost of the metro system (MTRC). Today, it is imitated by the main metro companies in China, but with important adaptations to the local context. There, the real estate developers are most often state-owned enterprises and not private companies (they are public–public cooperation). The R+P model can only be implemented in urban contexts where the state controls all or part of the land.
Asset management-based instruments	*Asset management* Management of real estate properties by the transport operator inside or outside its railway networks. Mostly used by rail operators.	The operator actively manages its properties to optimize the flow of rental income.	This model was initially developed by the Japanese private railways. It has spread widely to the point where most stations now have commercial premises of various kinds. This "rentier" model is tending to replace the development-based model in advanced economies with aging societies.

Table 6.1. *The main tools of LVC (source: elaboration by the author, based on Suzuki et al. 2015, Aveline-Dubach and Blandeau 2019, and Lincoln Institute 2018 (https://www.lincolninst.edu/sites/default/files/pubfiles/land-value-capture-policy-brief.pdf [Accessed January 2021]))*

Another categorization of LVC instruments, proposed by Suzuki et al. (2013), differentiates between *tax or fee-based instruments* and *development-based instruments*. The first category includes the indirect instruments mentioned above, plus the *tax increment finance* (TIF), a popular tool in the United States that allows municipalities to finance the redevelopment of blighted neighborhoods or investment in public infrastructure by capturing (often through bond financing) the future anticipated increase in tax revenues to be generated by the project (see Table 6.1). The second category of instruments takes more diverse forms, i.e. the sale of land charges or leasehold rights; joint public–private developments (especially for the construction of railway stations); the sale of building rights by local governments beyond certain regulatory limits; and the land readjustment and urban renewal projects, such as those carried out in Japan (Boxes 6.1 and 6.2).

Regardless of the typology chosen, most authors find a loss of interest for LVC tax instruments levied on property owners. Jeffrey Chapman (2017) argues that these tools recover only a small fraction of project costs. Their mixed results are mostly due to a growing voter reluctance to pay higher taxes (Alterman 2012) and difficulties in defining the boundaries of special perimeters for LVC taxation, which produce inequities among property owners (Medda 2012). In some cases, the tax burden can become unbearable for "asset-rich, cash-poor" local residents (Wolf-Powers 2019). As heirs to the Ricardo–Georgian land rent paradigm, these instruments remain most prevalent in Britain and the Americas. They have not found application in Northeast Asia outside the Taiwanese case.

On the other hand, some Asian countries have been major providers of *development-based* LVC instruments, as we have seen in the case of Japan. When large urban projects are carried out, the uplift in land value does not only result from the direct impact of public infrastructure or services (and in particular of accessibility gains for transit infrastructure), but also from changes in land use rules and income flows generated by the development project (Suzuki et al. 2015; see Figure 6.1). We are thus in the negotiated production of a place – a living environment, a social and economic environment – within which the increase in land value is no longer conceived as an unearned income but as the driving force of a public–private cooperation that rewards the risks taken by the partners (Aveline-Dubach and Blandeau 2019).

This entrepreneurial approach to value creation is gaining momentum. It takes place within a context of shrinking public budgets, which encourages state authorities to diversify their financial resources while maximizing revenues from their regalian rights (optimization of revenues from sales of public land, compensation for zoning revisions and increases in building rights). Because of the revenues it offers, the entrepreneurial approach is presented as an effective way to work towards decarbonizing cities through the development of sustainable mobility and the renewal of buildings (Granoff et al. 2016; Dunning and Lord 2020). It is thus actively promoted in developing countries by multilateral agencies (e.g. World Bank, UN-Habitat) as a "good practice" in urban planning. A substantial portion of the academic literature on LVC is based on expert work for these agencies, and takes a prescriptive and normative approach. This body of literature therefore pays little attention to the social and urban outcomes of LVC and tends to focus on the successes and challenges of its implementation.

Based on an overview of the conditions for successful value capture projects, Shishir Mathur (2019) emphasizes the need for a clear collaborative structure between the various government entities involved in the governance of the LVC. This is especially true for joint public–private development projects that require the approval, assistance and contribution of state institutions at various levels and jurisdictions. In the case of value capture to cofinance transit infrastructure, the challenge to LVC governance is even more critical, as the rail operator may not have the expertise to engage in real estate projects or may find its development activities contested by other actors. Mathur also emphasizes the importance of strong national regulation to limit the lobbying power of developers, but advocates pursuing a flexible approach to land use rules locally. Finally, like many authors, he recommends the broadest possible involvement of stakeholders in urban projects. However, the example of the East Asian countries discussed below shows that macro value capture is hardly conducive to participatory democracy and is perfectly compatible with authoritarian forms of power.

6.3. LVC strategies in East Asia

6.3.1. *Flexible and consensual LVC practice in Japan*

The Japanese state has been distinguished by a very assertive developmentalist strategy to support economic growth. From the earliest stages of capitalism (late 19th century), it had to mobilize scarce resources to make up for the industrial lag compared with Western countries (Muramatsu 1997). This led to the early adoption of an entrepreneurial strategy to finance urbanization, through the privatization of large public plots and the extensive use of private capital.

In this context, land readjustment quickly became "the mother of urban planning" (Sorensen 1999). This procedure was systematized with the implementation of large public projects for the reconstruction of damaged districts (Great Kanto earthquake in 1923, American bombings during World War II), the development of new towns in the 1960s and 1970s and even the construction in 2005 of a public railroad serving the city of Tsukuba to the east of Tokyo (Tsukuba Express), with about 20 stations. At the same time, smaller private land readjustment projects were carried out for the construction of residential areas on urbanization fronts. Local governments encouraged these initiatives to finance the development of the suburbs at low cost. The financial stakes were high in a country where land prices had long been the highest in the world. Land readjustment also offered a way of freeing public and private actors from the extreme fragmentation of property rights, which were moreover entangled and sacralized. However, this urban intervention tool is not a panacea. It is above all very time-consuming because of the need for consensual negotiation[4], but it also generates chaotic construction in peri-urban areas, since farmers are not obliged to build on their replotted land[5].

> The process of land readjustment (*tochi kukaku seiri*) involves the complete reshaping of land parcels to carry out a new development project. Land rightholders (landowners and land leaseholders) give up a portion of their land surface (typically 30%) to enable the construction of public infrastructure or facilities, as well as the creation of "reserve plots". The latter are sold to third parties (e.g. private developers, public institutions) in order to finance the cost of development. There are two types of land reajustment projects, those implemented by public operators (municipality or social developer) and those of private players (companies, association of landowners, individuals).

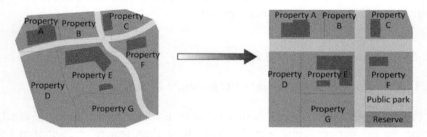

Public land consolidations may be carried out without obtaining the prior agreement of the rightholders of the land concerned. A land reajustment committee composed of representatives of the land rightholders, the urban development body and the local authorities must nevertheless be formed. These projects are generally on a large scale (about 50 hectares on average), often located in built-up areas, and their completion can take up to 10 years. Rather cumbersome to implement and not very consensual, they were mainly used for the reconstruction of cities after World War II and for the development of new towns during the 1960s and 1970s.

More numerous, private readjustment projects require the agreement of two-thirds of the rightholders of the area concerned. They are mostly carried out on the former agricultural zones of the urban fringes (which then become constructible), are smaller in size than public land reajustment and are completed more quickly (five years on average).

---

4. For private projects, the agreement of two-thirds of the land-rights holders is required, but in practice the broadest consensus is sought.
5. The readjustment projects on the urban fringes involve former agricultural land. Once the land is serviced, many farm owners keep it as is, so these parcels are very unevenly built.

Whatever the type of project, the general public cannot express its opinion on the land consolidation project, only the rightful claimants are authorized to make complaints to the prefect. However, appeals are rare: in the event of a disagreement with the project, the rightful claimants prefer to boycott the land reajustment committee, a much more effective way of blocking the project. As the land consolidation is not accompanied by any obligation to build, the regrouped plots often remain vacant on the urban fringes.

Box 6.1. *The land reajustment procedure in Japan (*tochi kukaku seiri*)*

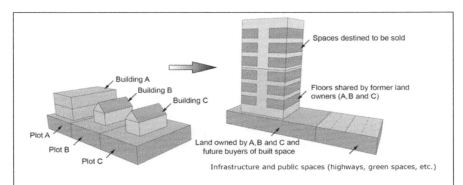

Urban renewal operations follow a principle very similar to that of land readjustment, to the extent that they could be described as "vertical readjustment". They also offer development opportunities without land acquisition, but their objective is primarily to increase building density. Land rights (full ownership and land leases) are no longer transferred to land, but to built-up surfaces. The rightful owners exchange their title deeds for built surfaces (housing, offices or shops) in proportion to the market value of their property before the start of the work.

As with land consolidation, urban renewal can be a private or public initiative. About one-third of the development cost is covered by public subsidies if the project contributes to the development of the road network and the construction of fire-resistant buildings. The balance of the financing is provided by the sale of a portion of the built-up surfaces to one or more investors, whether the project is initiated by a local authority or a property developer.

Box 6.2. *The urban renewal process in Japan (*toshi saikaihatsu*)*

In existing built-up areas, a law introduced in 1969 instituted a vertical land readjustment procedure known as "urban renewal" (*toshi saikaihatsu*; Box 6.2). This urban redevelopment method, which may also be a public or private initiative, is applied in areas where the land is restructured to construct high-rise buildings.

Densification of the built environment frees up land for the widening of roads and the creation of public spaces. Land-right holders (i.e. landowners and land leaseholders) can generally be relocated to the site by exchanging their property rights for a share of the new built-up surfaces worth the same amount as their original property, or they can opt for compensation of the same value. The significant increase in the floor area ratios (FARs) in these areas generates a surplus of built-up surfaces that are sold to third parties to finance the major part of the project cost, as in the case of land readjustment. Although it limits public investment, this procedure imposes significant delays in project implementation due to negotiations with multiple rights holders and temporary relocation operations. It also has socio-economic effects due to the eviction of real estate leaseholders (for residential or commercial purposes), who are not entitled to compensation under a land right.

Beginning in the 1980s, the authorities created several types of "special urban renewal areas" to make zoning and building rules even more flexible. These incentives for private investment were aimed at rapidly adapting Japan's major cities to international standards through the construction of large-scale buildings, the widening of major traffic arteries and the provision of urban amenities.

The urban fabric of Japanese cities has therefore been largely restructured through these urban renewal projects, in which solid public–private cooperation practices have been forged. Among the private actors, the railway groups stood out for their particularly intensive use of the two abovementioned tools of negotiated urban planning. On one hand, readjustment projects on the urbanization fronts guaranteed the route of their railroads – since they were not allowed to expropriate land-right holders – while allowing them to carry out residential development in suburban areas; on the other hand, urban renewal projects enabled them to rebuild their stations every 20–30 years as seismic technology improved, so they took advantage of these opportunities to increase the volume of their real estate assets under management by increasing building density. By deploying their rail networks in the suburbs of Tokyo and Osaka, these players have carved out vast areas of influence where they have diversified into three main sectors: real estate (residential development in the suburbs and asset management in major stations), retail (from convenience stores to department stores) and leisure (sports and hotel complexes, cultural facilities). These activities expanded outside their sphere of influence in the postwar period, transforming these companies into powerful groups (Aoki et al. 1997; Uda et al. 1997; Aveline 2003). Thus, when the state-owned JNR Railway was privatized in 1987, the six regional JR entities that emerged from it naturally adopted this business model.

Nowadays, rail provides approximately half of the passenger traffic in the Tokyo and Osaka metropolitan areas, where 45% of the national population is concentrated. Rail transport in the Tokyo and Osaka regions is provided mainly by two categories of private operators: the 13 suburban railway groups[6], which operate a total of 2,167 km of lines and 1,316 stations (700 in Tokyo, 616 in Osaka)[7] and the two regional groups JR East and JR West, which run a total of 2,900 km of lines and 750 stations in the Greater Tokyo and Osaka-Kyoto-Kobe regions (510 and 240 respectively).[8] All stations are equipped to varying degrees with facilities that ensure the continuity of multifaceted services in the transportation chain and generate real estate revenue streams. These strategies have prevented Japan's suburbs from becoming bleak dormitory towns in the absence of job deconcentration, which would have thwarted the interests of the rail groups.

However, the tremendous expansion of residential areas produced by the LVC was abruptly reversed when the country started to face a process of depopulation in the 2000s, combined with the bursting of a land bubble. Since then, Japanese metropolises have been experiencing urban shrinkage, driven by demographic aging and socioeconomic decline at their margins (Buhnik 2010; Ohashi and Phelps 2021). The result is the development of a structural vacancy of housing in the metropolitan peripheries, with 8.4 million dwellings unoccupied, representing 13.6% of the housing stock. Some of these constructions, mostly single-family houses, have seen their value fall to zero or even become negative (Kubo and Yui 2020).

Although the demographic and urban decline is reversing the rationale for planning policies and instruments, the authorities have not rethought theirs. They are pursuing a strategy of value creation and support for the real estate industry by encouraging urban renewal projects focused on the major railway stations, using the rhetoric of the "compact city" to justify an unprecedented intensification of building density in the urban renewal areas (Buhnik 2017). While this re-centering of urban production succeeds in stimulating investment in niche markets in "pockets of growth", it only reinforces the process of urban shrinkage and property devaluation in periurban areas.

---

6 For Tokyo, these are Tobu, Seibu, Keisei, Keio, Odakyu, Tokyu, Keikyu, Sosetsu groups; and Kintetsu, Nankai, Keihan, Hankyu and Hanshin for Osaka.
7 The data book of the major private railways 2020: https://www.mintetsu.or.jp/activity/databook/pdf/20databook_full.pdf [Accessed January 6, 2021].
8 7,401 km and 1,677 stations at regional level for JR East, 4,903 km and 1,174 stations for JR West [Group websites accessed December 2022].

Urban shrinkage particularly affects private rail groups, which are faced with a structural decline in passenger traffic and a reduction in the territorial base of their extra-rail activities. These groups are trying to maintain the attractiveness of their lines by developing new facilities and services, particularly for the elderly. But above all, they are accompanying the shift towards urban centers by taking advantage of the liberalization of urban planning and construction rules in the vicinity of their major stations to build multifunctional skyscrapers. They also invest in logistics facilities and manage multistory residential buildings. This accumulation of real estate assets provides them with long-term income streams to compensate for the loss of profit in traditional real estate development projects. The transit operators' expansionist strategy has thus evolved into an LVC model focused on property asset management in rail hubs (Aveline-Dubach 2015).

6.3.2. *An LVC regime based on land concessions in Hong Kong*

Unlike the Japanese case, where land rights are scattered among millions of private landowners, Hong Kong has a single land system[9] controlled by the government of the Hong Kong Special Administration Region (HKSAR). This situation is a legacy of colonial history. It dates back to the introduction of a public land grant system by the British Crown in 1843 to simplify property rights and spare the British taxpayer the cost of developing the colony.

This land tenure system, which was maintained as a public concession after the handover of Hong Kong to China in 1997, considerably facilitates the practice of LVC. It gives the HKSAR government the right to capture part of the increase in land values through lease contracts at different stages of the rental process. The crucial step is the auctioning of land for which the government sets a minimum lump sum corresponding to a given lease term (50 years since 1997, most often 75 and 99 years for earlier periods) associated with specific land use rules. Private developers bid for the *land premium* based on these conditions[10]. The developer who wins the auction must also pay an annual rent (*land rent*) during the rental period, but the amount is not related to real estate prices (3% of a rental value estimated by the administration). Thus, the value capture is essentially achieved through the *land premium*, which is similar to a land sale. The government then has the opportunity to increase its levies via the land premium according to the evolution of the real estate market in two specific cases: when the lease is modified and when it is renewed. The

---

9. With the exception of the land underlying Saint John's Episcopal Cathedral.
10. A "bid list" system was introduced between 2003 and 2013 to force the government to auction off land according to the needs of developers, rather than on the sites it selected itself according to urban planning objectives. This system was abolished in 2013.

first case occurs when lesses obtain a revision of their lease agreement to lift land use restrictions; the amount of the premium is calculated on the basis of the potential increase in land value. In the second case, lesses pay an additional premium in an amount equivalent to the market value of the land at the time the lease expires (Hong and Lam 1998).

This open arrangement has enabled the government to increase its value capture during a series of property booms which have put Hong Kong at the top of the world's ranking of most expensive cities. Land lease income has contributed nearly one-third of HKSAR's revenue in recent years, in addition to high property tax revenues that compensate for low corporate taxes[11].

But these are not the only benefits of the Hong Kong land regime. Since 1979, the HKSAR has also been able to build one of the most profitable rail infrastructures in the world, financed mainly through value capture. The MTRC metro company[12], which today operates 236.9 km of lines and 95 stations, was originally established as a statutory corporation (public company subject to profitability objectives) and was partially privatized in 2000. It had a difficult start due to stiff competition from private bus transport operated by large Hong Kong developers. To increase passenger traffic, it pursued a policy of low transport fares while expanding its ridership through station-centered real estate development projects.

However, as in Japan, the need for ridership soon gave way to the operation of income-producing properties. Inspired by the "business diversification model"[13] of Japanese railway groups, the MTRC developed its own LVC model in the 1980s, the R+P (Rail and Property). Much less diversified and more station-centric that its Japanese counterpart, the R+P diversification model also seeks to transform stations into attractive spaces through real estate development and varied commercial services related to rail. However, due to the strict control of land use by the government (less than 30% of Hong Kong's territory is open to urbanization), this model has resulted in particularly dense high-rise building projects. Those constructions above the stations consist of thick commercial slabs, known as "podiums", topped by office towers, residential units or prestigious hotels (Figure 6.2).

---

11. HKSAR (May 2018). Major source of government revenue [Online]. Available at: https://www.legco.gov.hk/research-publications/english/1718issf03-major-sources-of-government-revenue-20180530-e.pdf [Accessed January 5, 2021].

12. Mass Transit Railway Corporation, founded in 1972.

13. In Japanese: *takakuka keiei no moderu*.

Figure 6.2. *Podium urbanism in Hong Kong
(source: Natacha Aveline-Dubach, 2012)*

The MTRC financed the construction of its transit system through LVC by developing land for these major urban hubs. The government provided MTRC with low-cost, unserviced land with building rights for 50 years above and adjacent to its future stations. The MTRC built its railway facilities and sold the *land premium* for commercial use at a high price to developers through open or restricted tenders. In addition, it obtained a portion of the developers' profit in kind, in the form of built-up surfaces in large residential or business complexes (Cervero and Murakami 2009). But the effectiveness of the R+P was not solely based on these land and property revenues. Despite its laissez-faire rhetoric, HKSAR has strongly supported MTRC interests by organizing urban planning around transit corridors and restricting competition from alternative modes of transport (bus and automobile). As a result of the mutually reinforcing dynamics between rail and urbanization, the MTRC's share of passenger traffic in Hong Kong increased from 15% in 1981 to nearly 50% in 2020[14].

While the HKSAR government continues to support rail, it has put an end to the traditional R+P mechanism by ceasing to sell land to the MTRC. This major change was brought about by the reconfiguration of the local governance system following two major events in 1997: the handover of Hong Kong to China and the outbreak of the Asian financial crisis. The major Hong Kong developers, grown into powerful conglomerates after the withdrawal of British manufacturers, demanded a more advantageous sharing of the land rent along the transit corridors to overcome the financial crisis. Their aversion to the R+P model, of which the MTRC was the main beneficiary, was echoed by a then emerging civil society. The MTRC became the target of citizen mobilizations against "podium urbanism", which was considered unbearably dense and socially exclusive (limited public space, high-end housing). As a result of this criticism, the MTRC was deprived of its development revenues by the HKSAR governement. It responded by maximizing the income from its real estate assets, composed of properties in large complexes (Admiralty Center, Kornhill, etc.) and retail space in its stations. In 2019, the MTRC derived 60% of its profits[15] from these two categories of revenues. As in Japan, the business model of the R+P system has shifted to an *asset management-based* LVC approach that provides the rail operator with stable long-term income streams (Aveline-Dubach and Blandeau 2019).

6.3.3. *Optimization of the LVC by local governments in China*

Hong Kong's land tenure system served as a model for China's transition to a market economy. The state retained exclusive ownership of land, but devolved to

---

14. MTR (n.d.). Annual Activity Reports [Online]. Available at: http://www.mtr.com.hk/en/corporate/investor/financialinfo.html#02 [Accessed December 20, 2020]. Non-rail revenues collected within the infrastructure also include advertising revenues and broadband Wi-Fi access revenues.

15. EBIT (earnings before interest and taxes). Source: 2017–2019 MTRC activity reports.

municipal governments the right to exploit the proceeds of "land use rights" (LURs) in urban areas. Like *land premium*, commercial LURs are auctioned off to developers – private companies or state-owned enterprises – for varying terms depending on the land use (now ranging from 40 years for commercial uses to 70 years for residential). They can be renegotiated if the lease changes or expires but do not include a ground rent.

It is no coincidence that the first sale of land to a private developer in post-Maoist China took place in Shenzhen, a city bordering Hong Kong, in 1987. The institutional construction of land markets then progressed at a very uneven pace in China's city-regions, depending on the local constraints of the planned economy. However, in the late 1990s, local governments quickly moved towards optimizing land value capture (Tse 1998).

The catalyst for this change was the adoption of a major tax reform in 1994 aimed at consolidating state power by refocusing tax revenues. Local governments saw their share of tax revenue fall from 78% to 44%, while they were required to assume 70% of the country's budgetary expenditures (Zhu et al. 2019, p. 2). Prohibited from borrowing[16], they began to sell land massively to make ends meet. These policies were made all the more effective as the state organized the commodification of housing in the late 1990s through the abolition of the work unit housing allocation system and the establishment of mortgage credit channels.

A well-established mechanism of value capture has become widespread in the country, driven by the concomitant processes of economic and demographic growth in large cities: local governments "liberate" large public land parcels by compensating at low cost the land use rights of farmers in peri-urban areas and residents in urban renewal areas. These parcels are then auctioned off and sold to developers (private and public) at high prices to maximize the capture of value. The developers carry out real estate projects, mainly in the form of large residential blocks marketed to the middle classes (Wu 2015). The main driver of this system is the demand for housing acquisition by households. It is sustained by the proprietary ideology conveyed by the state as well as by the limited supply of financial investment vehicles that encourages households to place their savings in real estate, against a background of weak social welfare (Theurillat 2017; Aveline-Dubach 2020).

In addition to land use rights concessions, which provide on average about 50% of local tax revenues, value capture also takes the form of contributions to developers for the cost of public facilities and infrastructure, and even the

---

16. In 2014, local governments were allowed to issue bonds, but this did not reduce land sales or the issuance of Chengtou bonds.

construction of social housing. However, in order to finance large-scale infrastructure and urban development projects, local governments have created investment structures called Local Government Financing Platforms (LGFP). These structures issue so-called "Chengtou bonds" to finance their projects through private investment. They have state-owned enterprise (SOE) status and are held fully responsible for their debt, but in effect carry the implicit guarantee of local governments. The 2008 global crisis encouraged a rapid proliferation of LGFPs as the central state launched an ambitious economic stimulus package encouraging local governments to construct urban infrastructure. According to Huang and Du (2018), this had the effect of reinforcing land price overbidding (and consequently, the magnitude of value capture) by pushing local governments to inflate the value of the land pledged as collateral on the LGFPs to increase their borrowing capacity.

Among the infrastructure projects, the metro networks were particularly popular. At the turn of the 2010s, the state belatedly realized the ravages of urban sprawl, which was taking a dangerous bite out of agricultural land and contributing to deteriorating air quality by encouraging motorization. In 2011, the Ministry of Transportation put a "transit metropolis" program on the agenda to promote the development of subway systems in about 30 cities (Zhou 2016). Rail transit served the interests of local governments as an instrument of financial leverage (Shen and Wu 2020): by connecting new towns to urban centers, it monetized gains in accessibility and building intensification around new stations. Hence, the exponential growth of these infrastructures, with the number of cities with a built or planned metro network rising from 4 (146 km) in 2000 to 39 (6,300 km) in 2020[17].

However, the financing of rail networks via LGFPs has led to unsustainable debt for local governments, increasingly mobilizing "gray" (non-bank) finance with little state control (Huang and Du 2018). Thus, the R+P model has emerged as a more virtuous approach to financing these infrastructure projects. As in Hong Kong, this model is based on the transfer of land by the local government to the municipal metro company at very low cost. It has already been tried in the country's largest metropolises (sometimes on a single line) and is under consideration in several second-tier cities, more rarely in third-tier cities.

Shenzhen's experience is often cited as a particularly successful application of R+P on the Chinese mainland. However, this municipality has benefited from quite exceptional conditions to develop this model. First of all, it is worth mentioning the technological and commercial transfers from MTRC. In the early 2000s, the MTRC was approached by the local government of Shenzhen to build a metro network on the other side of the border, and saw the advantages of developing its R+P model in

---

17. https://www.camet.org.cn/english.htm [Accessed January 3, 2021].

China. However, no sooner had it launched the construction of a line (line 4) than it found itself in competition with the local metro company created in the meantime (the "Shenzhen Metro Company", SZMC), which took over its model and developed it on the rest of the local network (Aveline-Dubach and Blandeau 2019). The SZMC partnered with the country's leading private developer at the time, the Vanke Group, to develop real estate projects in and around its stations, thus benefiting from an exceptional level of expertise (Aveline-Dubach and Blandeau 2019). In addition, Shenzhen has a special status as a designated "Special Economic Zone" city, which gives it strong government support and entrepreneurial freedom (Wang et al. 2019).

In reality, the R+P model is difficult to adapt to Chinese cities due to a weak tradition of urban planning-transportation integration and institutional structures in silo (Doulet et al. 2017). Moreover, it does not rely on public–private cooperation as metro companies preferentially partner with state-owned developers (SOEs) to conduct their joint development projects (Xue and Fang 2017). This encourages corruption and creates moral hazard risk due to the credit facilities that both types of SOEs (metro company and developer) obtain from banks, of which the main ones are also state-owned. The SZMC was a forerunner in this direction, having de facto nationalized the giant Vanke by taking control of its capital in 2017[18].

Although R+P is a powerful tool for developing more sustainable rail-oriented urbanization, its application in the Chinese context is not without financial risks. Another danger is the overproduction of housing that LUR sales lead to. In addition to the moral hazard risks intrinsic to the model, the more general mechanism of LUR sales leads to a danger of housing overproduction. According to the latest official data, dating back to 2013 and therefore probably underestimated, there are 52 million empty dwellings in urban China, i.e. one in five[19]. This is due to the status of real estate as a near-exclusive investment vehicle in a society made up of more than 90% homeowners.

---

18. Financial Times (June 21, 2017). Available at: https://www.ft.com/content/d486259c-562b-11e7-9fed-c19e2700005f [Accessed January 24, 2021]. Vanke was the largest private developer in China. In 2017, its founding CEO stepped down and Vanke was quietly absorbed into Shenzhen's state-owned metro company, becoming its real estate arm.

19. China Households Finance Survey Data Talks, "Trends in the housing market and housing vacancy rate in urban China". This study, published very formally in 2014 by Southwestern University of Finance and Economics, is no longer available on the Web. It was based on interviews with 28,000 households in 262 townships. A more recent study based on nighttime lighting data (Tan et al. 2020) confirms rates of at least 20% in a large majority of cities (with the exception of first-tier cities), with a steeper vacancy gradient in the west than in the east and in the south than in the north. The northeastern region (former Manchuria) reports higher vacancy rates than other regions.

6.4. Conclusion

These three examples attest to the remarkable performance of macro-value capture in Northeast Asia. The large-scale practice of LVC has made it possible to shift the cost of urbanization largely to private investment, mainly by mobilizing household capital through land allocations and/or residential development operations supported by housing policies that encourage home ownership. Public funds have thus been able to focus on innovation and economic support policies, which have benefited greatly from infrastructure investment and in turn supported urban and economic growth. In this sense, macro value capture has served the interests of the "developmental state"[20] in two ways: by promoting technological innovation and by making residential production a pillar of growth. It should be noted that these strategies have been carried out by growth coalitions that are embedded in very contrasting land tenure regimes and political–institutional systems: a predominance of private initiative in Japan, a compromise between authoritarian executive and private interests in Hong Kong, and a prevalence of state entities in China. Equally diverse are the suburban landscapes generated by macro value capture: crumbling suburban fabric in Japan, vertical and compact complexes centered on railway stations in Hong Kong, clusters of multistory building blocks in China.

However, the success of these models is due to several common characteristics. Firstly, the high human density and growth of metropolitan areas ensures (ensued in the case of Japan) the profitability of real estate operations and investments requiring a high mobilization of fixed capital, such as subway networks. The state provides very substantial support for the modal prevalence of rail – a major value generator – through multisectoral measures. Secondly, these countries/territories have binding regulatory frameworks for zoning and construction, but urban development is fragmented and flexible in operational areas. Finally, a coordination framework (consensual or constrained) between the main beneficiaries of LVC ensures low conflict value sharing.

This success is not without undesirable consequences. Institutional arrangements organized around the creation and capture of value inevitably exert inflationary pressure on real estate prices. It is therefore not surprising that the countries/territories studied here have some of the most unaffordable residential values in the world. Tokyo was the most expensive city worldwide until the turn of the 1990s, followed by Hong Kong, which is now followed by Shenzhen, Beijing and Shanghai. Another undesirable effect of macro-value capture is residential

---

20. The notion of the developmental state, coined by the political scientist Charmers Jonson (1982) for the Japanese case, has been extended to several East Asian countries (including China) to characterize capitalist regimes with strong state control over economic development.

vacancy. In Japan, where this phenomenon is caused by the setbacks of the industrialization of suburban housing in the current context of a rapidly aging population, reflection on the measures to be taken has been placed at the top of municipal agendas (Buhnik and Koyanagi n.d.). Faced with the deterioration of uninhabited, worthless houses that threaten public safety, local governments are struggling to charge the cost of their necessary demolition to the heirs. In China, the future of these thousands of unoccupied collective condominiums incorporating household savings poses serious material, financial and environmental risks to urban societies. However, Chinese authorities are only just beginning to address vacancy, without it being explicitly put on the public agenda. Finally, the socially exclusive governance of the LVC should be highlighted: while in Japan the operations are carried out in a consensual manner with the landowners, this is by no means the case in China, where the occupants of the operational perimeters endure evictions that are often poorly compensated. As for those who do not have land rights, and more generally the inhabitants of the cities, they are suffering everywhere from the effects of gentrification and the intensification of the built environment without their voice being taken into account.

The LVC's business models, which are based on the anticipation of continued urban growth, are jeopardized by the demographic transition which is already affecting Japan and is expected to occur by 2030–2040 in China and Hong Kong. This coincides with the upcoming expiration of a majority of residential land leases in China (2030 in mainland China and 2047 in Hong Kong, respectively). The Chinese government has hinted at unconditional lease renewals for homeowners, although no official measures have yet been adopted. In Hong Kong, the government may try to increase recurrent revenues from land rents and property tax, but such levers do not exist in China; the generalization of a property tax, the measure most likely to offset the coming drop in LUR revenues, would risk being highly unpopular (Liu 2019). In the face of the current or future demographic downturn, the three countries/territories are pursuing a common policy of development and/or urban renewal centered on the railway/metro stations. Public and private rail operators are building high-density, multifunctional complexes in which they accumulate real estate assets to secure stable long-term real estate income streams while diversifying their services to local communities. It is not certain, however, that this shift in LVC business models will be sufficient to cover the cost of maintaining the rail networks, especially if recurrent pandemics challenge the hyper-mobility on which they are based.

6.5. References

Alterman, R. (2012). Land use regulations and property values: The "Windfalls Capture" idea revisited. In *The Oxford Handbook of Urban Economics and Planning*, Brooks, N., Donaghy, K., Knaap, G.-J. (eds). Oxford University Press, Oxford.

Aoki, E., Oikawa, Y., Noda, M. (1997), *Management and Culture of Private Railway Companies in Eastern Japan* [in Japanese]. Kôkon Shoin, Tokyo.

Aveline, N. (1997). Le remembrement urbain nippon : un modèle pour l'Asie ? *Daruma*, 1, 153–155.

Aveline, N. (2003). *La ville et le rail au Japon : l'expansion des groupes ferroviaires privés à Tôkyô et Osaka*. CNRS Éditions, Paris [Online]. Available at: https://books.openedition.org/editionscnrs/?lang=fr.

Aveline-Dubach, N. (2015). Stratégie des groupes ferroviaires privés face au déclin urbain dans les agglomérations de Tokyo et Osaka. In *Vieillissement et déprise urbaine au Japon les nouveaux défis de l'aménagement*, Aveline-Dubach, N. (ed.). La Documentation française, Paris.

Aveline-Dubach, N. (2020). China's housing booms: A challenge to bubble theory. In *Theories and Models of Urbanization*, Pumain, D. (ed.). Springer, Cheltenham.

Aveline-Dubach, N. and Blandeau, G. (2019). The political economy of transit value capture: The changing business model of the MTRC in Hong Kong. *Urban Studies*, 56(16), 3415–3431.

Bertolini, L., Curtis, C., Renne, J. (2012). Station area projects in Europe and beyond: Towards transit oriented development? *Built Environment*, 38(1), 31–50.

Buhnik, S. (2010). From shrinking cities to Toshi no Shukushō: Identifying patterns of urban shrinkage in the Osaka metropolitan area. *Berkeley Planning Journal*, 23(1).

Buhnik, S. (2017). The dynamics of urban degrowth in Japanese metropolitan areas: What are the outcomes of urban recentralisation strategies? *Town Planning Review*, 88(1), 79–93.

Buhnik, S. and Koyanagi, S. (n.d.). La vacance résidentielle au Japon : d'un problème d'accès au sol au souci d'y échapper. In *La ville inoccupée. Enjeux et défis des espaces urbains vacants*, Arab, N. and Miot, Y. (eds). Ponts des Chaussées, Paris.

Cervero, R. and Murakami, J. (2009). Rail and property development in Hong Kong: Experiences and extensions. *Urban Studies*, 46(10), 2019–2043.

Chapman, J. (2017). Value capture taxation as an infrastructure funding technique. *Public Works Management & Policy*, 22(1), 31–37.

Doulet, J.-F., Delpirou, A., Delaunay, T. (2017). Taking advantage of a historic opportunity? A critical review of the literature on TOD in China. *Journal of Transport and Land Use*, 10(1), 77–92.

Dunning, R.J. and Lord, A. (2020). Preparing for the climate crisis: What role should land value capture play? *Land Use Policy*, 99, 104867.

Granoff, I., Hogarth, J.R., Miller, A. (2016). Nested barriers to low-carbon infrastructure investment. *Nature Climate Change*, 6(12), 1065–1071.

Home, R. (2007). Land readjustment as a method of development land assembly: A comparative overview. *Town Planning Review*, 78(4), 459–483.

Hong, Y.-H. and Lam, A.H. (1998). *Opportunities and Risks of Capturing Land Values Under Hong Kong's Leasehold System*. Lincoln Institute of Land Policy, Cambridge, MA.

Huang, Z. and Du, X. (2018). Holding the market under the stimulus plan: Local government financing vehicles' land purchasing behavior in China. *China Economic Review*, 50, 85–100.

Johnson, C. (1982). *MITI and the Japanese Miracle: The Growth of Industrial Policy: 1925–1975*. Stanford University Press, Redwood City.

Knowles, R.D., Ferbrache, F., Nikitas, A. (2020). Transport's historical, contemporary and future role in shaping urban development: Re-evaluating transit oriented development. *Cities*, 99, 102607.

Kubo, T. and Yui, Y. (2020). *The Rise in Vacant Housing in Post-growth Japan*. Springer, Cheltenham.

Lam, A.H. (2000). Republic of China (Taiwan). *The American Journal of Economics and Sociology*, 59(5), 327–336.

Liu, Z. (2019). Land-based finance and property tax in China. *Area Development and Policy*, 4(4), 367–381.

Mathur, S. (2019). An evaluative framework for examining the use of land value capture to fund public transportation projects. *Land Use Policy*, 86, 357–364.

Medda, F. (2012). Land value capture finance for transport accessibility: A review. *Journal of Transport Geography*, 25, 154–161.

Mill, J.S. (2001). *The Principles of Political Economy. Book 5*, Volume 1. Batoche Books, Kichener.

Minerbi, L., Nakamura, P., Nietzk, Y.J. (1986). *Land Readjustment: The Japanese System. A Reconnaissance and a Digest*. Oelgeschlager, in association with the Lincoln Institute of Land Policy, Oakland.

Muñoz Gielen, D., Maguregui Salas, I., Burón Cuadrado, J. (2017). International comparison of the changing dynamics of governance approaches to land development and their results for public value capture. *Cities*, 71, 123–134.

Muramatsu, M. (1997). *Local Power in the Japanese State*. University of California Press, Oakland.

Ohashi, H. and Phelps, N.A. (2021). Suburban (mis)fortunes: Outer suburban shrinkage in Tokyo Metropolis. *Urban Studies*, 58(14), 3029–3049.

Oshima, K.T. (1996). Denenchōfu: Building the garden city in Japan. *Journal of the Society of Architectural Historians*, 55(2), 140–151.

Schiffrin, H. (1957). Sun Yat-sen's early land policy the origin and meaning of "Equalization of Land Rights". *The Journal of Asian Studies*, 16(4), 549–564.

Shen, J. and Wu, F. (2020). Paving the way to growth: Transit-oriented development as a financing instrument for Shanghai's post-suburbanization. *Urban Geography*, 41(7), 1010–1032.

Shoji, K. (2001). Lessons from Japanese experiences of roles of public and private sectors in urban transport. *Japan Railway & Transport Review*, 29, 12–18.

Smolka, M.O. (2013). *Implementing Value Capture in Latin America: Policies and Tools for Urban Development*. Lincoln Institute of Land Policy, Oakland.

Sorensen, A. (1999). Land readjustment, urban planning and urban sprawl in the Tokyo metropolitan area. *Urban Studies*, 36(13), 2333–2360.

Sorensen, A. (2000). Land readjustment and metropolitan growth: An examination of suburban land development and urban sprawl in the Tokyo metropolitan area. *Progress in Planning*, 53(2000), 217–330.

Suzuki, H., Cervero, R., Iuchi, K. (2013). *Transforming Cities with Transit: Transit and Land-use Integration for Sustainable Urban Development*. The World Bank Publications, Washington DC.

Suzuki, H., Murakami, J., Hong, Y.-H., Tamayose, B. (2015). *Financing Transit-Oriented Development with Land Values: Adapting Land Value Capture in Developing Countries*. The World Bank Publications, Washington DC.

Tan, Z., Wei, D., Yin, Z. (2020). Housing vacancy rate in major cities in China: Perspectives from nighttime light data. *Complexity*, e5104578.

Theurillat, T. (2017). The role of money in China's urban production: The local property industry in Qujing, a fourth-tier city. *Urban Geography*, 38(6), 834–860.

Trescott, P.B. (1994). Henry George, Sun Yat-sen and China: More than land policy was involved. *American Journal of Economics and Sociology*, 53(3), 363–375.

Tse, R.Y. (1998). Housing price, land supply and revenue from land sales. *Urban Studies*, 35(8), 1377–1392.

Uda, T., Asaka, K., Takechi, K. (1997). *Management and culture of private railway companies in western Japan* [in Japanese]. Kôkon Shoin, Tokyo.

Van der Krabben, E. and Needham, B. (2008). Land readjustment for value capturing a new planning tool for urban redevelopment. *Town Planning Review*, 79(6), 651–673.

Walker, T., Zhang, X., Zhang, A., Wang, Y. (2021). Fact or fiction: Implicit government guarantees in China's corporate bond market. *Journal of International Money and Finance*, 116, 102414.

Wang, J., Samsura, D.A.A., van der Krabben, E. (2019). Institutional barriers to financing transit-oriented development in China: Analyzing informal land value capture strategies. *Transport Policy*, 82, 1–10.

Watanabe, S. (1980). Metropolitanism as a way of life: The case of Tokyo, 1868–1930. In *Metropolis 1890-1940*, Sutcliffe, A. (ed.). University of Chicago Press, Chicago.

Wolf-Powers, L. (2019). Reclaim value capture for equitable urban development. *Metropolitics* [Online]. Available at: https://metropolitics.org/Reclaim-Value-Capture-for-Equitable-Urban-Development.html.

Wu, F. (2015). *Planning for Growth: Urban and Regional Planning in China*. Routledge, London and New York.

Xue, L. and Fang, W. (2017). Rail plus property development in China: The pilot case of Shenzhen. World Resource Institute [Online]. Available at: https://www.wri.org/publication/rail-plus-property-development-china-pilot-case-shenzhen.

Yamazaki, M. (1996). Asia, a civilization in the making: East Asia, The Pacific, and the Modern Age. *Foreign Affairs*, 75(4), 106–118.

Zhou, J. (2016). The transit metropolis of Chinese characteristics? Literature review, interviews, surveys and case studies. *Transport Policy*, 51, 115–125.

Zhu, X., Wei, Y., Lai, Y., Li, Y., Zhong, S., Dai, C. (2019). Empirical analysis of the driving factors of China's "land finance" mechanism using soft budget constraint theory and the PLS-SEM model. *Sustainability*, 11(3), 742.

7

The Dual Regionalization of Real Estate Financialization in Southeast Asia

Gabriel FAUVEAUD
*Departement de Géographie, Centre d'études asiatiques (CETASE),
Université de Montréal, Canada*

7.1. Introduction

Southeast Asian real estate markets have undergone profound changes since the late 1970s. Strong population growth, coupled with rapid industrialization and increasing rural–urban migration, has accelerated the emergence of large urban centers (McGee and Robinson 1995), mega-cities and mega-urban regions (Sorensen and Labbé 2020). The growing need for housing and office space, as well as the transformation of the demand due to the enrichment of a growing part of the population and the development of the tertiary sector, have been coupled with a rapid evolution of the production and exchange of real estate goods, as well as of changes in the regulatory frameworks of real estate markets. While these dynamics differ according to national situations, academic research has often emphasized how the liberalization and then the increasing neoliberalization of real estate markets have resulted in a growing privatization of urban production and planning. The spread of large-scale urban projects throughout the region has often been described as the emblematic example of these processes. (Douglass and Huang 2007; Fauveaud 2016; Harms 2016; Labbé and Boudreau 2011; Shatkin 2017).

However, when analyzing the overall changes in Southeast Asian real estate markets on a regional scale, from both a historical and a contemporary perspective, their transformations seem to stem from a complex and embedded set of factors requiring cross-cutting and multi-scalar analyses. As we will see below, while the evolution of the region's real estate markets proceeds from an increased commodification[1] of land and real estate resources over the last 40 years (Shatkin 2017), as well as from an increasing liberalization and financialization[2] of real estate markets, the political and economic adjustments and regulation processes that transform the logics of capital circulation and accumulation in Southeast Asia are far from being homogeneous. Such a reality emphasizes the particularly mobile and adaptable nature of the instruments and devices of globalized capitalism (Ong 2006), as well as the path-dependency of economic mutations on previous political and economic structures and patterns (Brenner and Theodore 2002).

In this chapter, we will see how the political and economic regimes, the economic strategies of real estate actors at national and regional scales, the rescaling of urban production and the changing logics of circulation and anchoring of capital flows in real estate set both general and specific conditions for the evolution of real estate markets in Southeast Asia and their increased financialization. In particular, we will see that these dynamics are driven by a "dual regionalization" of investment logics, which in this chapter refers to the growing internationalization of real estate processes that is taking place at the interface of intra-Asian and intra-Southeast Asian scales of urban production. On the one hand, we will see that real estate processes are increasingly emancipated from economic contingencies and regulatory frameworks that are national in scope. On the other hand, we will see that this dual regionalization is linked to the diversity of regional economic and political situations, revealing an uneven geography of real estate dynamics in Southeast Asia. This tension between divergence and convergence echoes not only the diversity of capitalisms in the region (Lafaye de Micheaux 2015), but also the specificity of the political–economic frameworks that condition the modes of capital accumulation in real estate.

7.2. The oligopolistic preconditions for the organization of real estate markets in Southeast Asia

During the 1980s, the influx of capital from the developed and emerging economies of East Asia was instrumental in the transformation of Southeast Asian

---

1. Commodification refers here to the process by which the production and exchange of real estate are mainly guided by their exchange value, rather than by their use value.
2. In this chapter, I define financialization as the increasing role of economic actors, practices and rationalities from the finance sector in the conduct of economic activities.

real estate markets. The revaluation of the yen in 1985 pushed Japanese companies to relocate their manufacturing industries to Southeast Asia, and to invest some of their capital in the region, notably through foreign direct investment (FDI). Korean, Taiwanese and Chinese companies quickly followed Japan's lead. During the 1980s, many countries in the region, primarily Malaysia, the Philippines and Indonesia, were largely impacted by the "Volcker shock"[3] and the falling prices of raw materials and agriculture. On the other end, the decay of the USSR's economy and of the Council for Mutual Economic Assistance – which organized the system of mutual aid and cooperation between brotherhood countries – pushed the socialist economies of Southeast Asia to reform their economies, as China has begun to do under Deng Xiaping's guidance. The influx of FDI from East Asia is therefore seen as an opportunity to compensate for the withdrawal of Soviet aid in the region, particularly for Vietnam, whose economy depended heavily on it. In order to support these investment flows, the countries of the region undertook national economic reforms that included the privatization of major state-owned companies and specific industrial sectors (Carroll 2020). Between the 1980s and the 1990s, Asia was the continent that received the largest share of global FDI, and the economies of Southeast Asia were considered to have the highest growth potential in the world.

These economic transformations had a strong impact on cities. The increasing industrialization of Southeast Asian developing economies, combined with strong population growth and an intensification of rural–urban migration, increased housing needs. The share of the urban population grew exponentially in Indonesia, the Philippines and Thailand from the 1970s, and then in Malaysia, Vietnam, Cambodia, Laos and Myanmar from the 1990s. The rise in the implantation of foreign companies from the 1980s onwards and the emergence of new consumer needs have also increased the demand for office and commercial space. Real estate has thus become an increasingly attractive sector.

The influx of capital from East Asian countries during the 1980s and 1990s, as well as the acceleration of urbanization, has opened up new opportunities for capital accumulation, especially for the large private or public–private conglomerates that prevail in the economic environment of many countries in the region. On the one hand, large conglomerates are diversifying their activities and investments by redirecting part of their activities into the real estate sector; on the other, new conglomerates specialized in real estate development are emerging, often relying on

---

3. The "Volcker Shock" refers to an aggressive U.S. monetary policy implemented from 1979 onwards by Paul Volcker, then the new chairman of the Federal Reserve. In order to control galloping inflation and in a context of economic stagnation, the U.S. Federal Reserve raised interest rates sharply for several years. Although this policy helped to curb American inflation from 1982 onwards, it will lead to a significant indebtedness for many developing countries.

capital accumulated in other economic sectors (e.g. agriculture, manufacturing). The prevalence of a "crony capitalism" model in Southeast Asia has also helped to set the characteristics of the oligopolistic organization of real estate markets in the region. According to Aligica and Tarko (2014), the notion of crony capitalism generally refers to a society where patronage dominates and political-economic relations are organized around hierarchical, family and clan ties structured by issues of loyalty and accountability. The authors also point out that crony capitalism refers more broadly to a "neo-mercantilist" system in which the public sphere is partially privatized by its strong interlocking with personal interests.

Crony capitalism is indeed particularly prevalent in Southeast Asia. In Indonesia, Suharto laid the foundations for a neo-patrimonial, clientelist and clannish organization of the state and the economy between 1965 and 1998. The strong state control over the economy was supported by an extensive network of large state-owned companies, as well as by the implementation of a broad clientelist network between large private companies and political actors. During the 1980s, some of the Indonesian conglomerates redirected a part of their capital into the property sector. The real estate activities of the Lippo Group, CIPUTRA and the Salim Group, which are among the most important national developers, benefited from their close relationship and collaboration with the Indonesian government, both under Suharto's leadership and after. In the Philippines, crony capitalism was built on the foundation of colonial land-based capitalism, which benefited an oligarchy notably composed of an elite of Chinese descent. (Brown 2007). While the political and economic clans have evolved over time with changes in regimes and governments, the neo-patrimonial system has been maintained. This explains the early existence of large economic conglomerates and the emergence of an oligopolistic land and real estate market in the 1980s (Shatkin 2008). During the 1980s–1990s, the growth of capital flows from Malaysia, Indonesia and China also increased the investment capacity of these developers. Large conglomerates such as Ayala Land and the Lopez Group are prime examples. In Malaysia, crony capitalism, which again has long-standing roots (White 2004), was reinforced by the implementation of the New Economic Policy from 1971 onwards. The latter has resulted in a redistribution of economic power in favor of the Malays (the *bumiputras*, or native Malays), at the expense of local elite groups who belonged to ethnic minorities, mainly Chinese and Indian. In Kuala Lumpur, the large-scale urban projects of Putrajaya and Cyberjya involved important Malay private developers directly linked to the government (Bunnell et al. 2002). In Thailand, the professionalization of real estate actors took place at a rapid pace between the 1980s and the mid-1990s (Renaud 2000). However, unlike in Indonesia or the Philippines, the strong collusion between economic elites, politicians and property developers has not resulted in the emergence of an oligopolistic property market. Rather, Thai crony capitalism has led to a highly speculative real estate market, which is barely controlled by the state and very open, as in many other economic sectors, to foreign investment (Charmes 2003). The capital accumulation strategies of elite groups through real estate speculation, combined with rapid financial deregulation, created the conditions for the formation of a speculative bubble, mainly in Bangkok, which finally burst in 1997. Finally, in Cambodia, the neo-patrimonial organization of the state is a key determinant in the organization of land and real estate markets. These are largely dominated by elite groups, families and conglomerates directly linked to the Cambodian People's Party and Prime Minister Hun Sen, who has ruled the country since the mid-1980s (Fauveaud 2015).

In short, "crony capitalism" and the neo-patrimonial organization of many countries in the region have structured the formation of rent-seeking economies since the 1980s, the decade in which intra-Asian capital flows accelerated. In this context, the real estate sector has been used as a powerful leverage to increase capital accumulation opportunities, to the benefit of political and economic elites, and large conglomerates well-connected to public institutions. These political and economic dynamics were also combined with the privatization of land tenure systems in a way that set the conditions for the long-term transformation of the logics of circulation and anchoring of real estate capital.

7.3. A privatization of land tenure

Since the 1980s, most Southeast Asian countries have been implementing public policies in favor of the privatization of land ownership and land-use rights. Driven and supported by key international development agencies, their main objectives are to promote greater efficiency in the functioning of real estate markets by strengthening land rights, developing finance (banking and financial services, access to financial markets, facilitation of foreign investment, etc.), encouraging the systematic use of private actors for urban development projects, as well as drastically reducing public support for access to housing (Rolnik 2019; Fauveaud 2020b).

This global push for greater liberalization of land and property markets has laid the foundation for a greater commodification of housing. While Brunei, Singapore and Malaysia have maintained advanced land registration systems since colonization, the situation is different in other Southeast Asian countries. Many western donors, led by the World Bank Group, initiated or supported various land reform programs from the 1980s onwards. According to the World Bank, these initiatives aimed to "make the transition from state ownership of property and land under command economies to private ownership under market-based economies."[4]. In Thailand, where the World Bank initiated one of the most ambitious land reform programs, there were three major projects financed in 1984, 1990 and 1994. In Indonesia, the World Bank supported the implementation of the Indonesia Land Administration Project between 1994 and 2001, and the Land Management and Policy Development Program between 2004 and 2009. In the Philippines, the World Bank has also been very active in the commodification of land resources since the 1970s (Borras Jr et al. 2009). In Cambodia, compared to other countries in the region, the forced collectivization of land by the Khmer Rouge slowed down the formalization of a private real estate market during the 1980s. However, the return of private property in 1989 allowed the rapid development of real estate markets during the 1990s-2000s, notably through the implementation, between 2002 and 2009, of the Land Management and Administration Project financed by the World Bank. This was aimed at mass land titling among socialist governments, Laos and Vietnam, while maintaining collective ownership of land, and privatized the use and ownership of buildings beginning in the 1990s, following the economic liberalization reforms that began in the second half of the 1980s. Myanmar, on the other hand, made this shift during the 1990s.

At the regional scale, while these land reforms have not led to widespread systematization of land registration and the eradication of informal land tenure, they have had important outcomes for urban land markets. The development of land titling[5] and its engineering, as well as the increased privatization of land and building properties, have accelerated the commodification of land and real estate, notably through the dissemination of new knowledge and practices related to the production and exchange of real estate (Fauveaud 2015). These policies also reinforced the legal distinction between formal and informal ownerships of real estate. Public institutions and private stakeholders used this new legal framework to accelerate the redevelopment of urban areas, as well as the development of periurban lands (Shatkin 2017). Ultimately, this favored an increase in land eviction.

The increasing normalization of real estate markets illustrates the instrumental role of states in the privatization of real estate markets. This has also resulted in the provision of large public land resources to local and international developers, and prefigures what Shatkin named the "real estate turn" in Asia, which for the author

---

4. See: https://www.worldbank.org/en/results/2013/04/15/land-policy-results-profile1 [Accessed February 10, 2023].

5. Land titling (also known as cadastral registration or land certification) refers to the establishment of a system of registration of land ownership through the production of title deeds, and a cadastral registration system indicating the exact measurements and locations of land lots.

refers to the neoliberalization of land and real estate policies, and the privatization of urban production in the region (Shatkin 2017). This has managed to situate private developers at the center stage of urban development processes in the region.

7.4. Regionalization and internationalization of real estate development

The internationalization and regionalization of real estate activities accelerated during the 1990s following the influx of international capital into the region and the liberalization of land and real estate markets. From the beginning of the 1990s, Olds (1995) emphasized an acceleration of the transnationalization of real estate investments within the Pacific region. This is notably driven by the restructuring of the international financial system, the internationalization of real estate markets, and the rising power of transnational companies. While the developed and emerging economies of Asia Pacific were integrated earlier into the globalization of real estate markets, Southeast Asia rapidly followed. Its potential for growth, the low prices of lands and the growing local demand attracted international investors and developers.

Developers from East Asia thus invested early in the region. Some Japanese developers and builders have been active in Southeast Asia since the 1960s. The Daiwa House Group, for example, an emblematic developer in Japan, founded joint ventures in Singapore in 1961 and in Thailand in 1964. Similarly, Mitsui Fudosan, one of Japan's largest developers, established a joint venture in Singapore in 1973. Others arrived later in the region. Mitsubishi Estate, for example, which opened an office in the United States in the first half of the 1970s, did not establish itself in Singapore until 2008. Japanese real estate investment in Southeast Asia finally rose in the late 2000s.

Korean builders were also able to export their expertise in Southeast Asia at an early stage. The significant investment capacity of Korean public companies specialized in large-scale residential development from the 1950s onwards (Gelézeau 2003) supported the internationalization of their activities from the 1970s onwards. Since the end of the 1980s, Korean companies operating in the construction sector, or in industrial activities – such as steel – have diversified their activities and turned to real estate development, mainly in Asia, to a lesser extent in North America and, more recently, in the Middle East. With Korean real estate markets facing supply saturation and demand stagnation, the internationalization of Korean firms in property markets has accelerated since the 2000s. For example, the Korea Land and Housing Corporation is a public company active in Vietnam, Indonesia and Myanmar, particularly in the construction of new cities, an expertise that it developed from its domestic market during the 1980s.

Similarly, Hyundai Development Company has been investing in real estate and infrastructure projects in Southeast Asia since the 1980s, notably in Brunei, Vietnam, Malaysia and Thailand, as has POSCO E&C, which has been very active all over the region since the 1990s.

The flow of capital and expertise towards Southeast Asian real estate markets has also relied on the financial specialization and real estate expertise of Singapore and Hong Kong, which have played, since the 1990s, the role of investment platforms for real estate players in the region (Haila 2000). Singaporean companies, many of which are state-owned, benefit from state support for the export of the "Singapore model" and have solid expertise in the construction of multi-functional projects and condominiums (Guillot 2005; Pow 2014). Companies such as CapitaLand, Keppel or City rely on both private financing, particularly by weaving partnerships with private equity funds, and the Singaporean state, which can financially and politically support these large national companies. Singapore also developed a major sovereign wealth fund in 1981, the Government of Singapore Investment Corporation. Now called GIC Private Limited, this fund leverages the Singaporean government's trade surpluses by investing in international real estate markets. By 2021, between 9% and 13% of the fund's capital was invested in the real estate sector[6]. In addition to being issuers, Singapore and Hong Kong represent important channels for real estate flows by hosting many subsidiary companies of international developers and investors. The development of their banking and business service sectors, as well as their attractive tax regimes, have made them veritable platforms and interfaces for Asian real estate investments, through which transits a significant portion of the incoming and outcoming flows of investments of real estate stakeholders.

Finally, the internationalization of real estate development in Southeast Asia has also been fostered by a regionalization of the investment and development strategies of large Southeast Asian conglomerates, reinforcing the intensity of intraregional real estate flows (Percival and Waley 2012). The Indonesian conglomerates Salim Group and Lippo Group, or the developer CIPUTRA, have been developing large-scale real estate projects throughout the region since the 2000s, whether in the Philippines, Vietnam or Cambodia. Similarly, Malaysian developers SP Setia, Gamuda, Guoco Land or IOI Properties are developing residential projects in Singapore, Vietnam and the Philippines. Thai developers, on the other hand, have a relatively small regional presence, although they do have projects in western markets, including the United States and Australia. Filipino, Cambodian and Vietnamese developers still have little international presence.

---

6. See: https://www.gic.com.sg/investments/investment-framework/ [Accessed February 23, 2021].

7.5. Towards a rescaling of real estate production and urban governance

The internationalization and regionalization of real estate activity, as well as the increased financial capacity of developers, have resulted in a rescaling of urban production. The generalization of large-scale urban projects, alternately called satellite cities, mega-urban projects or large-scale urban projects, is a particularly convincing example. In Southeast Asia, Shatkin (2017), following the work of Olds (1995), identifies their emergence between the mid-1980s and early 1990s in the major regional metropolises, mainly Metro Manilla, Bangkok and Jakarta. Urban megaprojects are real estate projects built in most cases for commercial purposes, aimed at generating a major profit for investors and developers. Their implementation relies on the developers' privileged access to large land resources located mainly on the outskirts of cities, but sometimes also in urban centers. In the vast majority of cases, these land reserves are made available by the states (private land in the public domain or public land), or the states facilitate the acquisition of land lots on a large scale by encouraging or compelling small owners to sell or transfer their plots. These projects are multifunctional in nature. Beyond the residential function, the developer may build commercial, office and leisure spaces, as well as public spaces. The urban planning of these projects can range from a simple land use blue print to a very sophisticated functional plan. The urban megaprojects are thought of as a whole more or less articulated to the existing city. The construction period, divided into phases, is long and can sometimes take more than 15 years. Conceived as specific urban projects, their design and organization reflect a desire to propose new, modern and innovative forms of urbanity. In this sense, these projects are the bearers of a "city project" built through institutional and commercial discourses on the forms of housing, lifestyles, consumption and entertainment. These projects thus contribute to the emergence of new urban practices and urban imaginaries. Finally, urban megaprojects require the implementation of new forms of governance adapted to the size of the projects, to their multifunctional nature and to the central role of private stakeholders in the management and organization of the project.

Since the 2000s, academic research has shown how urban megaprojects embody in an exacerbated way the diffusion and reappropriation of the model of the entrepreneurial city in Southeast Asia, where the state is put at the service of private urban actors. In this context, megaprojects are a consequence and a vector of greater privatization not only of urban production, but more broadly of the planning and transformation of metropolitan spaces, making real estate developers key actors of urbanization processes (Shatkin 2008; Dieleman 2011). However, the development processes of such urban projects are also very diverse, depending on the local contexts that condition their production.

	Convergence factors	Factors of divergence
Political and economic dynamics	– Privatization of production – Urban entrepreneurialism	– Nature of the political systems – Governance of populations and territories – Power relations between urban actors
Production strategies	– Big developers – Financialization – Major land acquisitions	– Identity of the developers – Production strategies and project management – Network of actors – Organisation of the local real estate market
Urban morphology	– Enclave – Urban fragmentation – Multifunctionality	– Degree of integration and openness of projects – Size and functional composition
Urbanity and city life	– Segregation – Individualism – Lifestyles shaped by the aspirations of the middle and upper classes	– Relationship to the city and the urban environment of the inhabitants – Community practices – Relation to public spaces
Project governance	– Privatization of governance – Corporatization and management approaches	– Legal frameworks – Political regimes – Power/domination relationships – Public/private relationships
Modes of territorialization	– Peri-urbanization – Redevelopment of central areas – Exclusion	– Pre-existing urban morphologies – Capacity of city dwellers to make their voices heard

Table 7.1. *Urban megaprojects: between converging and diverging modes of urban production (source: Gabriel Fauveaud)*

In Vietnam, urban megaprojects have been at the center stage of the new urban production strategies implemented by the state from the 1990s onwards. On the one hand, public authorities have relied on megaurban projects to answer the increase in housing needs. On the other, these projects have allowed public authorities to transfer their responsibilities for the production and management of housing to private actors. (Labbé and Boudreau 2015). However, this increasingly privatized urban development is taking place in close collaboration with the Vietnamese state, which is framing the production and governance of new residential areas. Moreover, as Harms (2016) has shown, the megaprojects also represent a particularly strong and operative embodiment of Vietnam's socialist discourse on the benefit of "urban civilization". In Indonesia, Leaf (2015) identifies their success by their ability to meet the social and political aspirations of upper socioeconomic groups eager to have access to a standardized living space embodying the social, economic and cultural modernity carried by Indonesian elites, especially institutional ones. Such an observation is not unique to Indonesia and could certainly be made in many other national contexts. In Cambodia, such projects are not part of a coordinated and supervised national urban strategy. Rather, they fall under the neo-patrimonial model of land rent capture by Cambodian elites and *tycoons*, allied or merging with important local or international real estate companies (Fauveaud 2016). Moreover, this urban privatization on a broad scale does not prevent the emergence of creative urban practices that challenge the privatized nature of such projects (Fauveaud 2020c). Such an observation also illustrates the often "porous" character of these projects (Harms 2015), which differentiates them from the western gated communities to which they are often equated.

Urban megaprojects also reflect a rescaling of urban governance. The latter is increasingly organized within the perimeter of the urban project, rather than within sub-municipal territories. For Douglass and Huang (2007), this privatization emphasizes the ever-increasing influence of the financial targets of developers and project managers over the production of the projects and the way they are managed. In this context, the inhabitant would become above all a consumer of space, and less and less a city dweller involved in local governance. However, this argument needs to be put into perspective. Indeed, the modes of governance of urban megaprojects are very heterogeneous. In Indonesia, Thailand and Malaysia, research shows that the governance of new urban projects has been almost completely transferred to private actors, particularly developers and management companies (Askew 2004; Dieleman 2011; Roitman and Recio 2020; Tedong et al. 2015). In other contexts, the state remains a key actor in project governance, whether in the planning or management of urban production in Singapore (Haila 2015), or in the more day-to-day governance of local residents as in Vietnam (Labbé and Fauveaud 2022). In Cambodia, the management of living areas within residential enclaves remains underdeveloped due to a lack of legal framework. The role of inhabitants, local institutions, and private stakeholders may thus vary from project to project. (Fauveaud 2015). In many cases, therefore, the key role of private actors in the urban fabric and management of living areas does not lead to a complete privatization of governance, but rather to an overlap and redefinition of the modes of action of city dwellers, private actors and public institutions (Labbé and Fauveaud 2022). The recent diffusion of new urban models, such as smart or sustainable cities, as well as the deployment of new technological and informational devices associated with them, raise new questions related to the spread of new political, economic and social modes of regulation that these types of models support.

Finally, it is important to emphasize that urban megaprojects, because of their important size, have significant environmental and social impacts. As drivers of peri-urbanization, they accelerate the loss of agricultural land and natural areas that are often essential to mitigating climate and environmental risks. Furthermore, urban megaprojects lead to an increase in land evictions and relocations of impoverished populations, whether by force, market pressure or direct injunction from political authorities (Leitner and Sheppard 2018).

7.6. Financialization of the regional real estate market

The privatization and rescaling of urban production has also been driven by the increased financialization of regional economies. Prior to the second half of the 1990s, real estate activities in Southeast Asia were mainly financed by domestic banks. The intensity of real estate speculation, poor banking management, and high exposure of banks to international monetary and financial fluctuations eventually led to the bursting of a speculative and real estate bubble in 1997 (Carroll 2020). Thailand and Indonesia were the most affected economies, followed by Malaysia and, to a lesser extent, the Philippines.

The financial crisis of 1997–1998 has pushed the financialization of the real estate sector in Southeast Asia. Starting in the 2000s, capital markets, where long-term debt (bonds) and equity (stocks) are traded, developed rapidly, particularly under the impetus of the International Monetary Fund. As Rethel (2018) notes, the development of capital markets was seen as a way to mitigate the weakness of domestic banking systems by diversifying sources of finance and financial actors. This development was supported by the promotion of new financial practices among individuals and the private sector in order to fluidify the flow of capital and strengthen the investment capabilities of economic actors.

State actors are at the heart of this financial integration processes. With the technical support of the International Monetary Fund, the ASEAN has become a strategic forum for the development, liberalization and harmonization of regional financial markets. Singapore plays a key role in this process. Indeed, since the early 2000s, the city-state has been striving to become the leading financial center in

Southeast Asia. It is thus the architect of the ASEAN Economic Community proposed in 2002 in Phnom Penh in order to strengthen regional economic and financial integration. Financialization has also relied on the deployment of data engineering aimed at collecting and disseminating information to better inform economic actors about regional economic dynamics (e.g. standards of living), legal contexts (e.g. access to property, setting up businesses, banking sectors), or even market trends (e.g. housing prices, supply and demand) (Fauveaud 2020b).

The development of the finance sector on a regional scale has impacted regional real estate markets. First, it favored the opening of real estate markets to financial stakeholders, such as insurance companies, pension funds and asset management companies. Second, financialization has facilitated and diversified the financing strategies of real estate stakeholders themselves. They no longer rely solely on banking markets; they also have access to financial markets via subsidiary financial companies, or via partnerships with investment companies. Moreover, financial integration has favored mergers and acquisitions, as well as the public listing of conglomerates involved in real estate activities. The effect of financialization is therefore to give rise to very large real estate companies with ever greater financing capacities, able to implement more ambitious projects.

The financialization of economies has also been supported by numerous initiatives aiming to increase financial inclusion, i.e. access to banking and financial services for a greater part of the population. The ASEAN, national central banks, international organizations such as the World Bank, as well as a wide range of public and private actors and economic associations are supporting and promoting the development of public policies and the dissemination of financial innovations. All of these seek to facilitate the use of banking and financial services by households, such as bank accounts, credit and mortgages. Such initiatives have been reinforced by significant efforts to digitize financial services, resulting in a greater fluidity of capital flows at both national and transnational levels. This financial inclusion promotes the use of mortgage credit, household participation in capital markets and speculative real estate investments, which in turn increase the capitalization of real estate, and particularly housing (Fauveaud 2020b).

Financialization has also opened up new opportunities for capital accumulation for real estate actors. They have diversified their activities by relying increasingly on the creation of asset portfolios through the creation of subsidiaries specialized in financial investments. Some of the main regional developers have created subsidiary companies in Singapore, Hong Kong and, more recently, in Mainland China (notably in Shenzhen). These companies, which are similar to investment funds, are responsible for leveraging part of the assets of their parent companies via the capital markets or by setting up partnerships for the purchase and management of commercial real estate (shopping centers, for example) or office buildings (high-rise buildings). These investments are also made through the creation of Real Estate Investment Trusts (REITs) that specialize in specific real estate sectors (mainly commercial, office and hotel). Often listed on the stock exchange, these funds bring together a varied shareholder base made up of banks, insurance companies, pension funds and large corporations, the majority of which are from the region and based in, or established in, major financial centers such as Singapore and Hong Kong.

In 2006, the Indonesian developer Lippo Group acquired the Singaporean real estate investment fund OUE in order to diversify its capital allocation, both in Indonesia and internationally. Lippo Group is developing its real estate portfolio through OUE and some of its subsidiaries and REITs. It does so mainly in the tourism and office sectors, as well as in healthcare real estate (hospitals, clinics), a sector in full development throughout the region. This real estate financialization is also taking place at national levels. For example, the largest Filipino developer, Ayala Group, which does not develop projects abroad, launched the country's first Real Estate Investment Trust in 2020, with 45% of its capital held by the state. In Vietnam, the Vinhomes Group, a subsidiary of the Vingroup company, has become the largest Vietnamese developer. Listed on the Ho Chi Minh City Stock Exchange in 2018, the Singapore government holds nearly 6% of the company's shares in 2019. Through its subsidiary Vinhomes Joint Stock Company (established in 2008), in 2019 Vinhomes managed 18 subsidiaries specialized in all activities related to the development, production and management of real estate assets and projects. In addition to property development, part of Vinhomes' revenue is generated from financial activities, whether through the Vietnamese capital markets (stocks and bonds), or through participation in investment projects in various sectors (e.g. telecommunications or infrastructure). Vinhomes was listed, in 2018, in Morgan Stanley's frontier markets equity portfolio.

The financialization of the economy and real estate markets in Southeast Asia is inducing changes in the way cities are developed. National, regional and international developers are focusing on real estate projects that are most suitable for speculative purchases, especially for a regional clientele looking for lucrative financial investments. The success of condominiums[7], multifunctional projects,

---

7. The term condominiums is commonly used in Southeast Asia to refer to high-rise apartment buildings that offer shared services to the residents, such as a swimming pool, a fitness center or a laundry room. From a legal standpoint, condominium refers to a co-owned building that distinguishes private ownership of the apartment from shared ownership, by quota, of the services and common spaces of the project. It is important to distinguish the condominium from the service-apartment, which the developer reserves exclusively for rental.

urban megaprojects and real estate products targeting the wealthiest clients can thus be partly explained by the accelerated development of financialized real estate speculation (Fauveaud 2022). These types of projects tend to push up real estate prices, while marginalizing other forms of real estate production that are nonetheless adapted and accessible to less wealthy socioeconomic groups for whom the cost of access to housing is increasingly weighing on their income.

7.7. China and the new geopolitics of real estate in Southeast Asia

The financialization of real estate goes hand in hand with the evolution of investment flows in the region, notably carried out by Chinese actors. (Fauveaud 2020a). Between 2012 and 2019, FDI in construction, from all origins and towards the Southeast Asian economies, increased by a factor of 3 on average, while that in real estate remained stable[8]. However, while China and Hong Kong issued just over 23% of total real estate FDI entering Southeast Asia in 2012, they issued nearly 47% of total such investment in 2019. At the same time, while intra-regional investment flows were prominent in 2012 (25%) and 2013 (40%), they account for just over 16% of FDI in 2019[9]. Chinese companies are thus becoming increasingly important in the region's real estate markets.

The intensification of the Chinese presence is reflected in a number of ways. First, Chinese investment has accelerated, particularly since the launch of the Belt and Road Initiative (BRI) in 2013. Since then, China's FDI in Southeast Asia has grown by 85% and their investment in the construction sector has grown by 33% (Tritto et al. 2020). In addition, the BRI has pushed the growth of large-scale investment and construction projects. If in 2005, 35 Chinese projects with more than USD 100 million of investment are recorded in the world, these projects largely increased during the year 2010[10], and Southeast Asia captured an increasing share of them. Between 2005 and 2007, Southeast Asia only captured between 5% and 10% of the total value of China's large-scale investments in the world. However, this share varied from 10% to 15% between 2008 and 2019, rising to more than 25% in 2020[11]. Since the 2000s, therefore, Southeast Asia has been hosting an increasingly substantial share of China's large-scale investment projects, within which real estate investments are more and more central. Chinese real estate investments of more than USD 100 million only appeared in Southeast Asia in 2009 and, at that time, represented only 4% of total large-scale Chinese real estate investments worldwide.

---

8. Source: ASEAN Statistics, https://data.aseanstats.org [Accessed August 30, 2021].
9. Source: ASEAN Statistics, https://data.aseanstats.org [Accessed August 30, 2021].
10. See: https://www.aei.org/china-global-investment-tracker/ [Accessed August 30, 2021].
11. See: https://www.aei.org/china-global-investment-tracker/ [Accessed August 30, 2021].

However, this share is growing rapidly, reaching 21% in 2019 and 45% in 2020, emphasizing the attractiveness of Southeast Asian real estate markets.

The bottom line is that not only are Chinese investments in Southeast Asian real estate markets growing rapidly, but the size of these investments is also increasing at a rapid pace. The year 2014, shortly after the publicization of China's new international geopolitical strategy, was a pivotal moment during which Southeast Asia became a strategic region for Chinese FDI in real estate.

While Singapore is the main destination for Chinese real estate investments, Malaysia, Indonesia and the Philippines are receiving a growing share of them. China has also become a major player in the development of major urban projects in the region, notably in the Philippines (New Clark City and New Manila Bay), Malaysia (Melaka Gateway and Forest City), Myanmar (New Yangon City Development) and Cambodia (Dara Satkor). These projects, which may or may not be officially recognized by China as BRI projects, are part of the development of Chinese expertise in large-scale urban projects (of the satellite city or smart city types) since the 1990s, particularly through the establishment of inter-state bilateral partnerships (with Singapore in particular) and private partnerships (via joint ventures) (Douay and Henriot 2016). The development of such projects in Southeast Asia also illustrates the ability of Chinese developers to export their skills in construction, urban planning and project management. Chinese companies have also benefited from the experience in real estate of Hong Kong-based companies to invest in Southeast Asian real estate markets. The implementation of the BRI, combined with the growing financialization of the Southeast Asian economies, has finally resulted in the diversification of asset portfolios of large Chinese companies, particularly those in real estate. The latter increasingly acquire strategic buildings in order to make a profit through rent, management fees and increased asset value. In this regard, Singapore is a prime investment location due to its stable real estate market and high-quality real estate assets. These investments are also carried out by large non-real estate Chinese companies – such as Alibaba, which acquired 50% of the Axa Tower in Singapore in 2020 – that diversify their capital portfolios in international real estate markets (mainly western, however). China tech companies such as Huawei are also becoming increasingly important partners in large-scale real estate projects, particularly for developing the technological devices used in urban mega-projects.

The evolution of Chinese real estate investment in Southeast Asia must be correlated with the broader transformation of China's economic and political strategies in the region. Shatkin (2019) has shown how Chinese sovereign loans in the urban infrastructure sector, particularly via state-owned or public-private banks (e.g. China Development Bank, China Exim Bank, Industrial and Commercial Bank of China, China Construction Bank), are paving the way for large-scale real estate projects by both local and international developers, particularly of Chinese origin. For the author, China is playing the role of a "shareholder state" seeking to export its investment and development capacities in the field of urban production (Shatkin 2019, p. 5). At the same time, Chinese real estate investments are also materializing within secondary cities and territories located on the periphery of large metropolitan areas and capital cities. In Cambodia, for example, Sihanoukville, the country's main port and a small city with a population of 250,000, has seen a massive influx of Chinese capital since 2015. These investments, which have profoundly transformed the landscape of the city, follow the establishment of a partnership between China and the Government of Cambodia in order to make Sihanoukville and its province a platform for logistics, trade and tourism especially open to Chinese actors. These investments have materialized in the construction of transportation infrastructure (e.g. airport, highways), large special economic zones, and casinos and hotels developed primarily by Chinese companies, including through joint investments with Cambodian companies. The construction of a large new city, Dara Satkor, which is supposed to house about 1.2 million people, is also planned in the western part of the province. In 2015, the project became the Cambodia–China Comprehensive Investment and Development Pilot Zone and was presented as part of the Belt and Road Initiative. The Dara Satkor example illustrates how real estate investments, when combined with infrastructure investments such as ports or special economic zones, can be linked to China's geostrategic ambitions in Southeast Asia, which are supported by the significant financing and negotiating capacity of Chinese companies. The Dara Satkor project, launched in 2008, was *subsequently* integrated into the Belt and Road Initiative, which also shows how Chinese companies are taking advantage of China's new geopolitics.

The integration of regional real estate markets has also been supported by the very strong increase in foreign investment by Chinese households seeking lucrative and fast-growing real estate markets. These transnational investments are driven by the explosion of real estate prices in China's major cities and metropolises over the 2000-2020 period, the increase in the cost of living, as well as the growth in the cost of services, particularly medical and educational ones. In addition, Southeast Asian countries are doing their utmost to capture these investment flows by facilitating access to property for foreign buyers, or by offering specific visas to attract foreign retirees or promote the purchase of second homes (e.g. Non-Immigrant O Visa in Thailand, MM2H program in Malaysia, Retirement Visa in Indonesia). Thailand, and mainly Bangkok, represents the top destination for real estate investments by

Chinese households in Southeast Asia, followed by Malaysia, Vietnam and the Philippines. As reported by Juwai Real Estate Agency for 2019[12], 50% of the condominium units purchased by foreigners in Bangkok would be purchased by Chinese buyers. In Ho Chi Minh City, Vietnam, 41% of luxury condominium units would be acquired by buyers from mainland China and Hong Kong, compared to only 21% by Vietnamese buyers. In the Philippines, the sale of residential units to Chinese investors is reportedly growing rapidly, with some developers declaring that they are selling more than a third of their newly produced units to Chinese buyers. In Jakarta, half of all condominium purchases are reportedly made by residents of mainland China or Hong Kong. In Phnom Penh, Chinese buyers account for the largest share of foreign buyers (Fauveaud 2020b). The growth of these transnational flows ultimately reinforces the mechanisms of real estate speculation and the exposure of domestic markets to the economic fluctuations of international markets.

7.8. Conclusion

Southeast Asian real estate markets have undergone profound transformations since the 1980s. A both contemporary and historical analysis has allowed us to better understand how the articulation of intra-Southeast Asian and intra-Asian real estate dynamics – which I have named the dual regionalization – has largely conditioned the evolution of real estate processes in the region. In this context, FDI, the action of regionalized real estate actors and the emergence of a capital market have played a crucial role in the evolution of real estate markets. Finally, these dynamics reflect both converging and diverging trends. On the one hand, the growth of commodification and capitalization of real estate, the real estate speculation, the financialization and the generalization of urban projects adapted to the acceleration of transnational capital flows represent underlying trends that affect many real estate markets in the region, particularly those of the bigger cities, as well as, and perhaps increasingly, cities located on the fringes of the major regional urban areas. On the other hand, these trends have not led to a homogenization of urban planning processes, the modes of governance of urban spaces, the political discourse that supports the development of the entrepreneurial city or the internationalization strategies of real estate actors. Detailed and empirically informed analysis is therefore essential to understand the complexity of the evolution of real estate processes in the region at both local and regional levels.

---

12. See: https://list.juwai.com/news/2019/11/top-10-chinese-picks-h1-2019.

7.9. References

Aligica, P.D. and Tarko, V. (2014). Crony capitalism: Rent seeking, institutions and ideology. *Kyklos*, 67(2), 156–176.

Askew, M. (2004). *Bangkok: Place, Practice and Representation*. Routledge, London and New York.

Borras Jr., S.M., Carranza, D., Franco, J.C., Manahan, M.A. (2009). Anti-land reform land policy? The World Bank's development assistance to agrarian reform in the Philippines. *Overseas Aid and Agrarian Reform Working Paper Series*, 11(11).

Brenner, N. and Theodore, N. (2002). Cities and the geographies of "actually existing neoliberalism". *Antipode*, 34(3), 349–379.

Brown, R.A. (2007). *The Rise of the Corporate Economy in Southeast Asia*. Routledge, London and New York.

Bunnell, T., Barter, P.A., Morshidi, S. (2002). Kuala Lumpur metropolitan area: A globalizing city–region. *Cities*, 19(5), 357–370.

Carroll, T. (2020). The political economy of Southeast Asia's development from independence to hyperglobalisation. In *The Political Economy of Southeast Asia*, Carroll, T., Hameiri, S., Jones, L. (eds). Palgrave Macmillan, Cham.

Charmes, E. (2003). Flux internationaux de capitaux et bulles spéculatives métropolitaines. Le cas de Bangkok et de la Thaïlande. In *Villes et citadins dans la mondialisation*, Osmont, A. and Goldblum, C. (eds). Karthala, Paris.

Dieleman, M. (2011). New town development in Indonesia: Renegotiating, shaping and replacing institutions. *Bijdragen tot de taal-, land-en volkenkunde/Journal of the Humanities and Social Sciences of Southeast Asia*, 167(1), 60–85.

Douay, N. and Henriot, C. (2016). La Chine à l'heure des villes intelligentes. *L'Information géographique*, 80(3), 89–102.

Douglass, M. and Huang, L. (2007). Globalizing the city in Southeast Asia: Utopia on the urban edge – The case of Phu My Hung, Saigon. *IJAPS*, 3(2), 1–42.

Fauveaud, G. (2015). *La production des espaces urbains à Phnom Penh. Pour une géographie sociale de l'immobilier*. Publications de la Sorbonne, Paris.

Fauveaud, G. (2016). Real estate productions, practices, and strategies in contemporary Phnom Penh. An overview of social, economic, and political issues. In *The Handbook of Contemporary Cambodia*, Brickell, K. and Springer, S. (eds). Routledge, Abingdon.

Fauveaud, G. (2020a). Les nouvelles géopolitiques de l'immobilier en Asie du Sud-Est : financiarisation et internationalisation des marchés immobiliers à Phnom Penh, Cambodge. *Hérodote*, 176(1), 169–184.

Fauveaud, G. (2020b). The new frontiers of housing financialization in Phnom Penh, Cambodia: The condominium boom and the foreignization of housing markets in the global south. *Housing Policy Debate*, 30(4), 661–679.

Fauveaud, G. (2020c). Reworking the meanings of urbanity in post-socialist Phnom Penh: Toward a commodification of urban centrality. In *Socialist and Post-Socialist Urbanisms: Critical Reflections from a Global Perspective*, Drummond, L.B.W. and Young, D. (eds). University of Toronto Press, Toronto.

Fauveaud, G. (2022). Géographies de la spéculation et urbanisation du capital dans le Sud Global : l'exemple de Phnom Penh, Cambodge. *Annales de géographie*, 746, 5–31.

Gelézeau, V. (2003). *Séoul, ville géante, cités radieuses*. CNRS, Paris.

Guillot, X. (2005). Flux économiques, transferts d'expertises et production immobilière haut de gamme en Asie orientale. *Geocarrefour*, 80(3), 171–181.

Haila, A. (2000). Real estate in global cities: Singapore and Hong Kong as property states. *Urban Studies*, 37(12), 2241–2256.

Haila, A. (2015). *Urban Land Rent: Singapore as A Property State*. John Wiley & Sons, Hoboken.

Harms, E. (2015). Porous enclaves: Blurred boundaries and incomplete exclusion in South East Asian cities. *South East Asia Research*, 23(2), 151–167.

Harms, E. (2016). *Luxury and Rubble: Civility and Dispossession in the New Saigon*. University of California Press, Oakland.

Labbé, D. and Boudreau, J.-A. (2011). Understanding the causes of urban fragmentation in Hanoi: The case of new urban areas. *International Development Planning Review*, 33(3), 273–291.

Labbé, D. and Boudreau, J.-A. (2015). Local integration experiments in the new urban areas of Hanoi. *South East Asia Research*, 23(2), 245–262.

Labbé, D. and Fauveaud, G. (2022). Institutional straddling: Negotiating micro-governance in Hanoi's new urban areas. *Environment and Planning C: Politics and Space*, 40(4), 933–949.

Lafaye de Micheaux, E. (2015). Recompositions économiques régionales. Une approche institutionnaliste de la diversité. In *Capitalismes asiatiques et puissance chinoise. Diversité et recomposition des trajectoires nationales*, Alary, P. and Lafaye de Micheaux, E. (eds). Presses de Sciences Po, Paris.

Leaf, M. (2015). Exporting Indonesian urbanism: Ciputra and the developmental vision of market modernism. *South East Asia Research*, 23(2), 169–186.

Leitner, H. and Sheppard, E. (2018). From kampungs to condos? Contested accumulations through displacement in Jakarta. *Environment and Planning A: Economy and Space*, 50(2), 437–456.

McGee, T.G. and Robinson, I.M. (1995). *The Mega-Urban Regions of Southeast Asia*. UBC Press, Vancouver.

Olds, K. (1995). Globalization and the production of new urban spaces: Pacific rim megaprojects in the late 20th century. *Environment and Planning A*, 27(11), 1713–1743.

Ong, A. (2006). *Neoliberalism As Exception: Mutations in Citizenship and Sovereignty*. Duke University Press, Durham.

Percival, T. and Waley, P. (2012). Articulating intra-asian urbanism: The production of satellite cities in Phnom Penh. *Urban Studies*, 49(13), 2873–2888.

Pow, C.P. (2014). License to travel: Policy assemblage and the "Singapore model". *City*, 18(3), 287–306.

Renaud, B. (2000). How real estate contributed to the Thailand financial crisis. In *Asia's Financial Crisis and the Role of Real Estate*, Mera, K. and Renaud, B. (eds). Routledge, London and New York.

Rethel, L. (2018). Capital market development in Southeast Asia: From speculative crisis to spectacles of financialization. *Economic Anthropology*, 5(2), 185–197.

Roitman, S. and Recio, R.B. (2020). Understanding Indonesia's gated communities and their relationship with inequality. *Housing Studies*, 35(5), 795–819.

Rolnik, R. (2019). *Urban Warfare: Housing under the Empire of Finance*. Verso Books, London.

Shatkin, G. (2008). The city and the bottom line: Urban megaprojects and the privatization of planning in Southeast Asia. *Environment and Planning A*, 40(2), 383–401.

Shatkin, G. (2017). *Cities for Profit. The Real Estate Turn in Asia's Urban Politics*. Cornell University Press, Ithaca.

Shatkin, G. (2019). Financial sector actors, the state, and the rescaling of Jakarta's extended urban region. *Land Use Policy*, 104159.

Sorensen, A. and Labbé, D. (eds) (2020). Megacities, megacity-regions, and the endgame of urbanization. In *Handbook of Megacities and Megacity-Regions*. Edward Elgar Publishing, Cheltenham.

Tedong, P.A., Grant, J.L., Wan Abd Aziz, W.N.A. (2015). Governing enclosure: The role of governance in producing gated communities and guarded neighborhoods in Malaysia. *International Journal of Urban and Regional Research*, 39(1), 112–128.

Tritto, A., Sejko, D., Park, A. (2020). *The Belt and Road Initiative in ASEAN*. Institute for Emerging Market Studies, Hong Kong.

White, N.J. (2004). The beginnings of crony capitalism: Business, politics and economic development in Malaysia, 1955–1970. *Modern Asian Studies*, 38(2), 389–417.

8

Real Estate in the Middle East: An Economy Shaped by Rents

Myriam ABABSA[1,2]
[1] UMR Géographie-cités, Aubervilliers, France
[2] Institut français du Proche-Orient, Amman, Jordan

8.1. Introduction

Since the 2000s, the major metropolises of the Middle East have been subject to the effects of the growing intervention of international financial markets in their financial and non-financial sectors (real estate, land). They have implemented major real estate projects that serve to attract international investors, improve their image and consolidate a class of entrepreneurs close to power (Hanieh 2016). This process began in downtown Beirut, rebuilt after the civil war by the private company Solidere. It has taken the form of the New Cairo project in Egypt; the new Abdali business center in Amman since 2004; *Marota City* in central Damascus since 2012, Abraj al-Bait in Mecca, *NEOM – The Line* in Saudi Arabia, and the downtowns of the UAE. These projects are largely financed by the sovereign wealth funds of the Gulf countries – Abu Dhabi Investment Authority and Kuwait Investment Authority in particular – which rank third and fifth worldwide in terms of financial volume. While their assets are mainly located in the United States[1], these SWFs are attracted by the advantageous tax conditions and low-cost land offered by the Middle Eastern

---

For a color version of all the figures in this chapter, see www.iste.co.uk/avelinedubach/globalization.zip.

1. Abu Dhabi Investment Authority (2021). 30–50% of investments are in North America [Online]. Available at: https://azcdewebp0003.azureedge.net/azstcwebp0002/azure/adia/media/2020/11/an-introduction-to-adia.pdf.

Globalization and Dynamics of Urban Production,
coordinated by Natacha AVELINE-DUBACH. © ISTE Ltd 2023.

states. Like private banks and pension funds, the sovereign wealth funds of the Gulf states seek to invest their surplus from hydrocarbon exports in real estate projects which are all the more lucrative because they are largely subsidized by the Arab states. This is how these actors convert their oil rent into land rent.

The former public or military land reserves created in the 1960s and 1970s are being reclassified as Central Business Districts, Development Corridors and Smart Cities to attract investors (Aveline-Dubach et al. 2020). These large-scale real estate projects are subsidized by governments, but mainly benefit private investors who support the authoritarian powers in place. Real estate investments mainly target the commercial sector (shopping malls) for 736 billion in 2021, more than residential (116 billion in 2021)[2]. Mortgage refinancing funds are being created, and bonds are being issued to finance social housing ownership programs. Land has become an investment vehicle for actors seeking increasing values that protects them from the negative effects of general inflation. Since 2016, a few listed real estate investment companies (*sunduq al istithmar al 'aqari* in Arabic, equivalent to Real Estate Investment Trusts) have been established by the Gulf states and then by Egypt, to offer regular rental income to investors, counting on the gradual increase in rents.

Speculative expectations about the real estate value of luxury developments are so high that buildings can be kept empty for years. One in five homes is vacant in Jordan and Lebanon (and one in three in Egypt), while many young people must cohabit with their parents (Hamilton et al. 2018). Arab cities thus suffer from a rampant housing crisis. Land accounts now for more than half of the prices of apartments in the formal market in the region's capitals. Land speculation benefits a few property owners and developers, but this is at the expense of the majority of inhabitants. In the absence of adequate fiscal instruments (such as capital gain taxes and vacant land taxes) and appropriate housing policies, land prices are rising faster than incomes and construction costs, making apartments unaffordable for modest households. Only the middle and upper classes (the top three income deciles) can use mortgages to access apartments in the formal sector, the cost of which now absorbs between seven and 10 years of their income, or even 14 in the case of Cairo[3].

---

2. Source: European Public Real Estate Association, see: https://prodapp.epra.com/media/EPRA_Total_Markets_Table_-_Q2-2021_1626682317868.pdf.
3. In Jordan, a 120-square metre apartment represented 6.6 years of the average income according to the Housing and Urban Development Corporation, i.e. 308 JD (375 euros) per square meter outside Amman and 600 JD (731 euros) in Amman. 70% of Jordanians earn less than 500 JD (610 euros) per month in 2020. In Egypt, an apartment in Cairo costs approximately 700 euros per square meter, while the average income is 500 euros per month. See: https://dailynewsegypt.com/2021/04/14/average-egyptian-family-to-make-annual-income-of-egp-109k-by-2025-fitch-solutions/.

The lack of control over land speculation is resulting in the expansion of informal settlements on agricultural land, and the presence of unoccupied land in the heart of the urban fabric, kept for speculative purposes. Faced with unaffordable or oversized land (of more than 500 m^2 in residential neighborhoods), about half of the residents of Middle Eastern cities live in informal housing, i.e. without transferable property titles (Ababsa et al. 2012). Rising land prices are forcing states to focus their social housing policies on public land reserves located on the urban periphery, far from employment and service areas.

Most of the work on the financialization of urban production focuses on large Western investment funds and concerns the major developed countries, the United States, the United Kingdom, Japan, Germany, France and some emerging countries (Brazil, South Korea, Turkey) (Marcel Delarcoque and Noisette 2017; Drozdz et al. 2020). They show that real estate and urban infrastructure now tend to be valued in terms of the risk/return trade-off, and no longer in terms of use value, according to the standards dictated by the financial industry (Banerjee-Guha 2010; Theurillat and Crevoisier 2013). Works addressing these issues in the Arab world link the financialization of economies and real estate to the authoritarianism of Arabian political systems and the strengthening of a ruling class that enriches itself at the expense of the public good (Mitchel 1999; Elsheshtawy 2010; Denis 2011; Hanieh 2016). In Egypt, Jordan, Lebanon, Saudi Arabia and Syria, different degrees of financialization and legal frameworks emerge depending on the size of the economies, on the level of economic development of the country, and the vitality of the middle classes. A few academic papers describe processes of financialization affecting commodities that were previously considered outside the sphere of influence of the financial industry: vacant land, privately constructed buildings and infrastructure are being transformed into financial assets by investment banks in several Middle Eastern countries (Gorton 2015; Denis 2018).

This chapter analyzes the growing importance of Arab sovereign wealth funds in the five Middle Eastern economies that are particularly subject to their investments in real estate and urban infrastructure: Egypt, Saudi Arabia, Jordan, Syria and Lebanon. It presents the housing crises in these countries. Since 2015, Saudi Arabia has undertaken taxing its vacant urban land in order to counter land/real estate speculation and thus finance its social housing policies. Lebanon and Syria have developed "territorial revenge" urbanism against opposition forces by targeting bombings or expropriations on land that houses opponents, only to offer it to investors close to political power (Krijnen and Fawaz 2010; Abu Zainedin and Fakhani 2020)[4].

8.2. The financialization of economies and real estate in the Middle East

From the time of their independence until the 1980s, the Arab states of the Middle East relied on the oil revenues of producer countries, either directly or indirectly (donations from Iraq to Jordan, for example). It provided them with abundant hydrocarbons at low prices. They developed their industry, which colonial Mandate powers had, until then, reduced, within the framework of planned economies. They regained control of their banking sector, set the interest rates of the Central Bank, within the framework of a pan-Arabian socialist ideology. Socialist states (Egypt, Syria and Iraq) also financed home ownership housing policies in the 1970s.

In the 1980s, the situation changed dramatically. Overburdened by debt, overcome by rapid population growth and lacking the capacity to create jobs, the Arab countries of the Middle East experienced severe economic crises. The social contract under which the state guaranteed citizens free health care and education, and graduates a job in the public sector (provided they eased their demands for democracy) was broken (Catusse 2006). Over-indebted countries were forced to follow structural adjustment plans imposed by the International Monetary Fund (IMF), which aimed at reducing public spending. Several food riots occurred: in Algeria and Tunisia in 1988, and Jordan in 1989. The structural adjustment policies supported by the IMF from 1987 onwards introduced greater private sector intervention in the economies, particularly in the real estate sector. In this context, Jordan was the first Arab country to initiate, in 1987, a housing policy encouraging public–private partnerships (PPPs) on low-cost public land, based on the "sites and services" model (plots of land that have been allocated and equipped, and put on the market).

From the 2000s onwards, states deregulated financial markets and privatized large national companies. They encouraged foreign investment in urban production by putting up for sale public pastoral or desert land in the metropolitan peripheries (Barthel and Verdeil 2008). The price of a barrel of Brent crude oil, which was approximately USD30, soared after the war in Iraq in 2003 and exceeded USD 110 in

---

4. I would like to warmly thank Natacha Aveline-Dubach for her help in the analysis of the financialization process, as well as Bruno Marot for his careful review of the Lebanese case.

2008. The main Arab banks doubled their assets (the Arab Bank in 2004) and invested in real estate, a sector that was all the more lucrative as public land was sold off by the state to a loyal entrepreneurial class. At the same time, the banking system was privatized in the 2000s (2006 in Egypt). The privatization of public assets was accompanied by the deregulation of credit and the creation of stock markets.

8.2.1. *Arab metropolises as engines of economic development*

Most Arab capitals adopted urban plans in the 1960s with public land reserves for future urban projects: Cairo's Urban Master Plan in 1953–1956, Beirut's Ecochard Plan[5] in 1963, Damascus' in 1964–1968, Amman's Civil Development Plan in 1968 and Mecca's Urban Plan in 1971 by Robert Mathew. The major metropolises are seen as engines of economic development because they concentrate capital, engineers and skilled personnel, as well as transport hubs. Each major city tries to develop a special economic zone in its periphery: in Syria near Aleppo and Damascus, in Jordan (industrial city of Sahab, south of Amman, industrial city of Irbid) and in Iraq (Al Mussayib south of Baghdad and in Basra).

In the 1990s, the World Bank encouraged foreign investment in the industrial, energy and urban development sectors. The World Bank's support for cities also took the form of financing road infrastructure (a circular highway in Amman), transport infrastructure (the Cairo metro, bus lanes in Amman) and water supply networks. The aim was to promote compact urban planning along road and rail transport routes (according to the policy of "Transit Oriented Development") and mixed forms of land use combining residential and commercial functions (Wahdan 2010).

In 2018, the World Bank launched a "maximizing finance for development" program[6], to mobilize private capital in economic growth policies to achieve Sustainable Development Goals by 2030 (Gabor 2018). The World Bank tends to encourage private investments in the outskirts of cities, especially as they take on the construction of essential infrastructure and services (roads, water and power

---

5. The French architect Michel Ecochard was in charge of urban planning in Mandatory Syria from 1938, and then in Morocco from 1946 (Verdeil 2012).
6. World Bank Group (2021). Maximizing Finance for Development [Online]. Available at: https://www.worldbank.org/en/about/partners/maximizing-finance-for-development [Accessed November 2021].

networks). Yet, the Middle East faces the major challenge of attracting the lowest amount of foreign direct investment (FDI) in the world. This is due in part to unstable governments, geopolitical conflicts and a lack of financial security for investors[7]. However, despite their low level, FDI contributes significantly to the financing of Arab economies: in 2019, it was equivalent to one-third of Egypt's GDP, 18% of Lebanon's and 10% in Jordan (see Table 8.1). These states also benefit from significant remittances from their diasporas, invested in the real estate sector. Egypt received USD 26.9 billion in remittances, Lebanon USD 6.3 billion, Jordan USD 3.9 billion and the Palestinian territories USD 2.6 billion in 2020[8].

	Egypt	Jordan	Lebanon	Palestinian territories
2008	27%	10%	17%	1%
2019	33%	10%	18%	1%

Table 8.1. *Share of foreign direct investment compared to GDP in 2008 and 2019 (source: OECD 2021, p. 43)*

8.2.2. Half of foreign investments are in real estate in the Middle East

On the eve of the global subprime mortgage crisis (2008), foreign investment flows to the Middle East totaled USD 77.8 billion, two-thirds of which went to Saudi Arabia (USD 39 billion), followed by Israel (USD 10.3 billion), Egypt (USD 9.4 billion), the UAE (USD 5.0 billion), Lebanon (USD 4.3 billion), Jordan (USD 2.8 billion) and Iraq (USD 1.8 billion) (see Figure 8.1). Investments fell with

---

7. The Middle Eastern states are indeed very poorly ranked according to the *Doing Business 2020* report: apart from the UAE, which ranks 16th worldwide for the ease of starting a business and registering it, followed by Israel (35th), Middle Eastern countries are at the bottom of the list with Saudi Arabia at 62nd, Jordan at 75th, well ahead of Egypt (114th), Lebanon (143rd) and the countries at war (Syria 172nd, Iraq 176th and Yemen 187th rank). Source: World Bank Group (2020). Doing Business: Comparing Business Regulation in 190 economies [Online]. Available at: https://documents1.worldbank.org/curated/en/688761571934946384/pdf/Doing-Business-2020-Comparing-Business-Regulation-in-190-Economies.pdf [Accessed November 2021].
8. The World Bank (n.d.). Personal remittances received (current USD) Middle East and North Africa [Online]. Available at: https://data.worldbank.org/indicator/BX.TRF.PWKR.CD.DT?locations=ZQ [Accessed November 2021].

the collapse of oil prices in 2014 (from USD 112 per barrel in 2010 to USD 42 in 2014)[9]. They shrunk to one-fifth in Saudi Arabia and were halved in Lebanon. Investments were maintained only in Egypt, thanks to the lucrative market of the construction of new cities and gas exploration (see Figures 8.1 and 8.3). Investments in the Middle East totaled USD 46.1 billion in 2019, of which 17.3 billion went to Israel, 13.7 billion to the UAE, 9 billion to Egypt, 2.2 billion to Lebanon and 4.5 billion to Saudi Arabia[10].

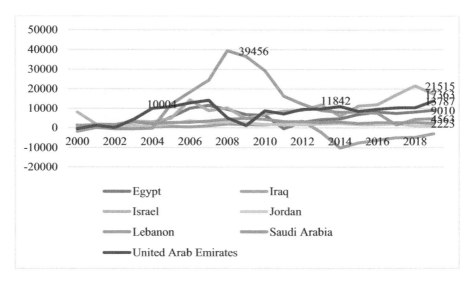

Figure 8.1. *Foreign direct investment flows to the Middle East (millions of USD) (2000–2019) (source: author based on World Bank 2020 data (World Data Bank, FDI Net Inflows, MENA))*

During the period 2003–2008, almost half of FDI to Arab countries was concentrated in the real estate sector (see Figure 8.2). However, with the discovery of gas fields in the Mediterranean off the coast of Israel in 2010, and Egypt in 2015, investments in hydrocarbons grew to one-third of FDI flows between 2013 and

---

9. World Energy Review (2021). Available at: https://www.eni.com/en-IT/global-energy-scenarios/world-energy-review.html [Accessed November 2021].
10. The World Bank (n.d.). Foreign Direct Investment, Net Inflows (BoP, current USD) [Online]. Available at: https://data.worldbank.org/indicator/BX.KLT.DINV.CD.WD?locations=ZQ [Accessed January 2022].

2019, bringing down the relative share of real estate investment (23%). Egypt, for example, attracted USD 20 billion of investment in its gas fields in 2017. Most of the investment in the mining sector comes from Eastern Europe, while 70% of the investment in real estate comes from Gulf countries (OECD 2021). Manufacturing investments make up 38% of the total, but are concentrated in Maghreb countries close to European markets and with a more established workforce.

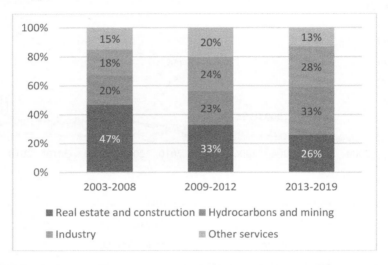

Figure 8.2. *Foreign direct investment in new subsidiaries by sector in eight countries in the Arab world (Morocco, Algeria, Tunisia, Libya, Egypt, Jordan, Lebanon, Palestinian Territories) (2003–2019) (source: OECD 2021, Greenfields FDI in MENA)*

The top FDI investors in the Middle East are the UAE, Bahrain, Saudi Arabia and Qatar (OECD 2021). Six Gulf Cooperation Council states (GCC, Saudi Arabia, Kuwait, UAE, Qatar, Bahrain and Oman) contributed 37% of these outflows of capital in the region from 2003 to 2019, followed closely by Asia Pacific (24%) and Europe (24%), compared to only 4% of investment from North America (Hanieh 2016). GCC FDI comes from the sovereign wealth funds of their member states, which invest in real estate and are major players in large-scale urban projects in Arab metropolises. The third and fifth largest SWFs in the world are Arabian: Abu Dhabi Investment Authority and Kuwait Investment Authority, followed by the two Saudi SWFs (see Table 8.2).

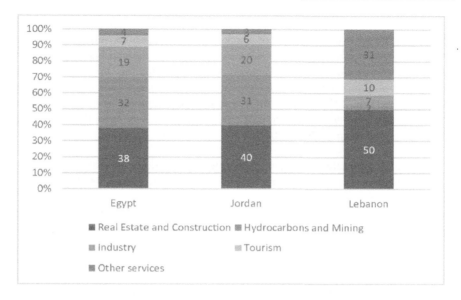

Figure 8.3. *Foreign direct investment in new subsidiaries by sector (2003–2019) (source: OECD 2021. Greenfield FDI by sector per MENA economy)*

Name of the sovereign wealth fund	Date of creation	Capitalization (USD in billions)	World ranking
Abu Dhabi Investment Authority, UAE	1976	697	3rd
Kuwait Investment Authority, Kuwait	1953	592	5th
SAMA Foreign Holdings, Saudi Arabia	1952	506	not classified
Public Investment Fund, Saudi Arabia	1971	320	8th
Qatar Investment Authority, Qatar	2005	320	11th
Investment Corporation of Dubai, UAE	2006	239	10th
Mubadala Investment Company, UAE	2017	229	13th
Libyan Investment Authority, Libya	2006	60	19th
Emirates Investment Authority, UAE	2007	45	25th
State General Reserve Fund, Oman	1980	22	38th

Table 8.2. *Ranking of Arab SWFs by capitalization in 2019 (source: https://english.alarabiya.net/business/economy/2019/08/28/Here-are-the-top-10-sovereign-wealth-funds-in-the-Arab-world; https://www.swfinstitute.org/profile/598cdaa50124e9fd2d05b242)*

Costas Lapavitsas (2013) shows that non-financial companies are financing themselves through the issuance of stock and debt securities rather than through traditional bank borrowing. At the same time, the industrial and banking sectors are becoming interconnected. Bank managers are participating in the management committees of companies, creating close links between large companies and finance (Krippner 2005, p. 201). In the Gulf countries, the categories of public and private are blurring due to the involvement of rulers and princes in several real estate and financial sectors (Hanieh 2011, 2016).

The main real estate investment companies in the Middle East are subsidiaries of Arab investment funds. These include Oger Lebanon, which is developing the investment portfolios of the Hariri family in Beirut. Saudi Kingdom Holding financed the construction of the Four Seasons Hotel in Beirut. The Qatari company Diar Real Estate Investments is very active in Egypt (with the New Giza, CityGate and Saint Regis Nile Cornich projects), as well as in Saudi Arabia with the King Abdullah Economic City. Damac Properties built a tower in Beirut as early as 2006, then in Amman in 2011. Finally, most cities have projects financed by real estate companies: Majid Al Futtaim, Kuwaiti Gulfinvest International, Abu Dhabi Investment House, Al Taameer Real Estate Investment Company of Kuwait. The board members of these companies are linked to the ruling families (Sinno 2017, p. 86). The Emaar Real Estate Investment Group, founded in 1997 in Dubai, is involved in the largest construction projects in Arabian cities. It was responsible for the construction of the Burj Khalifa tower, currently the tallest and most luxurious in the world, and the Dubai Mall. It has invested in the new city center of Amman (the Abdali project, studied below).

The case of the UAE illustrates the impact of entrepreneurial urbanism on the urban transformation of cities. The Gulf countries are in intense competition to attract international investment to their capital cities at the expense of their smaller cities (Wiedman and Salama 2019). Urbanized land and housing have become tradable commodities in international markets. The Dubai government allowed foreign capital to take shares in real estate holding companies as early as 1999, including Dubai Holding and Dubai World[11]. Urban governance is becoming entrepreneurial and subject to semi-public holding companies. Real estate markets are being deregulated to allow for development operations based on private real estate development to attract financial players. Municipalities develop land-use plans and guiding plans, while housing is in the hands of specific housing ministries, most of which work alongside local municipalities to develop new residential towns

---

11. Dubai Holding is the company that manages the personal assets of the Emir of Dubai and has been investing in major development projects in the UAE since 2004, while Dubai World is the investment company of the Dubai government founded in 1969.

on the outskirts of the capitals (Hamad Town and Issa Town in Bahrain). New property laws allow local people to buy undeveloped land and speculate on plots to expand residential areas, which was not allowed before the 2000s. Municipalities, meanwhile, have become key players in urban entrepreneurship through their zoning ordinances (physical planning, area structure plans and integrated urban areas), but they have lost control of their land by selling strategic locations to real estate investment companies (Wiedman and Salama 2019).

8.2.3. Capital invested in real estate and Arab real estate investment trust

Arab investments can be measured by the volumes of real estate companies listed on the stock exchange. Thus, USD 736 billion is in the commercial real estate sector in the Middle East (USD 293 billion in Saudi Arabia, USD 219 billion in the UAE, USD 68 billion in Egypt), far more than in housing, which was only USD 105 billion in 2021. These amounts include foreign direct investment. Note that REITs raised only USD 5 billion in the Middle East, and are mostly concentrated in Saudi Arabia (see Table 8.3).

Country	Unlisted real estate companies (USD in billion)	Listed real estate companies (USD in billion)	Listed REIT structures (USD in billion)	Number of companies (including REITs)
Egypt	68.5	5.5	-	34
Kuwait	62.8	8.2	0.09	36
Qatar	92.2	16.9	-	5
Saudi Arabia	293.3	40.7	4.8	28
UAE	219.9	33.9	0.15	16
Total	736.7	105.2	5.04	119

Table 8.3. *Amount of commercial real estate capital held by listed companies and REITs in the Middle East in 2021 (source: European Public Real Estate Association, https://prodapp.epra.com/media/EPRA_Total_Markets_Table_-_Q2-2021_162668231 7868.pdf)*

Arab REITs were established in 2016. These listed real estate investment trusts (*sunduq al istithmar al 'aqari* in Arabic) are saving instruments based on real estate rental. They deal only with formal, registered properties owned by structures listed in local stock exchanges. The income from the collected rents is distributed to shareholders, who prefer to acquire shares with assured income rather than invest larger sums in apartment units and assume the burden of rental management. REITs invest mostly in office and retail facilities, and much less in residential buildings, as the formal rental housing market is not well developed in the Arab world. However, governments are encouraging the development of these structures to finance the residential real estate sector.

As early as 2006, the Gulf states created Real Estate Active Funds in Dubai. The first Arab REITs were established in Saudi Arabia and Bahrain in 2016, Egypt in 2017, Oman in 2018, Qatar in 2020 and the UAE in 2021[12]. Saudi Arabia has 28 such real estate investment trusts, with a capitalization of USD 4.8 billion in 2021. In 2017, the first Egyptian REIT was opened by Bank Misr, announcing returns of 26%, which is considerable as the usual rates in the rest of the world are 3–5%[13]. Note that these REITs represent modest financial volumes compared to those in unlisted investment companies, which are USD 250 billion in 2020[14]. This is due to the low transparency of real estate investment in the region, which makes REITs unattractive. In the Jones Lang LaSalle (JLL) ranking[15], Middle Eastern countries fall into the semi-transparent or even opaque category (Saudi Arabia in 57th place, Egypt in 60th and Lebanon 87th out of 99 countries[16]).

Urban investments are now defined more by their financial characteristics (risk-adjusted returns and real estate capital gains) than by their physical attributes. Large real estate investment groups are in turn trying to build up land reserves by acquiring private and public land. In Egypt, the leading real estate developer TalaatMostafa Group (TMG) has built up a land bank of 50 million square meters, of which it has constructed some 8.5 million (Denis 2011).

> Since the mid-1990s, private developers have acquired title deeds and development permits for all public land within a 60-kilometer radius of Cairo. Supported by banks and multinational companies such as Solidere (Lebanon), Emaar (Dubai), Sama Dubai or al Maabar (Abu Dhabi), they have invested in megaprojects of private cities and towns (Denis 2011 p. 140).

---

12. See: https://menafn.com/1102366093/Real-Estate-Investment-Trusts-are-expected-to-grow-in-the-region.
13. Mokhtar (2017). The truth about the 26% interest on bank misr certificates. *Al Tahrir News* [Online]. Available at: https://tinyurl.com/y9nqovdy.
14. See: https://www.arabianbusiness.com/private-equity/460851-private-capital-investments-in-mena-region-projected-to-pick-up-this-year-after-28-fall-in-2020.
15. This ranking includes the existence of anti-money laundering regulations, transparency of tenders and the professionalism of real estate agents.
16. See: https://www.us.jll.com/content/dam/jll-com/documents/pdf/research/jll-and-lasalle-global-real-estate-transparency-index-2020.pdf.

8.2.4. Households' indebtedness for mortgages in the Middle East

The rapid increase in Middle Eastern land prices, which is higher than the increase in income, is pushing the middle classes in developed countries into debt by taking out real estate loans for more than 20 years. Investment advisory firms (PriceWaterhouseCooper, McKinsey Global Institute, Knight Frank) are drawing their clients' attention to the potential benefits of expanding developing urban regions, based on a middle-class demand for housing finance (Denis 2011). However, less than half of Middle Eastern citizens have a bank account: 44.7% of Lebanese, 42% of Jordanians, 32% of Egyptians and 20% of Iraqis in 2017 (compared to over 70% in the Gulf)[17]. In addition, having a bank account into which salaries are paid is not enough to obtain a home loan. The latter are often substantial – more than USD 20,000 – and require guarantors *(kafil)*, i.e. relatives who stand as guarantors. In 2010, only 15.5% of Middle Eastern residents could qualify for a home loan, and only 8.5% if we exclude the GCC countries and Israel.

Yet, despite the difficulty of taking out a home loan, mortgage markets have been expanding in major Arab countries since the 2010s. The increase in national mortgage debt has been interpreted as a sign of the financialization of the economy in the US and Europe (Aalbers and Haila 2018), as well as in the Middle East (Hanieh 2016), where the ratio of the household real estate debt to GDP ranges from 8 to 22% of GDP, but is still very low in Egypt at 0.3%. In 2016, real estate loans alone are equivalent to 21.3% of GDP in Lebanon, 22% of GDP in Kuwait, 15.1% in Jordan (they have doubled compared to 2013). They are rising sharply in Saudi Arabia: having increased from 2% to 7.9% of GDP between 2013 and 2016 (see Figure 8.4).

Since few households in the Arab world have the capacity to take out a home loan, most resort to moneylenders or tontines *(jamiyya* in Arabic). Members of the tontine agree to pay a fixed sum each month, decided in consultation with the other members, in exchange for an interest-free loan obtained in turn. Usually 20–30 people agree to pay a sum of money, usually between USD 100 and USD 300, for as many months as there are members, and then draw a random number to determine whether or not they will receive the loan that month (Ababsa 2020). Tontines are the most common means of accessing credit and savings in the Middle East. They are particularly common among working-class people, as well as among the middle classes. They play a primary role in daily life for a large proportion of the population, as well as for migrants and refugees (Tobin 2016). In 2011, half of all transactions in Egypt were conducted in cash: money from tontines and moneylenders, family loans and money laundering (Denis 2011, p. 152). The system

---

17. See: https://www.theglobaleconomy.com/rankings/percent_people_bank_accounts/MENA/.

responds to the Muslim imperative to avoid interest-bearing loans. It is seen as a way to save money, under the social control of the group.

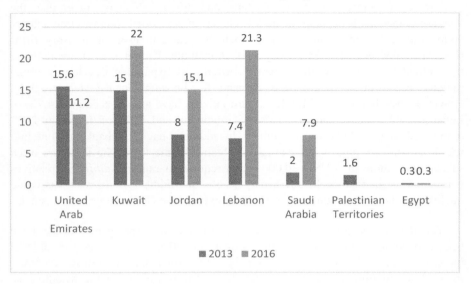

Figure 8.4. *Amount of home loans as a percentage of GDP in the Middle East (2013 and 2016) (source: World Bank 2013. MENA., Hofinet 2017, Regional Affordable Housing Project)*

The purchase of an apartment or a property constitutes a refuge in the context of economic and political instability. For those who can afford them, fear of the future is driving households to take out home loans. Real estate loans are expanding rapidly in Egypt, even though they only correspond to 0.3% of GDP. They have risen from LE 300 million (USD 42.8 million) in 2006 to LE 4.5 billion (USD 643.3 million) in 2011[18].

People in the Middle East prefer to take out Islamic loans (real estate and bonds – *sukuks*), which circumvent the prohibition of usury by backing the money with tangible real estate. Islamic law (*Sharia*) forbids profit by interest rate alone (*riba*), as the money must be invested in productive sectors. Islamic finance prefers to share the "profit and loss" of investments. Real estate loans take the form of *murabaha*, whereby a seller offers to buy an apartment for the bank, while they repay the capital and a margin defined at the beginning of the contract by both parties. This is a way

---

18. Oxford Business Group (2014). Egypt to lift Home Ownership Rates [Online]. Available at: http://www.oxfordbusinessgroup.com/news/egypt-lift-home-ownership-rates#.Uw8ury8oGJQ.twitter. (in Mokhtar 2017, p. 53).

of not paying interest every month, but at the end of the sale. Historically, commercial banks and Islamic banks have used *ifragh*, which involves the borrower transferring the title to the bank until the loan and interest are paid in full, as a kind of leasehold. The risk is that if the borrower defaults on the loan, they will lose all the drafts paid, because the borrower cannot sell a property that does not belong to them. The borrower must find a way to sell the remaining drafts at a low price.

In the Jordanian case, the growth of Islamic real estate loans is great: from one-third of the total real estate loans in 2010 (311 million JD – 378 million euros), they have increased to 1490 million in 2019 (37%). Each Jordanian bank has developed its own real estate leasing company, which allows borrowers to benefit from the 9% exemption from transfer and registration fees (i.e. 5%) and selling fees (4%). This is a way to apply an Islamic mechanism while cleverly avoiding taxation. The banks buy the apartments and lease them to the borrowers during the repayment period. At the end of the lease, the apartment is transferred to the buyers without the payment of registration and transaction fees (Ababsa 2021). Leasing companies can reduce apartment prices by 9%. Most Jordanians self-finance the construction of their homes through tontines or family money, as they do not have access to bank loans.

In Saudi Arabia, a new *Real Estate Mortgage and Financial law* was enacted in 2012 to attract foreign investors and expand the borrower base. It went into effect in 2014, but very slowly, with notaries keeping only manual records, but mostly because citizens are reluctant to take out real estate loans from banks whose interest rates are perceived to be inconsistent with religious *sharia* requirements. In May 2017, the Saudi central bank (SAMA) issued a circular that prohibits *ifragh*, requiring all real estate collateral to be registered as mortgages. It called for all outstanding *ifragh* contracts to be converted within three years to mortgages. Notaries then clarified that *tawarruq*[19] and *murabaha* mortgages and real estate loans were compatible with Islamic law.

8.2.5. *The legalization of informal settlements through the titling of "dead capital" (De Soto 2000)*

The majority of Middle Easterners self-build their homes: the middle classes add extra floors[20] while the working classes build informally, on cheaper outlying land.

---

19. *Tawarruq* (literally "cash generation") is a financial arrangement whereby cash is obtained from a bank through the sale of a financial asset to two intermediaries.

20. For example, in Jordan, only one-third of apartments were built with a permit between 2004 and 2015 (author's calculation for the Jordanian Housing Strategy, in Hamilton et al. (2018)).

The titling of informal property was advocated in 2000 by the Peruvian economist Hernando de Soto as a way to lift informal settlers out of poverty. According to him, registering their property would allow informal settlers to take out loans to start a self-employed activity. But it has been shown that, on the contrary, once registered, the property entered a real estate market that precisely excluded their owners: "In practice, titling does nothing to secure the right to the city for ordinary city dwellers insofar as the latter are never able to stabilize their position in the city with the increase in prices brought about by the commodification of their property" (Denis 2011, p. 154).

8.3. Egypt and Jordan: the squandering of public land and the construction of new cities

The rapid expansion of cities in the Arab world has similarities with other cities in the South. Since the 1990s, a private takeover of collective land assets has been taking place in the major Arabian metropolises. Whereas in the 1970s and 1980s there were evictions orchestrated by municipal authorities, there is now a more insidious dispossession by market forces. Private developers have acquired large tracts of land, with the support of banks and financial investment groups such as Solidere (Lebanon), Emaar (Dubai), Sama Dubai or al Maabar (Abu Dhabi). The land reserves of the municipalities or the Ministry of Defence within the cities, created in the 1960s and 1970s during the preparation of urban development plans, are gradually being sold or mobilized by the governments.

8.3.1. *The new cities of Cairo*

Faced with congestion in Cairo, Egypt began building new cities in the desert in the 1970s, at a time when new capitals were being constructed in the developing world: Brasilia, Chandigar, Gaborone, Abuja, Yamoussoukro, Astana in Kazakhstan and Naypyidaw in Myanmar (Sims 2014, p. 117). In 1979, the New Urban Communities Authority (NUCA) was created within the Ministry of Reconstruction (after the 1973 war) with the right to sell state land to finance the construction of new towns, and to manage building permits. The NUCA then became the country's fifth economic agent, after the Suez Canal Agency and the Oil Agency (Barthel 2011, p. 185). This led to a race to sell land at very low prices to people close to President Sadat, and later to President Mubarak, in new towns with no public transport network or employment center. Eighteen cities were built in this way in the first phase, including "Sadat City", "10 Ramadan" and "October 6". These urban entities are underpopulated compared to the initial project: 1.2 million inhabitants against the 6.7 million programmed in the mid-1980s. In the 2017 census, all the new cities are 74% empty (with 7 million inhabitants against the 27 million planned[21]). In 2017, the census indicated that one-third of the apartments in Egypt were empty, or 12.8 million units, of which 4.3 were under construction[22].

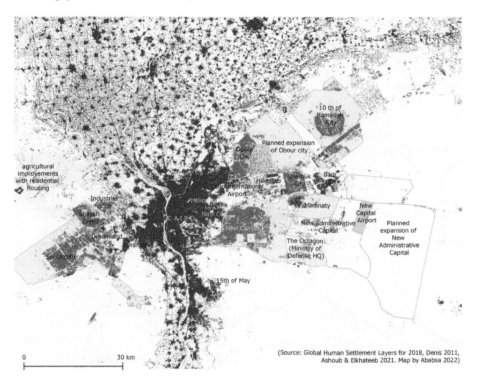

Figure 8.5. *Location of the main new cities in Cairo (source: Ababsa (2022))*

A second generation of satellite cities was launched in 1986 on the advice of the Ile de France Region Urban Planning Agency. The third generation of new cities was born in the year 2000, located in governorates other than Cairo (Tadamun 2015). In 2018, the president announced the start of the fourth generation of new cities. The 28 new cities have attracted members of the upper middle class, while the poor, lacking access to credit, have preferred to settle in informal settlements. This

---

21. See: https://egypt.unfpa.org/sites/default/files/pub-pdf/Egypt%20National%20%28AADPD%2B5%29%20Report%20MidNov18%20%281%29.pdf [Accessed October 2021]. They were already 63% empty in the 2006 census, compared to 25% of Cairo apartments (Sims 2014).

22. See: https://egyptianstreets.com/2017/10/03/egypts-vacant-housing-units-12-8-million-capmas/ [Accessed November 2021]. Confirmed by Shawkat (2020, p. 164).

has resulted in the destruction of 420,000 hectares of agricultural land in the Nile Delta and on the banks of the Nile over the past three decades (Singerman 2009; Mokhtar 2017, p. 9).

Presented as the solution to all of Egypt's urban problems, the new cities have mainly served to consolidate the class of entrepreneurs close to the government. Investment in real estate has been lucrative for real estate entrepreneurs since the 1990s, as desert land was developed at the expense of the state and sold at knock-down prices. 1200 km^2 of land were put up for sale: this is more than two and a half times the size of Cairo. 110 km^2 were built on between 1995 and 2007[23], at a rate of 8% per year, while the population was growing at no more than 2% per year (Denis 2011). The World Bank estimated that USD 1.5 billion (LE 26.4 billion) were invested in real estate from the 1980s to 2007, but in unreasonable projects, not adapted to local demand (Mokhtar 2017). A study conducted in 2016 by the independent Egyptian research group *10 Tooba*[24] shows that the budget planned in 2015–2016 for infrastructure in new cities is equivalent to that planned for the entire infrastructure costs of the rest of the country, in which 98% of the population resides (Denis 2018).

As elsewhere in the region, real estate strategies reflect the patronage of ministers in office. For example, in 2005, Housing Minister Al Maghraby allowed NUCA to sell 360 hectares to the Hesham Talaat Moustafa group at the very low price of LE 297/m^2 (16 euros/m^2), which expresses favoritism towards a business oligarchy. In the same year, 10,920 hectares (26,000 feddans) located in Ayat were sold at the price of agricultural land (LE 200 or 11 euros per feddan – 4168 m^2) to the Egyptian Kuwaiti Co, which then resold the land at a price of LE 100,000 (5,487 euros) per feddan for real estate projects to the Kuwaiti company, International Group for Real Estate Companies to build luxury housing (Mokhtar 2017).

Eric Denis has shown that public land in new towns, once serviced, was sold to Arab investors in many lucrative operations. These plots of land are "solid bank assets", the counterparty to the production of cash and loans (Denis 2018).

After the 2011 "Arab revolution", the Morsi government announced the introduction of a land tax to combat speculative retention of vacant urban land[25]. However, this was not implemented due to General Sissi's coup in 2013. In 2014, President Sissi announced the launch of a USD 14 billion, 1.5 million middle-class

---

23. World Bank Report (2007). Analysis of Housing Supply Mechanisms – Final Note.
24. See: https://www.10tooba.org/en/?page_id=4.
25. Al Arabiya (2011). The Egyptian economy loses USD 1.8 bn annually from land speculation [Online]. Available at: https://www.alarabiya.net/articles/2011/07/06/156363.html [Accessed April 2021].

housing program entrusted to the Emirates-based construction company, Arabtec. But the project was suspended in March 2015 in favor of building a new capital 30 kilometers east of Cairo, a gigantic project "the size of Singapore"[26]. The project's director, Ahmed Zaki Abdeen, unabashedly calls the project a financial operation (beyond real estate) because each square meter is sold at LE 7,000 (400 euros) to investors, who will resell it to affluent Egyptian households at LE 12,000 (675 euros) after the installation of roads and electricity networks. The rest of the population remains poorly housed in cramped apartments built by small informal entrepreneurs north of Cairo in the Nile Delta.

8.3.2. *The Abdali project, Amman*

A similar case of low-cost disposal of large-scale public land to investors was observed in Amman in the mid-2000s. This was the construction of the new Amman city center on former military land in Abdali, launched in 2004. This development project is emblematic of the neoliberal policy supported by the king, to which the main Arab real estate investment companies are contributing: Emaar and Saudi Oger, both of which are majority owned by the sons of the assassinated Lebanese prime minister Rafik Hariri. The project is located near the western neighborhoods of Shmeisani, the former business center of Amman built in the 1980s. Abdali is a real estate project with offices, hotels and shopping malls, as well as a new parliament building, covering an area of 384,000 m^2 (and 1.8 million m^2 built). In 2004, the real estate investment group Emaar signed a memorandum of understanding with Mawared (National Resources and Development Corporation), the Jordanian army's investment company, to develop its military land. In 2004, Abdali Investment and Development was established as a joint-venture between MAWARED (a state-owned company) and Saudi Oger (a Saudi real estate investment company) headed by Saad Hariri. In 2010, Saad Hariri's shares were sold to his brother Baha, who founded Horizon, his own private investment conglomerate[27]. The entire project would be worth USD 5 billion by 2021 according to the promotional website[28].

---

26. BBC Arabic (2015). Egypt announced the building of a new capital in the East of Cairo [Online]. Available at: http://www.bbc.com/arabic/business/2015/03/150314egyptplancairo [Accessed April 2021]. Cited in Mokhtar (2017).
27. In 2019, the shares of the companies were 81 million dinars of shares for Mawared, as much for Horizon and 6 million for Real Estate Company/Jordan, the Jordanian branch of the large Kuwaiti company (Kuwait Project Holding Company). See https://www.khaberni.com/news [Accessed April 2021].
28. See: https://abdali.jo/en/AboutAbdali [Accessed April 2021].

The Greater Amman Municipality (GAM) funded the road infrastructure cost of the project (Parker and Debruyne 2015). Private land was expropriated, including that of Talal Abu Ghazaleh, a media-savvy real estate entrepreneur who heads a private technical university. The latter initiated and lost a lawsuit against Mawared in 2008. GAM allegedly sold additional land to Mawared at a derisory price (14 times below the market price), in a form of direct subsidy to this military-private project, in complete opacity. The opposition press (Al Ghad) reported that the project's years-long delay required a government bailout in 2012 and 2014, a total of 52 million dinars converted into shares[29]. But the project is supported by the authorities, who see it as a way to attract Gulf consumers and boost employment. The first towers appeared in 2014, five years late, in a slowing economic climate.

Figure 8.6. *View of Amman towards the Abdali Towers. July 2021 (source: M. Ababsa)*

8.3.3. *Rental renewals and their current outcomes in Cairo and Amman*

Arab cities are highly segregated between run-down central districts, luxury residential areas and very dense informal settlements. The latter are subject to a great deal of coveting because they are often located near the old town centers. The central districts are deteriorating in part because rents have been frozen at very low levels for decades, which limits the owners' capacity to invest in renovation. Indeed,

---

29. See: https://jfranews.com.jo/article/33156.

as in some European and Asian countries, laws were enacted in the aftermath of World War II to protect tenants by freezing rents. In the Middle East, this was the case in Egypt, Lebanon and Jordan.

In Egypt, Law 121 of 1947 blocked rents signed for buildings built before 1944. Then in 1952, a law imposed a 15% reduction on rents signed after 1944. In 1962, a new law set new rents at 5% of the value of the property, plus 3% for building maintenance. The owners of buildings with blocked rents then demanded from their tenants the payment of a "key money" (*khiliw*), which was very high, more than one year of an average Cairo income. Although prohibited, this practice continued. Contracts signed before 1944 could be inherited for three generations provided that the grandchildren lived with the tenant. In 1971, two-thirds of urban families were tenants, or 2 million households. By 1976, 59% of urban apartments were rent-barred. But locked-in rents did not allow landlords to maintain the buildings. By 1975, 700,000 apartments, or 10% of the stock, were on the verge of collapse, but this did not stop some landlords from building additional floors (Shawkat 2020, p. 70). The Housing Act 49 of 1977 established new rents at 7% of the value of the building plus 3% for maintenance costs. A new law in 1981 allowed landlords to set rents for new buildings, and established that maintenance costs would be shared with tenants. But the wake-up call came with the 1992 earthquake that destroyed 5,000 homes (516 dead). Law 4 of 1996 removed all rent limits for new buildings, as well as for rent-stabilized units kept vacant. The old rents were maintained for fear of social destabilization.

This law led to the eviction of 610,000 tenants in 10 years, the majority in Cairo, who left to find housing in the informal sector (Shawkat 2017). Landlords did not find tenants and preferred to keep the units empty in many cases. While rent-blocked housing corresponded to 44% of urban apartments in 1996, this figure dropped to 28% in 2006 and 15% in 2017 (Shawkat 2020, p. 76). In order to stimulate the rental sector, a new rent regulation law has been under debate in parliament for the past two years. It is being pushed by President Sissi, who thinks it is unfair that an apartment in the city center "is rented for LE 20 (1.1 euros) per month when it is worth 5 million"[30]. The law under debate proposes a minimum rent of LE 200 (11 euros), with an increase of 10% per year to encourage landlords to rent out their properties.

In Jordan, the 1953 law guaranteed that rents would not be indexed to inflation. It was amended in 2000, and was to come into effect in 2010, just after the 2008 subprime crisis. Supported by landlords but opposed by users, its implementation was postponed several times from 2010 to 2013, only to be implemented in 2013.

---

30. See: https://english.ahram.org.eg/NewsContent/50/1201/422183/AlAhram-Weekly/Egypt/Justice-for-landlords.aspx.

However, that year also saw the arrival of a large wave of Syrian refugees (more than 1,000 per day), who competed with Jordanians in the rental market. The revised rent law of 2000 allows landlords to increase rents according to the length of time the property has been occupied. For tenancies less than 10 years old, landlords have been able to double the rents. The tenants' response has been to sign multi-year contracts to negotiate rents. But the law requires them to pay all annuities if they leave early. The pressure on tenants is great. Rents have doubled between the two censuses of 2004 and 2015. Two-thirds of rents remain below JD 200 per month (250 euros). They are higher in Amman where half of the rents exceed this amount. These rents are high compared to the minimum wage of JD 260 per month in 2021. Half of the employees registered with Social Security earned less than 500 JD per month in 2021.

All of these rent laws were modified in favor of landlords, so that they would renovate their dwellings, at a critical time when neighborhoods were degrading and insalubrity was becoming increasingly common. Rents that were set too low could eventually lead to the destruction of city centers. But the Arab states have not yet developed tools for capturing the land value generated by public investment (see Chapter 5). As we will see, Saudi Arabia is the only country in the Middle East to have mobilized the fiscal tool by introducing a tax on vacant land.

8.4. Saudi Arabia: tax innovation to finance housing

Saudi Arabia presents a unique case of a country that continues to build new cities, while investing in affordable middle-class housing programs on state-subsidized land. In 2016, Crown Prince Mohammed Ben Salman revealed an ambitious vision to prepare the kingdom for post-oil and decarbonization. *Saudi Vision 2030* plans to help 70% of citizens become homeowners by 2030, up from 47% currently. Outstanding home loans increased from 290 million Saudi riyals in 2017 to 502 million in 2020, and 623 by the end of 2021 (Deloitte 2020; Zawya 2022)[31]. The strategy is to tax vacant land to finance affordable housing policies while limiting speculative land retention. The *Saudi Vision* includes building new cities, housing and opening up to Western tourism around the Nabatean sites of Aloula in southern Jordan near the Red Sea. One of the new city projects seems particularly unrealistic: it is a city 170 km long and 1 km wide called *"The Line"*, planned for 1 million inhabitants and aims to use robots to provide transport, waste collection and cleaning services. Since cars will be prohibited, an underground express train will link the different islands. Its residents would be isolated in the desert, exposed to the sandy winds, which would not be slowed down by vegetation barriers.

---

31. See: https://www.zawya.com/en/business/banking-and-insurance/saudi-arabian-banks-mortgages-jump-27-to-170bln-in-q2-yaq1ikq7.

Alongside these huge projects, a housing policy was implemented in 2014 to produce 500,000 apartments. In 2021, 187 affordable housing projects were underway, representing only 233,000 apartments, far less than what is needed. The Saudi kingdom is in the midst of a demographic transition, with natural growth rates of 2% per year. But housing needs are high, especially for government employees and middle-income households. High land prices make up half the price of housing, and large areas of urban land are kept empty for speculation. According to the Bahraini firm Weetas, the cities of Jeddah, Riyadh and Makkah have a total of 1,100 vacant plots of land, covering an area of 411 km^2, held by residents seeking capital gain on land. Forty percent of Riyadh's urban area is vacant land.

As early as 2013, on the advice of the World Bank, Saudi Arabia has been debating the introduction of a new tax on private urban residential land[32]. This new regulatory tool, known as the "white land tax" was announced on March 23, 2015. It is part of a set of innovative policies designed to diversify the economy by reducing the dependence on oil (Wahbah et al. 2016; Zakaria et al. 2019). This new tax scheme aims to combat land speculation on subdivided land equipped with all urban amenities, while funding social housing policies. It is particularly ambitious: the law states that the tax will be used to finance housing policies for the middle classes, to curb land speculation and to "fight against monopolies" in the real estate sector.

Indeed, as of June 2016, tax is set at a high level of 2.5% of the market value of land. Saudi lawmakers were clever enough to present the law as Islamic and temporary; Islamic because it is positioned at the maximum usury rate, and temporary while the real estate markets are cleaned up, over a 10-year period. The tax is levied by the Ministry of Housing on private undeveloped land of more than 10,000 m^2 located within urban boundaries and categorized as residential or commercial. It is reserved for the exclusive financing of social housing. It came into effect in March 2017 for the four main urban areas of Riyadh, Jeddah, Dammam and Makkah. The first two-year phase covers undeveloped land over 10,000 m^2 owned by a legal entity or individual. The second phase, which started in 2020, covers spaces of more than 10,000 m^2 to be developed. The third phase will cover spaces over 5,000 m^2. The fourth phase will cover plots of land over 10,000 m^2 built within a real estate project. A total of 17 Saudi cities will be affected by this measure.

Between the announcement of the law and its implementation, a whole movement of selling and subdividing land for the benefit of the owners' children occurred to escape it. However, according to the International Monetary Fund, this tax is already showing positive effects: land prices were reported to have fallen at

---

32. Royal Decree M/4 of November 24, 2015, Decision No. 377 of June 13, 2016 of the Saudi Council of Ministers.

the time of implementation, forcing banks to review their mortgage policies (Oxford Business Group 2017). They have since resumed their rise. The tax reportedly brought in 1 billion Saudi riyals for the government in 2018 (223 million euros), with 70% of owners of vacant land paying it. The remaining 30% undertook to sell or build poor quality housing in a hurry, a negative effect that had not been anticipated. Those who were unable to do so sold their land. The payment of this tax was imposed on large landowners by a particularly authoritarian regime. Fines for perpetrators equals the amount of the tax, which is double the expected amount.

The authorities are aware that the tax alone will not make the land affordable. Indeed, even if prices were to fall by half, apartments on the market would remain unaffordable for the middle classes. To stimulate sales, the Saudi government has reduced the transaction costs of buying property: the newly introduced 15% VAT has been replaced by a 5% tax. The government has also provided subsidies to young first-time buyers to increase the amount of mortgages and facilitate the development of private property.

8.5. Lebanon and Syria: reconstruction policies as a means of consolidating elites

In contrast to these innovative policies in favor of affordable housing, Lebanon and Syria rely on real estate investments to consolidate their ruling classes around large projects for international elites, including investors from the Gulf states. Reconstruction sites and the rubble market (collection and sale of debris for embankment and port expansion) remain issues of political control in the service of consolidating regimes in power. Reconstruction was used as a pretext for the destruction of often informal neighborhoods, where political opposition had formed. These additional destructions are carried out to free up central lands that are expropriated for the benefit of large real estate projects. The old souks that were emblematic places of community cohesion and national culture have been replaced by sanitized projects, both in Beirut in the 1990s and in Aleppo since 2016 and Homs, while their inhabitants are displaced to the periphery.

8.5.1. *Lebanon, land of investor exemptions and subsidies*

Lebanon presents the extreme case of a country ruined by a rentier economic model that has benefited a handful of investors and corrupt leaders since the end of the civil war in 1990. The government encouraged the financialization of inner-city urban land through laissez-faire and tax exemptions to attract investors (Marot 2018). Real estate is one of the pillars of the national economy, driven by foreign investments and the Lebanese diaspora. The construction and real estate sector contributed 21% of GDP in 2014, making Lebanon a "real estate state" on par with Singapore and Hong Kong (Haila 2016; Marot 2020, p. 37).

The most emblematic operation of this model is the reconstruction of downtown Beirut by a private company, Solidere, in which Prime Minister Rafiq Hariri was one of the main shareholders. This had never happened before. Solidere obtained ownership of the city center, then gave compensation in the form of shares to the former owners and tenants (two-thirds) and sold a third to investors (Verdeil 2001; Schmid 2002; Nasr and Verdeil 2008). This expropriation process has been controversial. Some owners of repairable buildings were allowed to keep their property, while the land of religious communities (*waqfs*) was spared from confiscation and benefited from reconstruction. The Solidere society goes beyond the competence of the classical urban planning bodies. It uses its own construction standards, while benefiting from numerous state subsidies. The reconstruction of Beirut from 1990 onwards was a product of appeal for investors from the Gulf. The government of Rafiq Hariri offered them monetary stability (tying the Lebanese pound to the dollar), a guarantee by the Central Bank for deposits in private banks, and it issued short-term high-interest bonds, guaranteed by the state, for the benefit of investors.

Figure 8.7. *View of downtown Beirut, Solidere project, with the Hariri Mosque on the left. June 2019 (source: M. Ababsa)*

The Investment and Development Authority of Lebanon (IDAL) was established in 1994. It offers investors tax exemptions of up to 100% of registration and construction fees. In 2001, it became autonomous, no longer under the control of the municipal governement and reporting only to the Prime Minister's Office (Krijnen and Fawaz 2010). Lebanon has thus facilitated investments from Gulf countries and its diaspora. But some money flows from Iraq and the Middle East constitute laundering flows of illicit and unreported activities (Tierney 2017).

The transfer of urban planning power to the Solidere company has enabled significant private sector influence in the design of the 2004 real estate law. The latter allows for the construction of additional floors on existing buildings. The Federation of Real Estate Developers contributed to the revision of the law by facilitating the erection of towers.

Figure 8.8. *Beirut seen from the Hamra area towards the Northeast. April 2019 (source: M. Ababsa)*

Indirect subsidies offered by the Lebanese government to real estate developers have taken the form of a reduction in land taxes, an increase in floor area ratios (FARs) and a reduction in taxes on profits made by limited liability companies and joint stock companies in the real estate sector; investment companies (holding companies) are exempt from income tax; and real estate developers are allowed to declare land prices during 1992 even if they were acquired at a later date and have seen their prices rise (Krijnen and Fawaz 2010). Luxury apartment towers offer 375-square-meter apartments from USD 3,500 to USD 10,000 per m², when the minimum wage is USD 350. These towers are accessed by wide roads with small sidewalks that exclude half of Beirut's car-less population. Isolated from their social context, these buildings are the materialization of the financial networks in which the city is embedded (Krijnen 2018).

Figure 8.9. *Real estate projects by size in Beirut according to land prices (2000–2013) (source: Gebara et al. 2016)*

The city has experienced two phases of intense real estate construction (1992–1996 and 2003–2010) resulting in a surplus not adapted to the local market, but aimed in part at members of the Lebanese diaspora and Arab investors. The latter capture half of the Housing Bank's real estate loans (Marot 2018, p. 334). Due to the rising price of land in the city center, only companies can take out the necessary loans. Interest rates for builders are exorbitant: they range from 7% to 20% for loans in Lebanese pounds and from 6.8% to 11% for loans in dollars (Marot 2020, p. 38), which limits the attractiveness of real estate investment as a financial asset. Residential property prices doubled between 2003 and 2013, and have been declining since 2014. They remain very high at more than 4000 USD per m² in Beirut compared to half of that in the suburbs (Marot 2020). Figure 8.9 shows that the most expensive land (over 6,000 USD per m² in 2014) located in the corniche and within the Solidere project concentrates on the highest towers financed by diaspora and Gulf capital (Gebara et al. 2016).

The majority of the population has low incomes, debts, and for two-thirds, less than USD 10,000 per year (Marot 2020, p. 13). Half of the households do not have a bank account and a third were below the poverty line of USD 4 a day before the economic collapse of 2020. Unable to take out mortgages, they are reduced to living in the informal settlements that are developing around the main cities of Beirut, Tripoli, Saida and Tyre.

The rent control law passed in 1940 ensured a de facto social housing supply in the inner city for low-income households, with rents of only a few hundred dollars per year (Marot 2020). But after the war, the 1992 rent law liberalized leases by establishing two systems: those of frozen leases signed before 1992 and those that followed inflation after 1992. Now, a new rental law was passed in 2014 to gradually unfreeze rents over a 12-year period, but its application remains unclear. Beirut rents are now between USD 75 and 100 per square meter, which excludes modest households. This deregulation of rent was enacted to encourage landlords to renovate the housing stock and allow them to make new leases free of charge, or sell them at a better price to developers who demolish the buildings for land redevelopment. Its application occurred at the time of the arrival of Syrian refugees, leading to evictions of impoverished Lebanese people. A USD 1.5 billion compensation fund has been announced, but not funded on a permanent basis (Marot 2020). 100,000 households benefit from old rents, two-thirds of which are in Greater Beirut (Marot 2018, p. 338).

8.5.2. *Syria confiscates refugees' property and deploys a policy of territorial revenge*

Syria offers an even more radical case of the use of land for the benefit of a power elite, which began when Bashar Al Assad came to power in June 2000. In 2007, the president sold a public plot of land near Umayyad Square in central Damascus to the Emir of Qatar at a knock-down price for the Diar company, which is supported by a Qatari sovereign wealth fund (Vignal 2014). Six major real estate projects financed by Gulf countries were announced in Damascus in mid-2000, redirecting capital planned for Beirut to Syria after the assassination of the Lebanese prime minister. The largest project is Diar Damascus (USD 4 billion), followed by the Eight Gate project of the Emaar company (USD 1.5 billion), Khams Shamat of the Emirati group

Majid Al Futtaim, Kiwan project and Yaafour gardens. All of these projects were suspended during the war, as the Gulf countries supported the armed opposition.

With the recapture of Raqqa from the Islamic State in October 2017, the crushing of the opposition and the Covid-19 crisis, Gulf investors came back to Syria to take advantage of low-cost land. The vice president of investments for the UAE's Damac Group, a leader in the Arab real estate market, met with the heads of two Syrian real estate companies (one owned by the former minister of telecommunications and the other by a member of the Syriatel company) in Damascus in December 2018[33]. But the country is struggling to rebuild in the context of the Caesar Act passed by the U.S. legislature in December 2019 and implemented in June 2020, which imposes heavy sanctions on any investor contributing to Syria's reconstruction (apart from NGOs), particularly in the mining and real estate sectors. As a result, Chinese investments have dried up[34], as have those of the Gulf states. Only Russia and Iran have remained, as contracts for the exploitation of hydrocarbons were signed just before the sanctions were enacted.

The reconstruction of Syria is used by the regime as a pretext to expropriate residents of neighborhoods where the political opposition has organized, whether they are formal or informal neighborhoods. Decree 66 of 2012 allows for the displacement of residents of an informal neighborhood to carry out a real estate project. The recentralization of Syrian power is carried out through a legislative arsenal designed to confiscate land and expel populations in the name of "reconstruction" which rewards regime supporters and expropriates opponents. Property deeds in the city of Homs (the country's third largest city) were deliberately destroyed in 2013. Apartments in the retaken areas of the Damascus suburbs were assigned as early as 2014 to Alawite families, from the minority that has been in power in Syria since 1970. Syrian journalists and activists in Homs have accused the regime of deliberately bombing historic central neighborhoods to widen the artery leading to the *Homs Dream* real estate project, within a controversial new urban development plan that serves the regime's interests. Even areas of historic heritage are being sacrificed[35].

The Law on Removal of Rubble from Damaged Buildings allows real estate contractors to operate in the market. It is accompanied by manipulations of the

---

33. The Syria Report (2018). UAE Companies Showing Growing Interest in Syria, December 24 [Online]. Available at: https://goo.gl/B15ZRz.
34. In December 2018, the governor of Damascus hosted a delegation of Chinese investors China State Construction Company (CSCEC) and Hubie Zhuyuo Group.
35. See: https://www.independent.co.uk/news/world/asia/homs-syria-civil-war-damage-revolution-rebels-forces-assad-regime-damascus-a8164146.html.

property deeds of buildings and illegal changes in cadastral plans (Al-Lababidi 2019). In Damascus, informal settlements are being destroyed to be redeveloped in the form of large-scale real estate projects, in particular *Marota City* (12,000 apartments on 215 hectares[36]) or the *Basilia City* project (4,000 housing units on 880 hectares) in Kafr Soussa, the city where the General Intelligence offices are located. These projects are inspired by Solidere's achievements in Beirut. Marota City is a real estate project located on 215 hectares of land in Mazzeh and Kafr Sousseh, which plans to build 12,000 housing units, office towers, leisure centers and a new parliament. 232 buildings are to be erected, a third of which will benefit the Damascus governorate and the rest for wealthy individuals.

A 2015 decree allows Syrian municipalities and governorates to establish real estate investment companies to build commercial and residential projects on destroyed land. It was followed by the Urban Planning Law No. 10 of April 2, 2018, which allows municipalities to confiscate refugee land, just as Israel did with the iniquitous "absentee property" law. Notably, the Damascus governorate established its own real estate company, Damascus Cham Holding Private, in 2016 with a capital of USD 120 million, to build *Marota City* (see Figure 8.10). The construction of this new city is emblematic of territorial revenge urbanism on the opposition. The project is being implemented on land expropriated from thousands of opposition-supporting residents in the Khalaf al-Razi neighborhood (Abu Zainedin and Fakhani 2020). The main businessmen who became rich during the war (Rami Makhlouf, Samir Foz, Anas Talas) are now investing in the *Marota City* project (see Table 8.4).

Damascus Cham Holding was established in 2015, with very extensive powers. In particular, it has the right to create joint-stock firms, to collect taxes on the land it manages. *Damascus Cham Holding* proceeds with evictions and pre-emptions of public gardens (the Garden of the Bath Pioneers in Mazzeh), as well as covets central neighborhoods, such as the historic district of Hamrawi[37]. The price per square meter is advertised at USD 6,000. Decree 66 of 2012 authorized the destruction of the declared informal dwellings on this land to allow the implementation of urban planning projects by the Damascus governorate. The latter invested USD 2.4 million in infrastructure, one-tenth of the total project money (Al-Lababidi 2019). But U.S. sanctions have slowed funding.

---

36. The Syria Report (2020). Factsheet: Damascus Cham Holding, January 29.
37. The Syria Report (2018). Damascus Cham Holding acquires land, seeks to attract foreign investors for its landmark Marota City Project, December 17 [Online]. Available at: https://goo.gl/NXvMqA.

Company	Date of signing the contract	Capital of the company	Distribution of shares	Investors
Aman Damascus Joint Stock Company	July 2017	312 million USD	Aman Holding Group 51%/Damascus Cham Holding Company 49	Samir Foz
The Central Mall Company	December 2017	250 million USD	Tarazi 51%/Damascus Cham Holding Company 49	Mazen Tarazi
Developers Private Joint Stock Company	January 2018	20 million USD	Exceed Development and Investment LLC 51%/Damascus Cham Holding Company 49	Hayan Qaddour and Maen Haykal
Mirza	January 2018	51 million USD	The Talas Group 25% and Damascus Cham Holding Company 75%	Anas Talas
Bunyan Damascus Private Joint Stock Company	March 2018	33.7 million USD	Tamayoz and Apex companies 40% and Damascus Cham Holding Company 60%	Ahmad Jamal Eddine and his son, Nazir
Rawafed Damascus Private Joint Stock Company	March 2018	57.5 million USD	Wings, Ramac Projects, Ammar and Ultimate Trading 51%/Damascus Cham Holding Company 49	Rami Makhlouf

Table 8.4. *Major investors in Marota new town in Damascus in 2019 (source: Al-Lababidi (2019))*

From 2012 to 2016, 6,377 housing units holding approximatively 50,000 residents were gradually destroyed. The majority of the owners had built them without permits. They were offered two years' rent, and for those who had documentation, shares in the expropriated land. Many sold their shares. A rehousing operation was promised and has not yet been built. Damascus Cham Holding has reserved 68 lots within the project. In September 2019, 80% of the underground infrastructure (water, sewage, electricity) has been completed. But middle-class Syrians, who have been expropriated, cannot afford to buy apartments in this new neighborhood. The regime uses large real estate projects to consolidate the economic basis of its power, at the expense of a battered population (Abu Zainedin and Fakhani 2020).

Figure 8.10. *View of the Marota City project in southwest Damascus (source: Google Earth image of 4-08-2020 annotated by M. Ababsa in 2022)*

8.6. Conclusion

Cities in the Middle East are witnessing the financialization of their public and private properties. Luxury apartments and office towers are springing up, while often half of the floors are empty. One explanation for these apparent aberrations lies in the fact that the land is gaining in value because it is under-taxed. The financialization of cities is mediatized when pension funds from the Gulf buy port infrastructures, or engage in the construction of large projects and towers. But it takes other less visible forms, such as household debt and the sale of public land. The development of mortgage credit and household purchases are an important part of the land value system, as they ensure demand for acquisition.

Whether in Lebanon, Egypt, Jordan or Syria, large real estate projects serve the direct interests of an entrepreneurial class linked to the regimes in place. The latter use state subsidies to finance infrastructure and sell public land at low prices to investors, who support the regimes in place. In Egypt, it soon became clear that the investors did not have a direct plan to build new cities, but sought rather to speculate on future land rise. In Lebanon and Syria, large-scale real estate projects are being undertaken on the ruins of souks and central areas, leading to the exclusion of part of society.

Arabian cities show a growing contrast between the city centers which have been abandoned in favor of closed villa neighborhoods, and peripheral areas which are becoming denser. In turn, informal settlements are threatened with being razed in the name of environmental imperatives (seismic risk) or the renovation of obsolete buildings for real estate investments. Entrepreneurs and governments tend to push for the construction of new cities or more or less affordable housing on the outskirts of cities, on desert or pastoral land, in order to make quick capital gains, but which isolate future residents from employment areas and make them pay high transportation costs. Only Saudi Arabia has an ambitious policy of taxing vacant land to finance social housing policies and make apartments more affordable for its middle classes. The other countries prefer to let their upper classes speculate on the land, without worrying about the consequences of the housing crisis in the long term.

8.7. References

Aalbers, M. and Haila, A. (2018). A conversation about land rent, financialisation and housing. *Urban Studies*, 55(8), 1821–1835.

Ababsa, M. (2020). Diagnostic du secteur du logement abordable en Jordanie. Ifpo et AFD [Online]. Available at: https://www.ifporient.org/wp-content/uploads/2021/01/Ababsa-Diagnostic-du-secteur-du-logement-en-Jordanie.pdf.

Ababsa, M. (2021). Les politiques publiques de logement en Jordanie (1965–2019). In *Les politiques de logement social au Maghreb/Machrek et dans le Sud Global*, Sidi Boumedine, R. and Signoles, P. (eds). NAQD, Alger.

Ababsa, M., Denis, E., Dupret, B. (2012). *Popular Housing and Urban Land Tenure in the Middle East. Case Studies from Egypt, Syria, Jordan, Lebanon, and Turkey*. The American University in Cairo Press.

Abou Zainedin, S. and Fakhani, H. (2020). Syria's reconstruction between discriminatory implementation and circumscribed resistance. In *Contentious Politics in the Syrian Conflict: Opposition, Representation and Resistance*, Yahya, M. (ed.). Carnegie Middle East Center, Beyrouth.

Aveline-Dubach, N., Le Corre, T., Denis, E., Napoleone, C. (2020). Les futurs du foncier : modes d'accumulation du capital, droit de propriété et production de la ville. In *Pour la recherche urbaine*, Adisson, F. (ed.). CNRS Éditions, Paris.

Banerjee-Guha, S. (ed.) (2010). *Accumulation by Dispossession. Transformative Cities in the New Global Order*. SAGE Publications, Los Angeles.

Barthel, P.-A. (2011). Repenser les "villes nouvelles" du Caire : défis pour mettre fin à un développement non durable. *Égypte/Monde arabe, développement durable au Caire : une provocation ?* 8, 181–207.

Barthel, P.-A. and Verdeil, É. (2008). Experts embarqués dans le "tournant financier". Des grands projets urbains au sud de la Méditerranée. *Les Annales de la Recherche Urbaine*, 104, 38–48.

Deloitte (2020). Saudi mortgage market. A decade of reforms towards Vision 2030 targets [Online]. Available at: https://www2.deloitte.com/content/dam/Deloitte/xe/Documents/real estate/me_mortgage-finance-in-KSA.pdf.

Denis, É. (2011). La financiarisation du foncier observée à partir des métropoles égyptiennes et indiennes. *Revue Tiers Monde 2011/2 (No 206)*, 139–158.

Denis, É. (2018). Cairo's new towns. From one revolution to another. In *Cairo New Cities*, Angélil, M. and Charlotte, M.-B. (eds). Idea Book, Ruby Press.

Drozdz, M., Guironnet, A., Halbert, L. (2020). Les villes à l'ère de la financiarisation. *Métropolitiques* [Online]. Available at: https://metropolitiques.eu/Les-villes-al-ere-de-la-financiarisation.html.

Elsheshtawy, Y. (2010). *Dubai: Behind an Urban Spectacle*. Routledge, Abingdon.

Gabor, D. (2018). *Understanding the Financialisation of International Development through 11 FAQs*. Heinrich Böll Stiftung, Berlin.

Gebara, H., Khechen, M., Marot, B. (2016). Mapping new constructions in Beirut. *Jadaliyya* [Online]. Available at: https://www.jadaliyya.com/Print/33751 [Accessed November 2021].

Haila, A. (2016). *Urban Land Rent: Singapore as a Property State*. John Wiley & Sons, Chichester.

Hamilton, E., Mints, V., Acero, V., Jose, L., Ababsa, M., Tammaa, W., Xiao, Y., Molfetas-Lygkiaris, A., Wille, J.R. (2018). Jordan – Housing Sector Assessment – Housing Sector Review (English). Report, World Bank Group, Washington D.C.

Hanieh, A. (2011). *Capitalism and Class in the Gulf Arab States*. Palgrave Macmillan, Houndmills.

Hanieh, A. (2016). Absent regions: Spaces of financialisation in the Arab world. *Antipode*, 48(5), 1228–1248.

International Monetary Fund (2019). Saudi Arabia: 2022 Article IV Consultation – Press release and staff report. International Monetary Fund.

Krijnen, M. (2018). The spatial fix in Lebanon: Remittances, petrodollars, and the global financial crisis [Online]. https://mariekekrijnen.files.wordpress.com/2018/10/krijnen-the-financial-crisis-and-the-spatial-fix-in-lebanon.pdf.

Krijnen, M. and Fawaz, M. (2010). Exception as the rule: High-end developments in neoliberal Beirut. *Built Environment*, 36(2), 245–259.

Lapavitsas, C. (2013). *Profiting Without Producing: How Finance Exploits Us*. Verso, London.

Marcel Delarcoque, A. and Noisette, F. (2017). Urbanisation et financiarisation. Document préparatoire, journée de l'association des professionnels. AdP-Villes en développement.

Marot, B. (2014). The end of rent control in Lebanon: Another boost to the "growth machine?". *Jadaliyya* [Online]. Available at: www.jadaliyya.com/pages/index/18093/the-end-of-rent-control-in-lebanon_another-boost-t.

Marot, B. (2018). Growth politics from the top down. The social construction of the property market in post-war Beirut. *City*, 22(3), 324–340.

Mitchell, T. (1999). No factories, no problems: The logic of neoliberalism in Egypt. *Review of African Political Economy*, 26(82), 451–458.

Mokhtar, N.S. (2017). Between accumulation and (in)security: The real estate industry and the housing crisis in Egypt. Master's Thesis, American University in Cairo, AUC Knowledge Fountain [Online]. Available at: https://fount.aucegypt.edu/etds/1347.

Nasr, J. and Verdeil, É. (2008). The reconstructions of Beirut. In *The City in the Islamic World*, Jayyusi, S., Holod, R., Attilio Petruccioli, A., Raymond, A. (eds). Handbook of Oriental Studies, Brill.

OECD (2021). *Middle East and North Africa Investment Policy Perspectives*. Éditions OECD, Paris. DOI: 10.1787/6d84ee94-en.

Oxford Business Group (2017). Building activity in Saudi Arabia picks up as government launches new projects [Online]. Available at: https://oxfordbusinessgroup.com/analysis/catalyst-growth-introduction-white-land-tax-expected-engender-more-active-real-estate-market [Accessed November 2021].

Parker, C. and Debruyne, P. (2015). Reassembling the political: Placing contentious politics in Jordan. In *Contentious Politics in the Middle East*, Gerges, F.A. (ed.). Palgrave Macmillan, New York.

Schmid, H. (2002). The reconstruction of downtown Beirut in the context of political geography. *The Arab World Geographer*, 5(4), 232–248.

Schmid, H. (2009). *Economy of Fascination: Dubai and Las Vegas as Themed Urban Landscapes*. Gerbrüder Borntraeger, Berlin.

Shawkat, Y. (2015). Egypt's deregulated property market: A crisis of affordability. *Middle East Institute*, 2.

Shawkat, Y. (2020). *Egypt's Housing Crisis. The Shaping of Urban Space*. The American University in Cairo Press.

Singerman, D. (2009). *Cairo Cosmopolitan: Politics, Culture, and Urban Space in the New Globalized Middle East*. The American University in Cairo Press.

Sinno, M. (2017). L'internationalisation de la fabrique de la ville, vers un produit politique : les investissements immobiliers des pays du Golfe au Caire. PhD Thesis, Denis, E. (ed.). Université Paris 1 Panthéon-Sorbonne.

Tadamun. (2015). Egypt's new cities: Neither just nor efficient. *Tadamun: The Cairo Urban Solidarity Initiative* [Online]. Available at: http://www.tadamun.co/2015/12/31/egypts-new-cities-neither-just-efficient/?lang=en#.W_P705Mzbq0.

Theurillat, T. and Crevoisier, O. (2013). Sustainability and the anchoring of capital: Negotiations surrounding two major urban projects in Switzerland. *Regional Studies*, 48(3), 501–515.

Tierney, J. (2017). Constructing resilience: Real estate, investment, sovereign debt and Lebanon' transnational political economy. PhD Thesis, University of California, Berkeley.

Tobin, S. (2016). *Everyday Piety: Islam and Economy in Jordan*. Cornell University Press, New York.

Verdeil, É. (2001). Reconstructions manquées à Beyrouth : la poursuite de la guerre par le projet urbain. *Annales de la recherche urbaine – Villes et guerres*, 91, 65–73.

Verdeil, É. (2012). Michel Ecochard in Lebanon and Syria (1956–1968). The spread of modernism, the building of the independent states and the rise of local professionals of planning. *Planning Perspectives*, 27(2), 243–260.

Vignal, L. (2014). Dubai on Barada? The making of "globalised Damascus" in times of urban crisis. *Under Construction: Logics of Urbanism in the Gulf Region/edited by Steffen Wippel, Katrin Bromber, Christian Steiner*, 259–270.

Wahbah, Y., Moulay, A., Iqbal, M. (2016). Kingdom of Saudi Arabia White Land Tax, opportunities, implications and challenges for the real estate sector [Online]. Available at: http://www.ey.com/Publication/vwLUAssets/ey-ksa-white-land-tax/$FILE/ey-ksawhite-land-tax.pdf.

Wahdan, D. (2010). *Governing Livelihoods in Liberalizing States: A Comparative Study of Passenger Transport in Gurgaon, India and Sitta October, Egypt*. Lambert Academic Publishing, Saarbrücken.

Wiedman, F. and Salama, A.M. (2019). *Building Migrant Cities in the Gulf: Urban Transformation in the Middle East*. I.B. Tauris, London.

Zakaria, N., Ali, Z., Awang, M. (2019). White Land Tax: Evidence in the Kingdom of Saudi Arabia. *Journal of Accounting and Auditing: Research & Practice*, 2019, 218429.

9

Building Cities in West Africa: Construction Boom and Capitalism

Armelle CHOPLIN
Université de Genève, Geneva, Switzerland

In 2010, the international consulting firm McKinsey Global Institute (2010) published a report on the economic potential of African countries, then referred to as "lions on the move", an analogy similar to the Asian dragons (Pitcher 2012). It suggests that investing in Africa would be a worthy idea. In December 2011, the weekly magazine *The Economist* headlined "Africa Rising," heralding a boom in the African economy. In 2016, McKinsey reinforced this idea with "Lions on the move II: Realizing the potential of Africa's economies." A few years later, the term "growth(s)" is still written in the plural on the continent: demographic growth with a rate of 5% and 1.2 billion people; vigorous economic growth with double-digit rates and foreign direct investments in sharp increase; the strongest urban growth in the world as 50% of Africans are predicted to live in cities announced by 2030 (OECD/UNECA/AfDB 2022). African cities are seen as the last frontiers of capitalism and development (Watson 2014), perceived by international investors as the "last piece of cake" to be shared (Côté-Roy and Moser 2019). European, Indian, Brazilian, Turkish and Chinese people are investing, launching construction sites and building. New cities are springing up, and with them great hopes for economic development. The images of these futuristic projects, with their iconic architecture –

For a color version of all the figures in this chapter, see www.iste.co.uk/avelinedubach/globalization.zip.

Globalization and Dynamics of Urban Production,
coordinated by Natacha AVELINE-DUBACH. © ISTE Ltd 2023.

for example, Diamniadio in Dakar, Hope City in Accra, Konza in Nairobi or Eko Atlantic city in Lagos – are now being shown around the world (Watson 2014, 2020; Myers 2015; Van Noorloss and Kloosterboer 2018). Africa is experiencing a construction boom (Di Nunzio 2019), both in terms of infrastructure and housing, which translates into a high demand for concrete. In a few decades, Africa has become "the last great cement frontier" (White 2015) and this material, until recently still considered rare and reserved first for settlers and then for local elites, has spread among all strata of society (Choplin 2020, 2023).

This chapter proposes to explore the modes of urban production in Africa through its material make-up: cement and concrete. While it is increasingly difficult to grasp *those* who make the city, I propose here to focus on *what* makes the city, namely the building materials that constitute its foundations. I suggest focusing the analysis in particular on the cement industry and the concrete sector. Cement physically binds water and aggregates (sand, gravel or stone), which, after a few minutes of setting, turns into concrete. But cement also metaphorically links political issues, economic choices, social practices and environmental issues related to the urban environment. In order to grasp these different dimensions, the methodology chosen combines two approaches: the material turn (Ingold 2012; Schorch et al. 2020), which sheds light on materiality, and the *follow-the-things approach*, which makes it possible to trace an object from producer to consumer (Appadurai 1986; Cook 2004). This methodology, both multi-sited (Marcus 1995) and in motion like goods (Blaszkiewicz 2021), led me to West Africa, from limestone quarries to the plots of land in cities where bags of cement are opened to be made into concrete. In addition to the horizontal approach that follows the flows of materials, I also adopt a vertical, multi-scalar approach to capture the actors involved in the value chain at all levels: from the large cement groups and the state at the top, to the ordinary inhabitant at the bottom, who has their plot built, through contractors, real estate developers, government agencies and lessors, as well as masons, subcontractors and other intermediaries, who all, at their level, contribute to (de)regulating the market. The material flow approach is a relevant entry point for understanding other intangible flows, such as the circulation of capital, which is more complex to grasp.

This study examines the material production of the city from the West African corridor that links Abidjan (Côte d'Ivoire) to Lagos (Nigeria), via Accra, Lomé, Cotonou and Porto-Novo. Here, along this thin coastal strip wedged between the sea and the lagoon, a massive process of urbanization is at work, to the point of forming an urban corridor. If we focus on the 500 km between Accra and Lagos, more than 30 million people live, circulate, consume and… build. By 2050, statistics predict that there will be 50 million people (OECD/UNECA/AfDB 2022) (see:

http://africapolis.org)¹. The major cities that punctuate this corridor have been the subject of monographs (Gough and Yankson 2000; Gervais-Lambony and Nyassogbo 2007; Bertrand 2011; Ciavolella and Choplin 2018; Spire 2011; Dorier-Apprill et al. 2013; Sawyer 2016; Fourchard 2021), but I propose here to focus on the Abidjan–Lagos corridor as such. It provides an excellent example to grasp the new urban forms that are emerging and thus discuss the thesis of "planetary urbanization" announced by Lefebvre (1970) and then developed by Brenner and Schmid (2015).

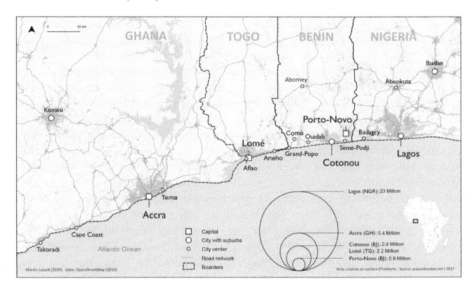

Figure 9.1. *The West African urban corridor*

This chapter first sheds light on the construction sector and the cement industry in West Africa, with particular attention paid to the actors who support the sector. It then explores the concrete urban forms that are taking shape, both along the corridor and within the city. In downtown areas and in a few strategic locations, towers and large projects are built within a few weeks. Elsewhere, housing programs described as "social" are built, supported by the state in search of private funds. Finally, in the peripheries, new urban areas are appearing, as a result of practices of self-building

---

1. This corridor connects major urban areas: Abidjan with 5 million inhabitants, Accra – 5.4 million, Lome – 2.2 million, Cotonou – 2.4 million, Porto-Novo – 900,000, Ibadan – 5 million, and Lagos, the largest city in sub-Saharan Africa with 23 million inhabitants in 2022 (source: https://africapolis.org/en).

day after day (Caldeira 2017; Gastrow 2017). Three types of habitat emerge; three temporalities; three modes of production. Of course, concrete is everywhere and links these different parts of the city, but there are respective money circuits, regimes of accumulation and actors. This chapter endeavors to reveal what is hidden *behind* cranes and towers under construction, financial arrangements and investment strategies, and foundations and finishes.

9.1. Construction boom and cement industry

"When construction goes, everything goes"... The old adage is more relevant than ever in Africa. More than 10 years after the 2008 global economic crisis and two years after the Covid-19 crisis, the construction and infrastructure sector is still growing. Cities are becoming the receptacles of this construction boom, produced by decrees and major projects, within showcase territories auctioned to the highest bidders. West African cities are following the entrepreneurial turn highlighted by Harvey (1989): managed as private companies, they are supposed to become smart, sustainable and/or green cities, by hosting new or satellite city projects. These projects inaugurate new links between capital, finance and real estate, as recently analyzed by Goodfellow (2017, 2020) in Ghana, Rwanda and Ethiopia. African land markets are becoming connected to international financial markets. Here, as elsewhere, the commodification of housing heralds a "new stage of capitalism" (Aalbers 2016). African cities are emerging as these new frontiers for private and real estate investment (Watson 2014; Gillespie 2020). Like Asian cities over the past two decades (Aveline-Dubach 2016; Shatkin 2008; Fauveaud 2020), they are being transformed by an increasing financialization of land and real estate policies.

The cement industry and the concrete sector accompany this financialization of cities and symbolize this new stage of capitalism, to the point of becoming its weapon of mass construction (Jappe 2020). Concrete is indeed a *spatial fix* that allows capital to anchor itself and capitalism to regenerate itself, to quote Harvey's (2001, 2016) theories. It is omnipresent in all constructions, in landscapes and in minds. Concrete boom goes with discourses of "Africa rising" (Ouma 2022) and "emergence" (Péclard et al. 2020). Cement production and consumption per capita is now taken as an index of development by donors and a symbol of growth, often compared to GDP. The world average is around 500 kg per capita per year (White 2015). The World Bank considers that a mature urban country, with a completed urban transition, would hover around approximately 400 kg per capita (White 2015; Byiers et al. 2017). In Africa, the kg cement/per capita ratio is still low, with an average of 115 kg and marked differences between countries: 121 kg in Nigeria,

180 kg in Benin, 211 kg in Ghana, 83 kg in Cameroon. With an annual increase in the consumption of 5% per capita, the room for improvement is immense (White 2015). This demand is generating a market that is becoming more structured, linked to the emergence of the middle classes and diasporas, as well as to the millions of poor people who consume and build. Forty (2012, p. 40), who has studied the history of concrete, reminds us that "reinforced concrete is one of the new technologies of poverty" that has enabled the democratization of construction by reaching poor populations, "with no professional or technical training". It lends itself well to standardization, with its mass manufactured blocks prefabricated since the 1950s. The concrete block has thus become the ingot of impoverished people.

The cement giants have understood the importance of capturing this new market: businesspeople, (Lafarge)Holcim, Heidelberg and Dangote are in fierce competition in Africa. No less than 10 cement plants have opened in the 2010s in West Africa, and others are expected to open soon. Cement is not new to Africa, but until recently, cement was mainly imported in the form of clinker, then ground and bagged in African ports. However, since the 2000s, because it is a heavy material and difficult to transport, the major groups have been investing heavily in Africa, where they have been opening more and more cement plants, this time integrated, which directly exploit West African limestone deposits. In addition, it was indeed too expensive to produce locally due to the lack of sufficient energy supply. In recent years, cement plants have built power plants on their own sites, most of them independent of the national grid. Cement is now produced entirely on site. Thus, cement, until then considered an emblematic product of colonial domination and synonymous with dependence, is becoming a mark of local national identities. Nearly 60 years later, cement has been "Africanized": local populations are proud to buy and consume cement "from the country", one of the few goods produced locally, alongside beer, iron and some agro-food products.

The figure of Dangote has played an important role in the "Africanization" of the material. In just a few years, this Nigerian businessman has become the main cement producer in Africa, and above all the richest man in Nigeria, as well as in Africa, with the 25th greatest fortune in the world (Akinyoade and Uche 2016). Founded in 1977, the group, which has 24,000 employees, heads more than 10 integrated cement plants and operates in 10 countries. Dangote has managed, in the space of two decades, to shake up a cement sector largely dominated by large private and foreign multinationals that have set up subsidiaries in Africa (Akinyoade and Uche 2016). Dangote is certainly the cement company that has most influenced the West African market, forcing it to be completely reconfigured in less than 10 years.

9.2. City-making: actors and sectors

"Building tomorrow's Africa today" ((Lafarge)Holcim Morocco) or *"Enriching the lives of Africans"* thanks to this material that has become *"vital and irreplaceable"* (Dangote), this is how cement companies present their activities on their websites. They propose to put a roof over the heads of the greatest number of people, to pave roads, to build schools and hospitals for the good of all, to the great delight of donors and politicians who see cement as a vehicle by which they can "emerge". These companies seem to put everyone in agreement, responding to the injunctions of both modernity and development. Hence, the immense enthusiasm and consensus around cement, which serves the interests of the most influential and wealthy, as well as those of the poor, who are promised a way out of poverty by pouring concrete.

Donors, cooperation agencies and technical and financial partners, such as the World Bank, the International Monetary Fund or the French Development Agency, largely support the cement industry. In its report *"Breaking Down Barriers: Unlocking Africa's Potential through Vigorous Competition Policy"*, published in 2016, the World Bank makes cement a key element to "boosting productivity, innovation and inclusive growth", just like fertilizers and telecommunications. Cement is presented as a source of significant profits, not only for large Western companies and developers now present in Africa, but also for all actors in the construction sector, and by the expected trickle-down effect, for households themselves. The World Bank insists on the competition that would force cement manufacturers to lower their prices. Cement is considered a "basic necessity", like bread or a bag of rice, and has a price ceiling in several countries in the region. Its production and marketing are subject to political support from donors, who until recently were not very concerned about the energy performance and environmental impacts of this highly polluting industry.

This benevolent stance by donors is related to the importance they now place on cities as drivers of economic development. UN-Habitat (2012, p. 6) has identified megaregions, urban corridors and city-regions (*megacity* and *mega-city region*) as major areas that can make a significant contribution to global economic production. The metropolitan level has thus gradually emerged as the preferred level of intervention in a globalized and neoliberal context (Brenner 2004). This observation, which was first made in the west, would also apply to Africa. At least that is what is implied in the 2009 World Bank report *"Reshaping Economic Geography"*, which considers cities as development opportunities and proposes growth by scale (Giraut 2009). The report explains that certain spaces, such as metropolitan areas or coastal zones, are necessary anchors for globalization and competitiveness, and that economic growth and its corollary, urban growth, are supposed to act as a lever for development in the surrounding territories, through a *trickle-down* effect. These principles were affirmed in the Sustainable Development Goals (SDGs) in September 2015 and at the UN Habitat III summit in Quito in October 2016. Development banks, such as the African Development Bank, the Islamic Development Bank and the French Development Agency, are financing large urban, transport and infrastructure projects in West African capitals. Roads are the backbone of this project, such as in the CORAL project (Corridor of Abidjan-Lagos), which is supposed to improve traffic flow and facilitate trade along the Abidjan–Lagos road axis, which concentrates 75% of the zone's economic activities (Banque Africaine de Développement 2016). It is along this corridor that cement circulates intensively, thanks to the support of states that consider it an essential commodity and are ready to implement advantageous customs policies by eliminating import taxes within the framework of ECOWAS[2]. By this rationale of regional integration, the African Union and ECOWAS largely support the Dangote company and its strategy, which they consider to be in line with their principles, since it aims to limit West Africa's foreign dependence. Cement is a reflection of reconfigurations with the state, the alliances and clientelism that influence the capitalist sector and the price of the product itself. No cement plant can be implemented without the solid support of a bank, donors and the state. The state must intervene to encourage foreign companies to invest in this sector, which is certainly profitable, but requires heavy investment (Akinola 2019).

Presidents themselves seek to assert themselves as builders, and to do this they win over voters with roads, pipes, paving stones and tar. They are generally confronted with two forms of time period: that of relatively short presidential terms and that of longer project cycles. Presidents are judged on their visible actions, and in particular the number of buildings that come up. They then tend to join with the state, which becomes a largely privatized investor (Hibou 1999), in search of emergening and profitable (urban) projects to support (Pitcher 2012, 2017; Péclard et al. 2020). Heads of state have, in becoming entrepreneurs themselves, developed closer ties with businessmen, especially cement and construction contractors. Since the 1990s, successive Nigerian governments, which are highly protectionist, have largely favored the establishment of Dangote's monopoly, by lowering taxes, selling back its shares to Dangote when the cement industry was privatized, and facilitating the export of its products (Akinola 2019).

---

2. The Economic Community of West African States (ECOWAS) is an intergovernmental organization created in 1975 to promote cooperation and integration among its 16 member countries. In particular, it facilitates the free movement of people and goods within the zone, in order to boost trade and economies.

The cement sector, and by extension the construction sector, highlights the alliances, co-optations and kinship between the political and private sectors, and informal practices, not to mention corruption, that are well known in the region (Blundo and Olivier de Sardan 2007). Concrete has become a political and geopolitical object of primary importance, intrinsically mixing business and politics. With the recent opening of new cement factories and a sector that is now entirely African, or at least presented as such, a whole urban political economy is being put in place, which feeds the local economy and allows the emergence and reproduction of elites and entrepreneurs. The actors in the urban fabric are numerous: the state and heads of state, of course, as well as developers and real estate agents, banks, diasporas, importers of building materials and construction companies, digital operators... All of them are making the city a huge construction site.

9.3. Concrete, towers and megaprojects

In the city centers of large African metropolises, luxury megaprojects and infrastructures, private or public–private, reserved for the elite, are emerging following the example of those now well-known and studied in Asia (Shatkin 2008; Goldman 2011) and in the MENA (Middle East and North Africa) region (Choplin and Franck 2010). They are indicative of new modes of urban production in which the city would be both a receiver and a producer of wealth (Watson 2014; Goodfellow 2017, 2020; Fält 2019). The announcement of these large projects makes it possible to demarcate zones, where foreign investors, with the support of the governments in place, deploy their operations according to their own rules. Following opaque land deals, these areas are generally sold for symbolic sums of money or are leased, with long leases that leave considerable room for maneuver. They escape local legislation and become "territories of the exception" (Roy 2011). In India, Goldman (2011) described this urbanism as "speculative": in the name of the strategy of building global cities, exceptional rules of dispossession emerge, redrawing the contours of relations between state, urban citizens, rights and conditions of access. States themselves are using the urbanization process to extend their power. In Asia, they support these projects by selling land, reclaiming land and privatizing urban planning (Shatkin 2008). In Asia, as elsewhere in Africa, we are witnessing the production of "new types of territory, authority and rights that fall outside the reach of existing public institutional frameworks" (Herbert and Murray 2015, p. 489). Beforehand, the spaces involved and coveted are usually cleared of potential street vendors, squatters and other poor inhabitants, following policies of decongestion and beautification, which lead to violent and recurrent evictions (Spire and Choplin 2018). These territories of exception exacerbate exclusion, injustice and segregation, as has been reported for African new towns (Van Noorloos and Kloosterboer 2018; Fält 2019).

In Nigeria, kilometers of concrete have been poured to cope with rising waters and coastal erosion. The dam is impressive: 8.5 kilometers long, 18 meters high, 10 of which are under water and eight of which are in the open air, and 100,000 concrete blocks. The project is justified by ecological necessity, as well as, and above all by economic necessity, as stated in the project document *Eko Atlantic Milestones: Shaping the Future*, signed by the then President of Nigeria, Goodluck, the Governor of Lagos and supported by the former American President Bill Clinton. The funds are totally private, coming from two wealthy Lebanese–Nigerian brothers and businessmen Ronald and Gilbert Chagoury. The project was supported by Bill Clinton and his Foundation, in exchange for funds received from R. Chagoury (Côté-Roy and Moser 2019). More than 100 million tons of the sand were dredged from the seabed and dumped to produce a polder and accommodate the new, yet widely reviled, city of Eko Atlantic (Acey 2018; Mendelsohn 2018). This artificially created 10 million m^2 area is supposed to host a "Global City – World Class Design", where "good living meets great business". Access to it will be controlled and limited, a veritable gated community in the heart of Lagos.

Some 300 kilometers away, Ghana's capital city is also undergoing many transformations. The coastline has been cleared to accommodate the Marina Drive Project, a vast luxury residential, business and commercial area in a $1.2 billion public–private partnership (Fält 2019). Nearby, a new Chinese-funded fishing complex is slated to open in the historic core of Jamestown, causing evictions in May 2020. Downtown, the Octogon project, a luxury residential and commercial complex, has now taken the place of an informal vendor market after bitter resistance (Spire and Choplin 2018). Heavy road improvements have been launched by the government to ease traffic flow, particularly at the Nkruma Circle interchange. Several projects are also planned for the outskirts of Accra, around Tema and Prampram, such as Hope City, announced since 2013 as the future technology park of Ghana. The Ningo-Prampram project for the urban extension of Greater Accra is supposed to accommodate 1.5 million inhabitants, with the support of UN-Habitat, international consultants and local leaders, demonstrating the global connections of this space (Grant et al. 2019). A few miles north, Appolonia City is designed to soon accommodate 88,000 residents. So far, only a few houses have been sold. According to Fält (2019), this project reflects the emergence of a "privatized urbanism" in which a whole constellation of actors is evolving, from the state to the traditional authorities and real estate developers. Fält points out the contradiction between this mega-project, which targets an international elite, and the model officially presented as a sustainable and inclusive project.

In Benin, a smart city, named Sèmè City, is supposed to be built just outside of Cotonou, a few kilometers from Nigeria. The Sèmè City Development Agency is directly linked to the Presidency of the Republic. The future *smart city*, whose slogan is "innovation made in Africa", is supposed to counterbalance the "skills desert" and the mismatch between the job market and graduates of the national university. The project is supposed to create 200,000 jobs and welcome 40,000 "learners" from all over Africa, especially from neighboring Nigeria. Among the training courses offered, an African City Lab has been set up jointly by EPFL, Nkrumah University (Ghana), Mohamed VI Polytechnic University (Morocco), the University of Cape Town (South Africa) and the University of Rwanda. The Lab also offers online MOOCs (Massive Online Open Courses) on urban issues. The Sèmè City project has received a lot of media attention in Benin, supported by the head of state, and even more outside Benin, without local elected officials having been informed. The territory selected was taken out of the regime of communal laws and placed under the control of the presidential agency. The Singaporean group Surbana Jurong was commissioned by the Beninese government to develop the city's future master plan. This consulting firm is well known in Africa for having developed the Kigali Masterplan 2050 (Michelon 2016; Goodfellow 2017; Bock 2018). Rumors say that during his first trip to Rwanda, Beninese President Talon sought advice from President Kagame on urban management, as Kigali is now perceived as the best managed and cleanest city in Africa. The Surbana Jurong group was suggested to him. This example illustrates the circulation of models, from Singapore to Cotonou, via Kigali, reminding us of the extent to which urban models, ideas and currents of thought circulate throughout the world and on the African continent. It shows how "mobile" urbanism is, through those models that aim to modernize the city and make it more competitive, carrying with them so-called good practices and serving to support neoliberal reforms (McCann and Ward 2011; Parnell and Robinson 2012; Soderstöm 2014; Peck and Theodore 2015). In this case, the connections between the political regimes of Benin, Rwanda and Singapore are transposed into the synthetic images produced from the Asian city-state. The Asian model of success has thus traveled, first to Kigali, now labeled as the model African city and the "Singapore of Africa", and then to Cotonou, which Benin's leaders dream of transforming into "Kigali-on-the-sea."

Figure 9.2. *Sèmè City (source: Surbana Jurong 2017)*

These different projects show that the city is now seen as a new marketing asset. It is becoming a political support and a capitalist tool, as shown by the advertising panels that are flourishing in the streets and show future real estate projects that are as pharaonic as they are hypothetical (De Boeck and Baloji 2016). The latter often remain at the stage of "fantasy" and computer-generated images, produced by international groups that copy and paste skyscrapers (Watson 2020). Nearly 10 years after the announcement, there is no trace of Hope City; in Eko Atlantic, the towers can be counted on the fingers of one hand; as for Sèmè City, the Agency's offices decorated with 3D images of the Singaporeans remain located in an annex of the Presidency of the Republic. Some of these projects are ephemeral or on standby, which makes it difficult to gather information and monitor the actors involved. In the meantime, whether real or virtual, they play a performative role, showing a "Dubaization" of the African city (Choplin and Franck 2010, p. 193; Di Nunzio 2019, p. 378). In many cities, these hypothetical projects are supposed to be developed on large land reserves, in strategic positions (downtown, waterfront...). While waiting for them to be built, these plots of land have been allocated to foreign investors, following transactions facilitated by a lack of regulation, in exchange for modest sums or very advantageous long leases. The city, as it is taking shape, and its opaque links with the world of finance, serves the construction and real estate sectors.

9.4. "Social" housing programs

In parallel with the large private projects aimed at the elite, so-called "social" housing programs are regularly launched by the governments in place. They are based on agreements between the state, the private sector and banks, encouraged by international donors who support the affordable housing policy. Since 2012, the FSD (Financial Sector Deepening) Africa group, which specializes in housing markets, has been funded by the United Kingdom through UK Aid, which has a mandate to develop financial markets across sub-Saharan Africa. The think tank "Center for affordable Housing Finance in Africa," based in South Africa, is supported and funded by: UK Aid, FAD (French Agency of Development), Cities Alliance, FSD Africa and the Mastercard Foundation. The WAEMU (West African Economic and Monetary Union – UEMAO) and the World Bank are also supporting the development of this affordable housing sector, which reveals close links between donors, banks, governments in place and the local elites and diasporas that are targeted by these programs.

Somewhat surprisingly, banks have had little presence in the real estate sector in West Africa to date. The low development of local banking systems, combined with the predominance of informal employment and the absence of regular, short-term income, explains the low rate of bank penetration. This leads to prohibitive interest rates, which are an obstacle to taking out real estate loans. Individual projects are poorly supported by the banking sector. In Benin and Togo, loan rates are approximately 12–13%, sometimes reaching 25% (compared to an average of 2.5% in Europe today). The poorest cannot qualify for a bank loan, while the richest and especially members of the diaspora prefer to pay in cash, whether to buy land or pay for construction work, in order to avoid any dispute with other potential buyers.

Banks' interest in the real estate sector is recent, as Gillespie (2020) shows in the case of Ghana and Goodfellow (2020) in East Africa. As the latter observed in Addis Ababa and Kigali, West African banks are essentially offering loans for major economic players and companies approved by the banks themselves. But more than that, they tend to play a major role in social housing programs launched by West African presidents. In the Ivory Coast, Alassan Ouattara launched his Presidential Program for Social and Economic Housing (*Programme présidentiel de logements sociaux et économiques*, PPLSE) in 2013. In Benin, Patrice Talon launched his "20,000 social housing program" in 2018. In 2020, Macky Sall promised the Senegalese 100,000 social housing units within five years, while Faure Nassigbé is promising 20,000 to the Togolese people. As N'goran et al. (2020) have shown, based on the case of Côte d'Ivoire and the 150,000 housing units promised, these projects are part of the discourse of emergence and the redeployment of the state through social housing policies. These projects reveal interesting financial arrangements, placing private investment at the center: "The state is no longer the direct contributor as it was in the 1970s-1980s, but rather a market regulator" (N'goran et al. 2020). The state guarantee limits the risks and thus allows interest rates to be lowered, at least in theory. In the case of the Côte d'Ivoire, however, the results are mixed: the state is struggling to regulate the market and, on the contrary, has made it possible "to expand the sphere of political patronage to the private sector" (N'goran et al. 2020).

Ten kilometers north of Cotonou, in Ouédo, in the commune of Abomey Calavi, trucks loaded with sand come and go. The neighborhood is supposed to host the "20,000 social and economic housing program", the 40th and latest flagship project launched by the Talon government in 2019. On a 235-hectare site, more than 4,000 buildings and 10,000 homes will be built, mainly apartments (7,310) and villas (3,539). The promotional video shows that an administrative city is also supposed to be built, to which commercial and leisure facilities and green spaces are to be added. The financing comes from the West African Development Bank (100 billion for 3,035 housing units), the Islamic Development Bank (43 billion for 2,145 housing units), the National Social Security Fund (90 billion for 3,099 housing units) and private partners. A real estate and urban development company (*société immobilière et d'aménagement urbain*, SIMAU) has been created to implement the social housing program and the ministerial city. The shareholders mentioned on the website are: "*the state of Benin, BOAD (Banque Ouest Africaine de Développement, insurance companies and local banks*", as well as the Duval Group, a French company specialized in real estate and investment, already present in Cameroon, Togo, Senegal and Côte d'Ivoire. In December 2019, a contract was signed between SIMAU and the Spanish company PN HG, which has set up a subsidiary in Benin, to build the first set of 1,735 housing units over 18 months in 2020.

From the promotional videos, financial arrangements and private actors involved, it is obvious that these programs are "social" in name only. They reflect new modes of urban production, in which the private sector has become predominant. The presidential construction programs give primacy to real estate developers, investment companies and pension funds, development banks, international banking groups and private foundations. These projects raise questions about the government's choices to offer these opportunities to the private sector without being able to regulate them completely. They also question the role of official development assistance, whose primary goal is to reduce poverty, but which, in this case, contributes to financing and subsidizing housing for the upper classes.

These programs and the intervention of these new actors are part of the neoliberal turn taken by the cities. They are also indicative of the connection of African real estate markets with global finance. Of course, unlike what is observed in Asia (Aveline-Dubach 2016; Fauveaud 2020), the financialization of real estate is only in its infancy in Africa. However, these examples of programs, whether so-called social or mega-projects, show that real estate is becoming a financial asset. The links between political powers, the banking sector and private investors, and more generally, the circulation of capital in the city, need to be analyzed in even greater detail. For, beyond the satisfaction of leaders, who congratulate themselves on attracting capital and seeing buildings rise from the ground, the results raise questions. Private actors, and indirectly the state, are participating in the production of fragmented cities. These projects allow the authorities and their private partners to appropriate land resources, by reclassifying the public domain and taking over private land thanks to the regalian rights used to expropriate at low cost. Far from the ideal of the inclusive and just city that the model is supposed to set out, this contributes to the land rent capture exercised by private actors associated with the state, which delegates the responsibility of implementing social housing policies (N'goran et al. 2020).

Figure 9.3. *Container for retail cement sales in the outskirts of Cotonou (source: © Choplin 2017)*

9.5. Self-build and incremental urbanization

In the distant outskirts of Abidjan, Accra, Lomé, Cotonou, Porto-Novo and Lagos, concrete is omnipresent, accompanying the urbanization front that seems to retreat endlessly. However, unlike the large private initiative projects and the social housing programs promoted by the state, the city is erected here on the backs of inhabitants, who, with few resources, pile up concrete blocks, often of inferior quality. The construction sites are directly supervised by the inhabitants, who practice self-construction (Caldeira 2017; Gastrow 2018). In places, we can still glimpse bits of sheet metal and wood, stigmata of poverty and remnants of a slum that has recently been sealed and hardened with cement.

This urbanization is above all incremental (Van Noorloos et al. 2020), the result of a city that is built day by day, as money flows into ordinary households. For ordinary people, who have little access to the banking system or are wary of taking out loans from a bank, buying bags of cement and building brick by brick is a way of hoarding money (Archambault 2017). This explains the omnipresence of hardware stores and cement dealers. Building materials, a sign of an imminent construction site, as well as a sign indicating the name of the owner are usually stored in the middle of the plots.

These building materials can remain stored on the plots for weeks or even months. The building work can be spread out over many years depending on the regularity of income of the owner. The purchase of concrete-reinforcing bars must be added to the cement bricks, then the roof sheets, as well as the screens and windows. It is still necessary to find a reliable mason and to come and visit the site regularly to make sure that the work is progressing. As Norbert sums up, a little fatalistically:

> Everyone is looking for their "home" ("son chez" in French). As soon as you start working, you want your home, so you tighten your belt. You save up little by little to get the plot of land first and then build your house. Finally, often, you finish all that when you get to retirement and that's when you die, when you take possession of the property (Interview, Cotonou, December 2016).

Building allows an individual to access a certain social status, that of owner of a built plot. *"Building is part of the dreams of most Beninese city dwellers. It is a measure of social success and of the place that the individual deserves among his or her own people"* (Chabi 2013). Through the hardness and durability of concrete, the inhabitants dare to project themselves and take a long-term view, which traditional local materials such as wood or straw do not allow. A young architect, Romaric, explained: *"When I propose these materials to my clients, they refuse. They say it's for the bush*" (Interview, Porto-Novo, January 2017). These materials are also connotative: in the city, straw and bamboo are reminiscent of illegal occupations. Acquiring bags of cement and building with concrete takes on a particular meaning in neighborhoods marked by great economic precariousness, which is accentuated by recurrent heavy rains. During the three months of annual floods that can wash away everything, concrete is the only thing left. As soon as they can, households plaster the dirt floor with cement and then put up cement walls. Unlike mud houses, which must be rebuilt after each rainy season, cement houses require little maintenance, because *"Brick does not rot"*, as the Ivorian proverb says. Sheet metal also tends to replace straw roofs, which rot quickly and are flammable. In this situation of uncertainty, the use of concrete means an end to the hassle and extra cost of maintenance. However, everyone agrees that concrete, which retains heat, is not at all suited to the humid tropical climate.

In the face of recurrent evictions and forms of dispossession in the region (Gillespie 2016), using permanent materials and building in concrete is also a way to express demands for greater integration into the city and lay the foundation for claiming urban citizenship. For Morton (2019), in the case of Maputo, where cement has long been reserved for settlers only, building with cement can be interpreted as a political act of defiance against the powers that be. Building in concrete allows us to establish our presence in the long term and break away from insecurity. No longer accepting destitution in materials such as bamboo and sheet metal, no longer being at the mercy of eviction policies and rains, building hard, laying the foundations, climbing to higher ground: all these are material and political acts that symbolize the fact of existing, of being legitimate to stay here. In this sense, cement materializes the right to be in the city and to stay there – a first stone towards a "right to the city" (Lefebvre 1968).

9.6. Conclusion

Along the corridor that runs from Abidjan to Lagos, cement and concrete are present everywhere: in the gray color, in the bags on the plots or the bricks for sale on the sides of the road, in the minds of individuals. Thanks to its different lives – political, economic and social – concrete opens up possibilities to grasp the urban production, its temporalities and the different, changing forms it takes. This concrete corridor that takes shape is made by capital and politics, as well as and above all by millions of individuals who try to access property, build and therefore exist. It is also the result of arrangements, of intertwined logics of informality and survival, as well as of close links with politics. In Lagos, Porto-Novo, Cotonou, Lomé or Accra, and between and around these poles, heads of state build, private companies invest and the actors of the building industry put the city under construction. As for the inhabitants, they experiment and redefine city-making in its forms, temporalities and materialities, and this through their relationship with cement and concrete, which link, connect, manufacture and destroy individuals and spaces. This research has allowed us to explore some facets of this urban corridor (Choplin 2020; Choplin and Hertzog 2020), but it leaves some questions unanswered.

The widespread use of cement and concrete construction indeed raises many environmental challenges. The cement industry is one of the most polluting in the world: it contributes to 8% of global anthropogenic greenhouse gas emissions (IPCC 2022). In addition, increasingly recurrent collapses (the Genoa Bridge in Europe and buildings in Africa) call into question its longevity, especially in Africa (Smith 2020). Its obsolescence is programmed (Harvey 2016; Jappe 2020) and controversies are multiplying to question the systematic use of this material. The question of energy efficiency and environmental sustainability of cement industry projects is more acute in Africa, where concrete is hardly adapted to the hot climate, and its widespread use implies the use of air conditioning. Initiatives, such as that of the Burkinabe architect Francis Kéré, who received the Pritzker Prize (the highest distinction in architecture) in March 2022, or the Fact Sahel + network, which brings together architects, masons and engineers who promote bio-sourced materials, are launched to find alternatives to all-concrete. Cement manufacturers themselves say they want to think about setting up less energy-intensive production processes, and some are hesitantly supporting the development of green cement. In the meantime, the 'Concrete City' (Choplin 2023), as it is unfolding in West Africa, and elsewhere, invites us to reflect on our urban futures and, more broadly, on the habitability of our urban spaces and of the planet.

9.7. References

Aalbers, M.B. (2016). *The Financialization of Housing: A Political Economy Approach*. Routledge, London. doi: 10.4324/9781315668666.

Acey, C. (2018). Rise of the synthetic city: Eko Atlantic and practices of dispossession and repossession in Nigeria. In *Disassembled Cities: Social and Spatial Strategies to Reassemble Communities*, Sweet, E.L. (ed.). Routledge, Abingdon and New York.

Akindès, F. and Kouamé, S.Y. (2019). L'immixtion "par le bas" des technologies digitales dans la vie urbaine africaine. *Afrique contemporaine*, 269–270(1), 87. doi: 10.3917/afco.269.0087.

Akinola, A.O. (2019). Rent seeking and industrial growth in Africa: The case of Dangote's cement industry. *The Rest*, 9(1), 6–17.

Akinyoade, A. and Uche, C. (2016). Dangote cement: An African success story? African Studies Centre Leiden, ASC Working Paper 131/2016, 1–40.

Appadurai, A. (1986). *The Social Life of Things: Commodities in Cultural Perspective.* Cambridge University Press, Cambridge and New York. doi: 10.1017/CBO9780511819582.

Archambault, J. (2018). "One beer, one block": Concrete aspiration and the stuff of transformation in a Mozambican suburb. *Journal of the Royal Anthropological Institute,* 24(4), 692–708. doi: 10.1111/1467-9655.12912.

Aveline-Dubach, N. (2016). Land and real estate in Northeast Asia, new approaches in an era of financialization. *Issues & Studies*, 52(4), 11. doi: 10.1142/S101325111602001.

Banque Africaine de Développement (2016). Rapport Annuel 2016. Département Infrastructures, Villes et Développement Urbain. Report, BAD.

Bertrand, M. (2011). *De Bamako à Accra. Mobilités urbaines et ancrages locaux en Afrique de l'Ouest.* Karthala, Paris.

Blaszkiewicz, H. (2021). Using the flow regimes framework to de-hierarchise the analysis of commercial movements: Case studies from the central African Copperbelt. *Transactions of the Institute of British Geographers.* doi: 10.1111/tran.12439.

Blundo, G. and Olivier de Sardan, J.-P. (2007). *Etat et corruption en Afrique.* Karthala, Paris. doi: 10.3917/kart.blund.2007.01.

Bock, S. (2018). *Translations of Urban Regulation in Relations between Kigali (Rwanda) and Singapore.* LIT Verlag, Münster.

Brenner, N. (2004). *New State Spaces: Urban Governance and the Rescaling of Statehood.* Oxford University Press, Oxford.

Brenner, N. and Schmid, C. (2015). Towards a new epistemology of the urban? *City*, 19(2–3), 151–182. doi: 10.1080/13604813.2015.1014712.

Byiers, B., Karaki, K., Vanheukelom, J. (2017). Regional markets, politics and value chains: The case of West African cement. *European Centre For Development Policy Management*, 216 [Online]. Available at: www.ecdpm.org/dp216.

Caldeira, T.P. (2017). Peripheral urbanization: Autoconstruction, transversal logics, and politics in cities of the global south. *Environment and Planning D: Society and Space*, 35(1), 3–20. doi: 10.1177/0263775816658479.

Chabi, M. (2013). Métropolisation et dynamiques périurbaines : cas de l'espace urbain de Cotonou. Geography PhD Thesis, Université de Nanterre, Paris.

Choplin, A. (2020). Cementing Africa: Cement flows and city making in the west African corridor (Accra-Lomé-Cotonou-Lagos). *Urban Studies*, 57(9), 1977–1993. doi: 10.1177/0042098019851949.

Choplin, A. (2023). *Concrete City. Material Flows and Urbanization in West Africa.* Wiley, Oxford.

Choplin, A. and Franck, A. (2010). A glimpse of Dubai in Khartoum and Nouakchott: Prestige urban projects on the margins of the Arab World. *Built Environment*, 36(2), 192–205. doi: 10.2148/benv.36.2.192.

Choplin, A. and Hertzog, A. (2020). The West-African corridor, from Abidjan to Lagos: A Mega-city region under construction. In *Handbook of Megacities and Megacity-Regions*, Labbe, D. and Sorensen, A. (eds). Edward Elgar Publishing Ltd, Cheltenham.

Ciavolella R. and Choplin A. (2018). *Cotonou(s). Histoire d'une ville sans Histoire*. Cahiers de la Fondation Zinsou, IRD, Cotonou.

Cook, I. (2004). Follow the thing: Papaya. *Antipode*, 36(4), 642–664. doi: 10.1111/j.1467-8330.2004.00441.x.

Côté-Roy, L. and Moser, S. (2019). Does Africa not deserve shiny new cities? The power of seductive rhetoric around new cities in Africa. *Urban Studies*, 56(12), 2391–2407. doi: 10.1177/0042098018793032.

Datta, A. (2021). Fast urbanism: Between speed, time and urban futures. *Transcient Space and Societies*. doi: 10.34834/2019.0017.

De Boeck, F. and Baloji, S. (2016) *Suturing the City. Living Together in Congo's Urban Worlds*. Autograph ABP, London.

Di Nunzio, M. (2019) Not my job: Architecture, responsibility and inequalities in an African metropolis. *Anthropological Quarterly*, 92(2), 375–402.

Dorier, E., Tafuri, C., Agossou, N. (2013). Porto-Novo dans l'aire métropolitaine littorale du Sud-Bénin : quelles dynamiques citadines ? In *Porto-Novo : patrimoine et développement*, Mengin, C. and Godonou, A. (eds). Publications de la Sorbonne, Paris.

Fält, L. (2019). New cities and the emergence of "privatized urbanism" in Ghana. *Built Environment*, 44(4), 438–460(23). doi: 10.2148/benv.44.4.438.

Fauveaud, G. (2020). The new frontiers of housing financialization in Phnom Penh, Cambodia: The condominium boom and the foreignization of housing markets in the global south. *Housing Policy Debate*, 1–19. doi: 10.1080/10511482.2020.1714692.

Forty, A. (2012). *Concrete and Culture: A Material History*. Reaktion Books, London.

Fourchard, L. (2021). *Classify, Exclude, Police: Urban Lives in South Africa and Nigeria*. Wiley, Oxford.

Gastrow, C. (2017). Cement citizens: Housing, demolition and political belonging in Luanda, Angola. *Citizenship Studies*, 21(2), 224–239. doi: 10.1080/13621025.2017.1279795.

Gervais-Lambony, P. and Nyassogbo, G. (eds) (2007). *Lomé : dynamiques d'une ville africaine*. Karthala, Paris.

Gillespie, T. (2016). Accumulation by urban dispossession: Struggles over urban space in Accra, Ghana. *Transactions of the Institute of British Geographers*, 41(1), 66–77.

Gillespie, T. (2020). The real estate frontier. *International Journal of Urban and Regional Research*, 44(4), 599–616. doi: 10.1111/1468-2427.12900.

Giraut, F. (2009). Les ambiguïtés de la nouvelle doctrine spatiale de la Banque mondiale. *Cybergeo: European Journal of Geography* [Online]. Available at: http://journals.openedition.org/cybergeo/22695.

Goldman, M. (2011). Speculative urbanism and the making of the next world city: Speculative urbanism in Bangalore. *International Journal of Urban and Regional Research*, 35(3), 555–581. doi: 10.1111/j.1468-2427.2010.01001.x.

Goodfellow, T. (2017). Urban fortunes and skeleton cityscapes: Real estate and late urbanization in Kigali and Addis Ababa. *International Journal of Urban and Regional Research*, 41(5), 786–803. doi: 10.1111/1468-2427.12550.

Goodfellow, T. (2020). Finance, infrastructure and urban capital: The political economy of African "gap-filling". *Review of African Political Economy*, 47(164), 1–19. doi: 10.1080/03056244.2020.1722088.

Gough, K.V. and Yankson, P.W.K. (2000). Land markets in African cities: The case of peri-urban Accra, Ghana. *Urban Studies*, 37(13), 2485–2500. doi: 10.1080/00420980020080651.

Grant, R., Oteng-Ababio, M., Sivilien, J. (2019). Greater Accra's new urban extension at Ningo-Prampram: Urban promise or urban peril? *International Planning Studies*, 24(3–4), 325–340. doi: 10.1080/13563475.2019.1664896.

Harvey, D. (1989). From managerialism to entrepreneurialism: The transformation in urban governance in late capitalism. *Geografiska Annaler. Series B, Human Geography*, 71(1), 3–17. doi: 10.2307/490503.

Harvey, D. (2001) *Spaces of Capital: Towards a Critical Geography*. Routledge, New York.

Harvey, D. (2016). *Abstract from the Concrete*. Sternberg Press, Berlin.

Herbert, C.W. and Murray, M.J. (2015). Building from scratch: New cities, privatized urbanism and the spatial restructuring of Johannesburg after apartheid: Privatized urbanism in Johannesburg after apartheid. *International Journal of Urban and Regional Research*, 39(3), 471–494. doi: 10.1111/1468-2427.12180.

Hibou, B. (1999). *Priviatizing the State*. Columbia University Press, New York.

Ingold, T. (2012). Toward an ecology of materials. *Annual Review of Anthropology*, 41(1), 427–442. doi: 10.1146/annurev-anthro-081309-145920.

IPCC (2022). Climate Change 2022: Mitigation of Climate Change. Contribution of Working Group III to the Sixth Assessment Report of the Intergovernmental Panel on Climate Change. Cambridge University Press, Cambridge and New York. doi: 10.1017/9781009157926.

Jappe, A. (2020). *Béton : arme de construction massive du capitalisme*. Echappée, Paris.

Lefebvre, H. (1968). *Le droit à la ville*. Anthropos, Paris.

Lefebvre, H. (1970). *La révolution urbaine*. Gallimard, Paris.

Marcus, G.E. (1995). Ethnography in/of the world system: The emergence of multi-sited ethnography. *Annual Review of Anthropology*, 24, 95–117.

McCann, E. and Ward, K. (2011). *Mobile Urbanism: Cities and Policymaking in the Global Age*. University of Minnesota Press, Minneapolis.

McKinsey Global Institute (2010). Lions on the move: The progress and potential of African economies. Report, McKinsey Global Institute, McKinsey & Company [Online]. Available at: https://www.mckinsey.com/featured-insights/middle-east-and-africa/lions-on-the-move.

Mendelsohn, B. (2018). Making the urban coast: A geosocial reading of land, sand, and water in Lagos, Nigeria. *Comparative Studies of South Asia, Africa and the Middle East*, 38(3), 455–472.

Michelon, B. (2016). *Douala et Kigali, villes modernes et citadins précaires en Afrique*. Karthala, Paris.

Morton, D. (2019). *Age of Concrete. Housing and the Shape of Aspiration in the Capital of Mozambique*. Ohio University Press, Athens.

Myers, G. (2015). A world-class city-region? Envisioning the Nairobi of 2030. *American Behavioral Scientist*, 59(3), 328–346. doi: 10.1177/0002764214550308.

N'goran, A., Fofana, M., Akindès, F. (2020). Redéployer l'État par le marché : la politique des logements sociaux en Côte d'Ivoire. *Critique internationale*, 89(4), 75–93.

OECD/UNECA/AfDB (2022). Africa's urbanisation dynamics 2022: The economic power of Africa's cities. Report, West African Studies, OECD Publishing, Paris. doi: 10.1787/3834ed5b-en.

Ouma, S. (2020). "Africapitalism" and the limits of any variant of capitalism. *Review of African Political Economy* [Online]. Available at: https://roape.net/2020/07/16/africapitalism-and-the-limits-of-any-variant-of-capitalism.

Parnell, S. and Robinson, J. (2012). (Re)theorizing cities from the Global South: Looking beyond neoliberalism. *Urban Geography*, 33(4), 593–617. doi: 10.2747/0272-3638.33.4.593.

Peck, J. and Theodore, N. (2015). *Fast Policy: Experimental Statecraft at the Thresholds of Neoliberalism*. University of Minnesota Press, Minneapolis [Online]. Available at: http://data.rero.ch/01-R008167689/html?view=GE_V1.

Péclard, D., Kernen, A., Khan-Mohammad, G. (2020). États d'émergence. Le gouvernement de la croissance et du développement en Afrique. *Critique internationale*, 4(4), 9–27. doi: 10.3917/crii.089.0012.

Pitcher, A. (2012). Lions, tigers, and emerging markets: Africa's development dilemmas. *Current History*, 111(745), 163–168.

Pitcher, A. (2017). Entrepreneurial governance and the expansion of public investment funds in Africa. In *Africa in World Politics: Constructing Political and Economic Order*, 6th edition, Harbeson, J.W. and Rothchild, D. (eds). Westview Press, Boulder.

Roy, A. (2011). Slumdog cities: Rethinking subaltern urbanism. *International Journal of Urban and Regional Research*, 35(2), 223–238. doi: 10.1111/j.1468-2427.2011.01051.x.

Sawyer, L. (2016). PLOTTING the prevalent but undertheorised residential areas of Lagos. Conceptualising a process of urbanisation through grounded theory and comparison. PhD Thesis, ETH Zürich. doi: 10.3929/ethz-a-010898517.

Schorch, P., Saxer, M., Elders, M. (eds) (2020). *Exploring Materiality and Connectivity in Anthropology and Beyond*. UCL Press, London. doi: 10.2307/j.ctv13xpsp9.

Shatkin, G. (2008). The city and the bottom line: Urban megaprojects and the privatization of planning in Southeast Asia. *Environment and Planning A: Economy and Space*, 40(2), 383–401. doi: 10.1068/a38439.

Smith, C. (2020). Collapse. Fake buildings and gray development in Nairobi. *Focaal*, 86, 11–23. doi: 10.3167/fcl.2020.860102.

Söderström, O. (2014). *Cities in Relations: Trajectories of Urban Development in Hanoi and Ouagadougou*. Wiley, Oxford.

Spire, A. (2011). *L'Etranger et la ville en Afrique de l'Ouest*. Karthala, Paris.

Spire, A. and Choplin, A. (2018). Street vendors facing urban beautification in Accra (Ghana): Eviction, relocation and formalization. *Articulo – Journal of Urban Research*, 17–18. doi: 10.4000/articulo.3443.

UN-Habitat (2012). State of the world's cities report 2012/2013: Prosperity of cities. United Nations Human Settlements Programme (UN-Habitat).

UN-Habitat (2018). The state of African Cities 2018: The geography of African investment. Report, United Nations Human Settlements Programme (UN-Habitat).

Van Noorloos, F. and Kloosterboer, M. (2018). Africa's new cities. The contested future of urbanisation. *Urban Studies*, 55(6), 1223–1241. doi: 10.1177/0042098017700574.

Van Noorloos, F., Cirolia, L.R., Friendly, A., Jukur, S., Schramm, S., Steel, G., Valenzuela, L. (2020). Incremental housing as a node for intersecting flows of city-making: Rethinking the housing shortage in the global South. *Environment and Urbanization*, 32(1), 37–54. doi: 10.1177/0956247819887679.

Watson, V. (2014). African urban fantasies: Dreams or nightmares? *Environment and Urbanization*, 26(1), 215–231. doi: 10.1177/0956247813513705.

Watson, V. (2020). Digital visualisation as a new driver of urban change in Africa. *Urban Planning*, 5(2), 35–43. doi: 10.17645/up.v5i2.2989.

White, L. (2015). The case of cement. In *African Investing in Africa: Understanding Business and Trade, Sector by Sector*, McNamee, T., Pearson, M., Boer, W. (eds). Palgrave Macmillan, Hampshire.

Conclusion

Towards a Financialization of the Urbanity[1]

Olivier CREVOISIER[1] and Natacha AVELINE-DUBACH[2,3]

[1] *Université de Neuchâtel, Switzerland*
[2] *UMR Géographie-cités, CNRS, Aubervilliers, France*
[3] *CNRS@CREATE, Singapore*

Throughout the beginning of the 21st century, real estate has played and still plays a considerable role in the economy. This was not the case beforehand. Can we thus identify and understand what has happened in the past 25–30 years? While real estate in the broadest sense has always been an economic sector representing an overriding social issue, it was first and foremost a local affair with regard to construction companies, political regulations and the needs and aspirations of the population. Today, it is a much more central component of global capitalism, which is spread across all continents. Global crises are now linked to its dysfunctions, as has been demonstrated throughout this book.

To understand this change, we have adopted the proposal of Adkins et al. (2021), according to which a "particular logic of [property] asset inflation" has been constructed by government policies over the last two decades, to compensate for the stagnant returns of labor and for the erosion of welfare provision, resulting in new types of inequalities between households (see Chapter 3). Indeed, if the regime of capital accumulation is still characterized by the centrality of financial markets

---

1. The authors thank Thierry Theurillat, Denise Pumain and Anaïs Merckhoffer for their fruitful comments.

Globalization and Dynamics of Urban Production,
coordinated by Natacha AVELINE-DUBACH. © ISTE Ltd 2023.

(Boyer 2000) and the continuous rise of stock market indices – despite periodic crises – this regime has been renewed since the beginning of the 2000s by relying on real estate (see Chapter 1). Thus, we are not so much witnessing a financialization of real estate as an accommodation of market finance to the particularly interesting characteristics and attributes of real estate.

C.1. The emergence of the international dimension of real estate

Until the 1980s, real estate was an emblematic branch of local activity, driven by industrial development and commercial services or by tourism. Even the large-scale urban restructuring projects of the 1980s in Manhattan or in central Tokyo were the consequence of the extraordinary development of American or Japanese companies. Our common sense tells us that "when real estate goes, everything goes". In other words, it has only been since all other activities have grown that real estate began to take off. Real estate extended the cycles but was dependent on the rest of the economy, whose growth was propagated locally.

While the Japanese real estate crisis of 1992 had profound consequences in Southeast Asia and provoked aftershocks in several advanced and emerging economies (Renaud 1997; Aveline and Li 2004), real estate was still only a "trailer" sector. However, the perspective changed radically with the bursting of the "Internet bubble" in 2000–2002. This financial crash made the dotcoms look like a random lottery which benefited only a very few lucky people (Srnicek 2018). Having lost confidence in the stock market, investors turned to other markets to place accessible capital at low cost, at a time when the policy interest rates of central banks (Fed, BCE) were reduced to exceptionally low levels to mitigate the banking debacle. Real estate then became a strategic asset. Financiers and bankers considered it to be the least risky asset, to the point that it was used as a guarantee for its own production. During the 2002 crisis, the response to reassure investors was to introduce as many real estate securities into portfolios as possible to restore confidence in the markets.

The tangible results of this "convention" demonstrate that banks have continually created a huge amount of real estate debt, guaranteed on the objects produced by the investment. Thanks to this convention of reduced risk, real estate has been instrumentalized by finance to restore confidence and reconstitute the basis for accumulation based on credit creation.

C.2. Real estate, a highly sought-after asset

The attraction of real estate investment has been strongly stimulated by the aging of the population in the major advanced economies. The need for retirement savings has encouraged the proliferation of institutional investors, which allocate a significant share to real estate – notably pension funds, which control nearly half of the world's institutional real estate investments[2]. As mentioned above, households are also strongly encouraged to invest in real estate, either directly or through financial vehicles. This strong demand for property investment tends to create a structural imbalance between real estate development and the effective demand of end-users for built space. China presents a particularly emblematic example of such a mechanism: as the savings of economic actors have been concentrated in real estate, especially in residential property, it is estimated that at least one housing unit in five is vacant in China's urban areas (Aveline-Dubach 2019).

Households that have acquired real estate in the central areas of major cities and tourist regions have experienced unprecedented asset appreciation over the past two decades. Other players have been the major beneficiaries of asset inflation: banks and real estate actors, of course (see Chapter 2), as well as governments at various levels. The latter have seen their tax revenues increase, as well as their ability to capture urban rent through land value capture instruments. Some governments are recycling their oil revenues (Middle Eastern countries, Norway) or their trade surpluses (China, Singapore) into real estate through sovereign wealth funds (see Chapter 8).

National states and local governments are the main architects of the financialization of real estate and the privatization of property development projects – combining with the sale of public land and social properties, as well as the deregulation of rental leases – to develop their financial industry and cofinance their ambitious urban (re)development projects. As we have seen in this book, the World Bank plays an important role in circulating these neoliberal approaches in emerging countries.

C.3. The diversity of capital accumulation dynamics in real estate

These processes have contributed to the development of a *"financialized real estate-driven regime"* (Aalbers 2017), which has, on the one hand, general characteristics that can be traced back to the process of accumulation – and in

---

2. See: https://docs.preqin.com/newsletters/re/Preqin-RESL-September-16-Pension-Funds-Investing-in-Real-Estate.pdf [Accessed March 3, 2022].

particular the creation of credit money – and, on the other hand, characteristics that vary accross space. Financialization has served to spread American–British, and later Western, capitalism throughout the world. However, it is very unevenly distributed around the planet. As the contributions to this book show, the gradient and the ways in which finance has penetrated real estate are largely determined by the geo-economic and geopolitical risks of the target countries of the investment. Thus, we can observe a strong anchoring of global finance in the North American and Western European real estate markets, as well as in certain East Asian countries where the level of economic advancement allows for diversification in several sectors – with a growing appetite among investors for the logistics and residential sectors (see Chapters 4 and 5). In these countries, investment strategies combine expectations in terms of yields and capital gains, in varying proportions depending on the expected risk-adjusted returns.

In contrast, global financial investments are more conservatively placed in the South. While finance is substantially anchored in urban production in the Middle East, it comes mainly from regional investors, notably the sovereign wealth funds of oil-producing countries. Here, as in other regions of the South, financial investment is little concerned with rental yields and seeks rather long-term capital gains. The strategy consists of maximizing capital gains by acquiring low-cost land in strategic sites (demolition of slums or public land sold at a discount) where large public investments are planned (see Chapter 8). The hopes of "dubaization" (see Chapter 9) underlying the orientations of local public action in some of these cities reflect the notable change in national growth strategies: from a sector with dynamics induced by economic activities, real estate has become a driving sector of the whole economy, capable of creating the infrastructure for growth ex-nihilo.

China best embodies the productivist objectives of these urban strategies, but has the singularity of having voluntarily preserved its urban production from the uncontrollable movements of global finance. The financing of urbanization in China mobilizes mainly domestic capital, through bank credit and idiosyncratic investment vehicles (Theurillat et al. 2016), but also via the large-scale capture of land rent by local governments – defined here as "macro-value capture" (see Chapter 6). The same is true in the "Belt and Road Initiative" corridor (see Chapter 7), especially in Africa and Southeast Asia, where the construction of cities and special economic zones by Chinese operators – property developers and infrastructure builders/operators – is taking place with little recourse to globalized real estate financial vehicles (Andujar 2020).

C.4. From sectorial and induced real estate to the integrated and driving production of urban construction

Whether or not it is stimulated by financial investment, the considerable rise of real estate is marked by a change in scale and a densification of the urban fabric, with the generalization of multifunctional megaprojects in metropolitan centers or in new urban cores well connected to the existing city. These dynamics are associated with profound changes in urban governance, marked by a shift in power relations in favor of private interests (Swyngedouw et al. 2002).

The concrete form of Fordist capital accumulation was the large-scale industrial firm, while that of financial accumulation is characterized by the continuous rise of stock prices and market capitalization. Today, large neighborhoods and entire cities created by a single gigantic coordinated project, often over many years, could constitute the concrete form of a new mode of real estate accumulation.

In the past, the (sectoral) economies of location preceded the economies of agglomeration and the development of the city. Today, the production of the urban built environment (real estate and infrastructure investment by large entities capable of building integrated neighborhoods, industrial zones or event entire cities) in many cases precedes the development of urban activities and (sectoral) income growth (see Chapters 4, 5, 7, 8, and 9). It is from the global cities that sectoral developments and their distribution around the world are organized.

The financialization of real estate started in the centers of the largest globalized cities, as well as in the most famous tourist resorts. Today, it operates where the people with the highest incomes, the highest fortunes and probably also the highest skills are located.

The returns on these investments are therefore not the *result of* the city's economic success and its successful integration into globalization. These investments *precede* and in part *make possible* the development of activities and the presence of selected populations in the city. It is therefore a *bet* on the redeployment of a district area in a metropolis, or even on the success of a new city. The Spanish urban production of the 2000s, intended for retired people from Northern Europe, was a gamble – in this case a failed one. From this perspective, the rise in real estate prices observed in the largest centers seems to be a set of bets won not on this or that property, but on the urban dynamic as a whole and on the success of its insertion into globalization. In this sense, we are probably witnessing the financialization of urbanity more than the financialization of real estate assets.

C.5. The financialized urban construct as a concrete scene of the global city

In short, the financialization of urban production can be seen as an acceleration of the overcoming of industrial society and its productive specializations. The same observation can be made for the GAFAMs (Google, Apple, Facebook, Amazon and Microsoft), whose stock market values have grown spectacularly in the past two decades. These two sectors are now at the center of capital accumulation, and the development of both would not have been possible without the close interaction with market finance and the actors in the banking and monetary system.

The financialized urban construct, on the one hand, and the industrialization of informational and symbolic interactions on a global scale by digital platforms, on the other hand, are articulated and outline a global system in the making. In short, all our "real", concrete activities have, in one way or another, a correspondence on digital platforms. This duality between concrete (constructed) and symbolic (digitalized) scenes (Guex and Crevoisier 2015) reveals how, starting from the *global city*, large platforms industrialize all the immaterial relations between beings and between beings and objects on a world scale. From its center, Amazon offers a set of generic services (management of stocks, supplies, deliveries, invoices, financial management, etc.) to companies scattered across the planet, which enable it to draw income from a very wide range of activities. Beyond these functional and informational activities, the GAFAM platforms have enabled a generalized connection to a *symbolic scene* on which information is exchanged, controversies are developed, opinions are built and *storytelling* finds its resonance.

C.6. Social consequences and the need for rethinking public policies

Unlike commodity-based capitalism, the business model of both financialized real estate and platforms is based on a flat rate. Users pay a subscription, a rent or an entrance fee. In other words, they pay for a right of access to a physical and/or digital stage, which itself gives them the opportunity to perform a large number of activities. It is up to the user to imagine these activities, to invest skills, time, energy, other material or immaterial means in them, in order to obtain personal well-being (e.g. by attending cultural programs in a big city) or an income (e.g. thanks to a business service platform located in Silicon Valley). But in the meantime, flat rents are running, securing income streams that, for the time being, validate the assumption that future real estate incomes will pay for the high amounts invested.

The fundamental institution of capitalism is the primacy of the capital income over all others: even when crisis strikes, even when businesses have to close and workers lose their jobs, the capital income remains due. The closure of shops and restaurants during the Covid-19 crisis was a bitter reminder of this fundamental institution: landlords not only had the right to demand payment of rent, but very few waived it.

Real estate capitalism constitutes an advance which will have to be repaid either by rent increases or by property capital gains. Simply being in a place – living in a building, visiting an attraction, going to work, etc. – can be seen as a rent-capturing experience, a package that everyone pays for, as a precondition and independently of the actual use or non-use of the benefits provided by the city. Having largely surpassed commodity-based capitalism, the contemporary economy presents itself as a bundle of rights that allow for the capture of monetary flows generated by the desire or necessity of populations to live in cities. The bet is that the increase in the density and variety of experiences available in cities makes them more value-generating and more desirable to live in and visit. But how far can the revenues and property prices generated by the rehabilitation/regeneration of cities grow? And how can we believe that this development will take place without strong tensions between the populations and activities that will have more means to pay these rents and the others?

In this context, urban policies must develop effective land strategies to maintain and articulate the plurality of activities, populations and interests that constitute urbanity. The tools for capturing land value can be virtuous, provided they are not used on a very large scale as in certain East Asian countries (see Chapter 6).

In Europe, narrow growth coalitions undermine the social and environmental justice that maintains the city's long-term value. Particular attention should therefore be paid to the *wider urban milieus* (Crevoisier and Rime 2021), i.e. the more or less coordinated and organized sets of actors – inhabitants, businesses, tourist operators, media, cultural actors, etc. – that make up the city, its diversity and its value in the long term.

C.7. References

Aalbers, M.B. (2017). The variegated financialization of housing. *International Journal of Urban and Regional Research*, 41(4), 542–554.

Adkins, L., Cooper, M., Konings, M. (2021). Class in the 21st century: Asset inflation and the new logic of inequality. *Environment and Planning A: Economy and Space*, 53(3), 548–572.

Aveline, N. and Li, L.-H. (ed.) (2004). *Property Markets and Land Policies in Northeast Asia. The Case of Five Cities : Tokyo, Seoul, Shanghai, Taipei and Hong Kong*. Maison Franco-Japonaise/Center for Real Estate and Urban Economics, Hong Kong and Tokyo.

Aveline-Dubach, N. (2019). China's housing booms: A challenge to bubble theory. In *Theories and Models of Urbanization*, Batty, M. and Pumain, D. (eds). Springer, Cham.

Boyer, R. (2000). Is a finance-led growth regime a viable alternative to Fordism? A preliminary analysis. *Economy and Society*, 29(1), 111–145.

Crevoisier, O. and Rime, D. (2021). Anchoring urban development: Globalisation, attractiveness and complexity. *Urban Studies*, 58(1), 36–52.

Esposito Andujar, A. (2020). Figures d'un urbanisme aspirationnel. Les villes secondaires d'Asie du Sud-Est à l'heure de la Belt and Road Iniative. *Urbanités* [Online]. Available at: http://www.revue-urbanites.fr/usea-esposito/.

Guex, D. and Crevoisier, O. (2015). A comprehensive socio-economic model of the experience economy: The territorial stage. In *Spatial Dynamics in the Experience Economy*, Lorentzen, A., Schrøder, L., Topsø Larsen, K. (eds). Routledge, Abingdon.

Renaud, B. (1997). The 1985 to 1994 global real estate cycle: An overview. *Journal of Real Estate Literature*, 5(1), 13–44.

Srnicek, N. (2018a). *Capitalisme de plateforme : l'hégémonie de l'économie numérique*. Lux, Montreal.

Srnicek, N. (2018b). *Platform Capitalism*. Polity Press, Cambridge.

Swyngedouw, E., Moulaert, F., Rodriguez, A. (2002). Neoliberal urbanization in Europe: Large-scale urban development projects and the new urban policy. *Antipode*, 34(3), 542–577.

Theurillat, T., Lenzer Jr., J.H., Zhan, H. (2016). The increasing financialization of China's urbanization. *Issues & Studies*, 52(04), 1640002.

List of Authors

Myriam ABABSA
UMR Géographie-Cités
Aubervilliers
France
and
Institut français du Proche-Orient
Amman
Jordan

Natacha AVELINE-DUBACH
UMR Géographie-cités
CNRS
Aubervilliers
France
and
CNRS@CREATE
Singapore

Armelle CHOPLIN
Université de Genève
Geneva
Switzerland

Olivier CREVOISIER
Université de Neuchâtel
Switzerland

Jean DEBRIE
Université Paris 1 Pantheon-Sorbonne
and
UMR Géographie-Cités
Campus Condorcet
Aubervilliers
France

Gabriel FAUVEAUD
Departement de Géographie
Centre d'études asiatiques (CETASE)
Université de Montréal
Canada

Adeline HEITZ
LIRSA
Conservatoire National des
Arts et Métiers (CNAM)
Paris
France

Renaud LE GOIX
Université Paris Cité
and
UMR Géographie-Cités
Campus Condorcet
Aubervilliers
France

Julie POLLARD
LAGAPE
Institut d'études politiques
Université de Lausanne
Switzerland

Nicolas RAIMBAULT
Nantes University
and
UMR Espace et société
France

Thierry THEURILLAT
Institut du Management des Villes
et du Territoire (IMVT)
Haute École de Gestion-Arc (HES-SO)
Neuchâtel
Switzerland

Index

A, B

affordability, 47, 48, 58, 60, 63–65
Africa, 63, 119, 182, 213–218, 220, 222, 224, 226, 229
Amman, 177, 178, 181, 186, 195, 196, 198
Asia, 127, 129, 134, 136, 149, 154, 156, 157, 160, 161, 169–172, 184, 220, 226
  East Asia, 79, 129–131, 137, 149, 154, 156, 157, 161
  Southeast Asia, 131, 155–159, 161–163, 166–172
Beirut, 177, 181, 186, 200–204, 206

C, D

Cairo, 177, 178, 181, 188, 192–197
capitalism, 4, 8, 16, 55, 73, 131, 137, 156, 158, 159, 213, 216
cement industry, 214–216, 218, 219, 229
China, 9, 14, 16, 18, 28, 129, 130, 135, 142, 145, 146, 148–150, 157, 158, 167, 169–172, 205
city-port relationship, 106, 107
commodification, 50, 111, 112, 146, 156, 159, 160, 172, 192, 216
concrete, 4, 29, 38, 73, 214–218, 220, 221, 227–229
construction, 12, 13, 15, 19, 29–31, 33, 38–40, 49, 51, 54, 63–65, 75–79, 83, 93, 130, 133–135, 137–144, 146–149, 161–163, 169–171, 178, 181, 183, 186, 191–193, 195, 201–203, 205, 206, 208, 209, 213–220, 223–225, 227, 229
Damascus, 177, 181, 204–208
deterritorialization, 4, 9
development, 5–9, 12, 15–21, 27–41, 49, 54, 58, 61, 73–78, 80, 83, 85–94, 96–98, 105, 106, 110, 112, 113, 115, 117–119, 129, 131–145, 147–150, 157, 159–172, 181, 186, 188, 192, 195, 200, 202–208, 213, 216, 218, 224, 225, 229
  economic, 74, 75, 82, 83, 85, 134, 149, 179, 181, 213, 218
  sustainable, 39–41, 119, 181, 219
  urban, 6, 8, 12, 13, 15–21, 29, 34, 85, 92, 112, 138, 147, 149, 159, 161, 165, 178, 181, 192, 205, 225
developmental state, 149
docklandization, 105, 106, 109–111, 115–117

E, F

economic growth, 137, 181, 213, 219
Europe, 18, 27, 36, 79, 105, 133, 184, 189, 224, 229

financing of real estate, 29, 30, 34, 36, 41, 49, 51, 85, 169, 226

H, I

home ownership, 16, 47–54, 57, 58, 60–62, 64, 180, 190
Hong Kong, 13, 15, 129, 135, 142–147, 149, 150, 162, 167–170, 172, 201
housing, 14, 29, 30, 32, 33, 35, 36, 38–41, 47–58, 60–65, 87, 88, 90, 94, 111–115, 132, 133, 139, 141, 145–150, 155, 157, 159, 163, 164, 167, 169, 178–180, 186–191, 194, 195, 197–200, 204, 206, 207, 209, 214–216, 224–227
  affordable, 16, 37, 38, 41, 61, 133, 190, 198–200, 209, 224
  policies, 48–50, 53, 61, 62, 149, 178–180, 198, 199, 224, 225
  social, 15, 38, 53, 54, 147, 178, 179, 199, 204, 209, 224–227
infrastructure, 4, 6, 17, 19, 74, 78, 79, 85, 88, 96, 106, 107, 109–113, 117, 118, 127, 129–138, 143, 145–147, 149, 162, 168, 170, 171, 179, 181, 194, 196, 206, 208, 209, 214, 216, 219, 220
intermediate logistics, 75, 79, 93–97
investment funds, 6, 9, 13, 15, 19, 31, 63, 83, 167, 168, 179, 186

J, L

Japan, 13, 14, 48, 88, 129–131, 136, 137, 139–141, 143, 145, 149, 150, 157, 161, 179
land
  consolidation, 138, 139
  regime, 143
large projects, 200, 208, 215, 220
logistics
  facilities, 74–80, 82–91, 93–98, 142
  real estate, 36, 75, 80, 82–84, 86–89, 92–96

M, N

markets, 3–21, 28, 35, 40, 41, 48–58, 60–63, 65, 82, 83, 110, 141, 155–162, 166–168, 170–172, 177, 180, 184, 186, 189, 216, 224
  finance, 3–7, 9–13, 15–21
  land, 146, 160, 216
  real estate, 12, 14, 18, 19, 21, 27, 28, 30, 54, 65, 97, 155–162, 166–172, 199, 226
  regimes, 48, 49, 51, 54, 57–60, 62, 63, 65, 129
  stratification, 50
Middle East, 161, 177–180, 182–184, 186–191, 197, 198, 202, 208, 220
neoliberal urban policies, 18
North America, 27, 36, 39, 79, 105, 109, 110, 118, 119, 132, 133, 161, 177, 184

P, R

Paris, 13, 18, 33, 57, 58, 73, 79, 80, 83, 84, 88–91, 93, 95, 96, 113–116
  region, 18, 33, 34, 80, 84, 88, 90, 96
platform, 11, 62, 63, 74, 87, 88, 95, 119, 132, 147, 162, 171
policy instruments, 37, 38
port metropolises, 106, 111, 117, 118, 120
privatization, 16, 17, 50, 83, 85, 112, 137, 155, 157, 159, 160, 163–166, 181
proprietary ideology, 146
public action, 90, 92, 112, 128
real estate
  debt, 48, 51, 65, 189
  developers, 23, 27–31, 34–39, 82, 84, 88, 90, 96, 135, 163, 202, 214, 222, 225
  development, 12, 18, 19, 27–33, 35–37, 39, 41, 58, 134, 142, 143, 157, 161, 162, 186
  inflation, 49, 65
  production, 163, 169

regionalization, 108, 155, 156, 161–163, 172

S, T

social inequalities, 47, 49, 60, 65
standardization, 93, 106, 111, 112, 116, 118, 217
suburbanization, 61, 75
terminalization, 106–108, 117–119
territories, 4, 11, 18, 32, 37, 117, 149, 150, 164, 165, 171, 182, 184, 216, 219, 220

U, V, W

urban
    environment, 93, 110, 164, 214
    governance, 13, 17–19, 163, 165, 186
    production, 3–5, 8, 11, 14–16, 19–21, 24, 25, 34, 49, 61, 82, 111, 118, 141, 155, 156, 161, 163–166, 171, 179, 180, 214, 220, 225, 228
    projects, 13, 14, 18, 29, 35, 49, 88, 96, 106, 111, 118, 120, 132, 136, 137, 155, 158, 163–165, 170, 172, 181, 184
    rent, 4, 6, 7, 12–15, 19–21
    restructuring, 236
urbanization, 3, 4, 17–19, 74, 75, 79, 82–85, 92, 97, 127, 129, 137, 140, 143, 145, 148, 149, 157, 163, 164, 166, 214, 220, 227
value capture, 127, 129, 137, 142, 143, 146, 149
    land (LVC), 20, 127–131, 133, 135–137, 141–146, 149, 150
    macro-, 129, 137, 149, 150
warehouse, 74–79, 87, 88, 91, 93–98, 112, 115

Printed and bound by CPI Group (UK) Ltd, Croydon, CR0 4YY
19/12/2023